A Lost Heroine
of the Confederacy

A Lost Heroine

of the Confederacy

THE DIARIES AND LETTERS OF

Belle Edmondson

Edited by
Loretta and William Galbraith

University Press of Mississippi
Jackson and London

Center for the Study of Southern Culture Series

Copyright © 1990 by the University Press of Mississippi
Manufactured in the United States of America
The paper in this book meets the guidelines for permanence and dura-
bility of the Committee on Production Guidelines for Book Longevity
of the Council on Library Resources.

Print-on-Demand Edition

Library of Congress Cataloging-in-Publication Data

Edmondson, Belle, 1840–1873.
     A lost heroine of the Confederacy: the diaries and letters of Belle Edmondson /
edited by Loretta and William Galbraith.
          p.   cm.—(Center for the Study of Southern Culture series)
     Includes bibliographical references and index.
     ISBN 978-1-60473-393-8
          1. Edmondson, Belle, 1840–1873—Diaries. 2. Edmondson, Belle, 1840–1873—
Correspondence. 3. United States—History—Civil War, 1861–1865—Secret ser-
vice. 4. Tennessee—History—Civil War, 1861–1865—Secret Service. 5. United
States—History—Civil War, 1861–1865—Personal narratives, Confederate. 6.
Smugglers—Tennessee—Memphis—Diaries. 7. Smugglers—Tennessee—Mem-
phis—Correspondence. 8. Spies—Tennessee—Memphis—Diaries. 9. Spies—
Tennessee—Memphis—Correspondence. 10. Memphis (Tenn.)—History. I. Gal-
braith, Loretta. II. Galbraith, William. III. Title.
IV. Series.
E608.E238   1990
973.7'86'092—dc20
[B]   90-19314
                                                                            CIP

British Library Cataloguing-in-Publication data available

To the memory of
Susan Tate Bray Williams,
Emri leDavis,
and
Betty Lou Stidham

Contents

12. A Journey Homeward / 1864 Diary: September   175

13. Return to Waverley / 1864 Diary: October
    and November   181

14. A Wedding and Two Battles / 1864 Letters   188

    Bibliography   217

    Index   229

Preface

When we lived in Mississippi, we became interested in that state's architecture, history, and literature. Waverley, a plantation home in Clay County, seemed to embody all of these disciplines. The handsome Greek Revival structure was being restored after standing vacant for almost fifty years. With the assistance of its new owners, we began a study of Waverley. In our attempts to document the mansion's past, we discovered the Civil War diary of a young woman who had taken refuge there in 1864. That woman was Belle Edmondson from West Tennessee.

Belle's diary gave us insight into daily life at Waverley during the latter part of the war, as well as a feeling for the young woman who kept that journal. Her account was intensely personal and very revealing. We discovered that she had fled her home near occupied Memphis to escape imprisonment. Belle's story was so compelling that our Waverley research evolved into a search for this lost Confederate heroine.

Picking up Belle Edmondson's trail after she left Waverley was difficult. We knew very little about her, her family, or her home. Our only lead was a Mary B. West of Memphis who had donated the diary to the Southern Historical Collection at the University of North Carolina. Mary B. West's name appeared in the Memphis city directory until 1972. We contacted colleagues who remembered her but knew nothing of relatives or possible heirs. They knew only that she was unmarried and was known as Brodie West, a name of which she was proud. Brodie is an unusual name, and we remembered that Belle had mentioned a "Brother Brodie" a few times in her 1864 diary.

In our search for Miss West's obituary, we discovered her mother's. Mary Brodie Crump West was a pioneer social worker in Memphis and first cousin to E. H. "Boss" Crump. Then we realized that Brother Brodie and Major Crump from Belle's diary were the same person. Mary Brodie Crump West, born in 1865 and mother of Mary

B. West, was the daughter of Belle's sister Helen, who married Major Brodie Crump. Their wedding at Lochinvar was described in Belle's 1864 diary.

Our next lead was an 1863 map of Memphis and vicinity drawn by a Federal officer. We found a copy in the Memphis Public Library's Local History Room. The map charted an area outside the city where property was listed by owners' names. On that map was the name Edmondson and the names of neighbors Belle had mentioned in her diary. Superimposing that map over a current one helped us pinpoint the general location as what is now called Whitehaven. Major roads, some with unchanged names, still run in the same directions.

While examining area histories, we found *Tales of Old Whitehaven*, a book written by Anna Leigh McCorkle in 1967. Miss McCorkle mentioned Belle's father, Andrew Jackson Edmondson, in her book. We also learned that Belle's home was a farm called Elm Ridge. When we called Miss McCorkle, we found her to be in failing health but cooperative and interested in our work. She knew of the diary's existence but had not seen it. She was able to provide us with the names of two women who proved to be excellent sources of information.

The first person was related by marriage to the Perkins family who figured so prominently in Belle's diary. This lady shared family papers and lore with us. The other person was one of Belle's collateral descendants. The family genealogist and historian, this charming lady was a godsend. From her we learned when Belle died and where she was buried, as well as the mysterious nature of her death. It was also through her intercession that we made contact with Edmondson family descendants throughout the country who lent us old photographs, Belle's album, documents, and family Bible records.

Our best find came one rainy afternoon in Memphis when another family member allowed us to look through an old trunk in her attic. There, carefully labeled and tied in fading pink ribbon, was a box containing Belle's Civil War papers. This material brought the pieces of Belle's life together, and we felt we had unearthed what Daniel Aaron once called the buried details of history.

Belle's writing seemed to convey a cry of pain, a plea for understanding, a feeling of loneliness and alienation from the rest of her family. After she arrived at Waverley, the tone changed, and she seemed happy and at peace.

Anyone who has ever travelled through Memphis on Interstate

240 has passed beautiful Elmwood Cemetery. Two large statues are especially noticeable from the highway: the stern figure of a man in a frock coat and an angel apparently waving to passing traffic. Belle is buried nearby in the Edmondson plot, her grave shaded by a giant magnolia and carpeted with wild strawberries in the spring. When we drive past Elmwood, we can't help but say, *"Sit tibi terra levis* (Light lie the earth upon thee)."

We owe so much to so many people we can never enumerate them all. We are especially grateful to Belle's niece Susan Tate Bray Willams who preserved the papers over the long years and to Sue Tate's grandchildren, Betty Lou Stidham and Emri leDavis Stidham, both deceased in 1990. We also thank Charlotte Adee Edmondson Elam who took us in hand and headed us in the right direction. She opened doors for us in more ways than one.

Other Edmondson family descendants who deserve our gratitude are Sidney and Lillian Newcomb for the use of Belle's photograph album and for the gift of her wartime photograph; Tate Dashiell Coggins who lent photographs, gave encouragement, and became a good friend along the way; and Georgia and the late Hugh Edmondson and Ferdinand Farrow Edmondson.

We also thank Kate Pinckney for the Perkins family material and photographs; the late Anna Leigh McCorkle who introduced us to Charlotte Elam and Kate Pinckney; Donna and Robert Snow of Waverley who placed their papers at our disposal; Doctors Janis and Forrest Tutor of Lochinvar, whose doors were always open to us; and Daniel Williams for his support in so many special ways.

Much gratitude is owed to Bill Ferris at the Center for the Study of Southern Culture at the University of Mississippi. He was never too busy to meet with and advise us. We also thank Professor Leonard Curry at the University of Louisville's History Department, our mentor who spent long hours with Belle; Professor Leon Driskell, English Department, University of Louisville; Professor Carl Ryant, History Department, University of Louisville; Professor Martha Swain, History Department, Texas Woman's University; and Dr. John Simon, editor of the Ulysses S. Grant Papers, Southern Illinois University, who took an early interest in Belle.

Special thanks to Richard Schrader, Reference Archivist of the Southern Historical Collection, University of North Carolina; Ljilja Kuftinec, librarian, Inter-library Loan Department, University of Louisville; Martha Irby, Interlibrary Loan Department, Mississippi

State University Library; and to the countless archivists and historians we met and contacted during our long search.

We give special thanks also to our typist, Virginia Callan. And last, but not least, we thank our children, who edited our prose in the book and drew maps, and other family members, friends, and co-workers who endured the quest with us. Some who loved us are not here to see Belle in print. Light lie the earth upon them, too.

Introduction

The Civil War has been called a "spy conscious" war. It was the first war in which many women actively participated as spies, couriers, and smugglers, especially in the Confederacy. But the scarcity of records makes it difficult to learn of the illegal activities of southern women. What documents did exist were lost or deliberately destroyed as the Union Army approached Richmond. Years after the war, Jefferson Davis discouraged any revelations about the South's spies.[1]

Of the few published accounts by or about women spies, some are of the "cloak and dagger" genre and are of scant value in any study of espionage by southern women. Two authors of notable memoirs were Rose O'Neal Greenhow and Belle Boyd. The latter, a highly visible young spy who operated in western Virginia, wrote a sensational and popular narrative that was first published in England in 1865.[2]

In the Western Confederacy, an area that may have received less attention from its own government than it has from historians, another young woman named Belle performed daring service for the southern cause. This Belle also had a "burning zeal and inventive mind." Unlike her counterpart, Belle Edmondson did not write a book or give dramatic readings about her exploits. The fact that she died unsung may have been a result of the family's postwar friendship with Jefferson Davis.[3]

1. Harnett T. Kane, *Spies for the Blue and Gray* (Garden City, NY: Doubleday and Co., Inc., 1954), 12, 15; Oscar A. Kinchen, *Women Who spied for the Blue and the Gray* (Philadelphia: Dorrance and Co., 1972), vii; Edwin C. Fishel, "The Mythology of Civil War Intelligence," *Civil War History* 10 (1964): 344, 352–53.

2. Ishbel Ross, *Rebel Rose: Life of Rose O'Neal Greenhow, Confederate Spy* (New York: Harpers and Brothers, 1954); Belle Boyd, *Belle Boyd in Camp and Prison*, ed. Curtis Carroll Davis (New York: Thomas Yoseloff, 1968); Jane A. Martin, et al., eds, "The Siren of the Shenandoah," *Spies, Scouts and Raiders* (New York: Time-Life Books, Inc., 1985), 48–49; Curtis Carroll Davis, "The Spy Memoir as a Social Document," *Civil War History* 10 (1964): 385–400.

3. Mary Elizabeth Massey, *Bonnet Brigades* (New York: Alfred A. Knoff, 1966), chap. 5 passim; Martin, *Spies*, 10. For further comment on how the Western Confed-

Belle Edmondson did, however, leave behind a body of personal papers that document her intelligence work for a company of scouts, as spies were called by both sides. When captured, scouts, even in civilian clothes, were more likely to be treated as prisoners of war than to be executed. This changed later in the war, as Belle's 1864 diary indicates. Male gallantry and the double standard probably saved women spies from death, though not from prison.[4]

Belle Edmondson's papers, in addition to providing a record of espionage and smuggling by a woman, supply other significant information. Her descriptions of travels in "Dixie" point up the importance of topography in the war. The west-running streams of west Tennessee and north Mississippi, however sluggish and meandering, were at times genuine barriers that kept the Federals in Memphis and the Confederates thirty miles to the south.

The papers also contain highly readable accounts of the stresses on and conflicts within a family living between the lines of opposing armies, of close relationships with slaves, and of soldiers' lives in military camps. Details of life in and around wartime Memphis, a subject that lacks primary sources, are especially interesting.

Isabella Buchanan Edmondson (Belle) was born in 1840 in Pontotoc, Mississippi, six years after the Chickasaws ceded the rest of their land at the Treaty of Pontotoc. These Indians were removed west of the Mississippi River in 1839.

The years before Belle's birth were hectic in Pontotoc. The newly opened Indian lands came at the height of the cotton boom. The combination of cheap land and ample paper money led to what Joseph Baldwin called "flush times."[5]

Farmers, planters, merchants, entrepreneurs, and land speculators swarmed into Pontotoc for these sales. Mississippi was consid-

---

eracy fared with Richmond, see Shelby Foote, *The Civil War: A Narrative* 3 vols. (New York: Random House, 1974), 3:1064; and Thomas L. Connelly, *Autumn of Glory: The Army of Tennessee, 1862–1865* (Baton Rouge: Louisiana State University Press, 1971), 535.

4. Among Belle's papers were seven certificates of disability and twenty-one medical furlough certificates, which may have been used by scouts for identification if captured while not in uniform. John Bakeless, *Spies for the Confederacy* (Philadelphia: John B. Lippincott Co., 1970), 212–213; Kane, *Spies*, 12–13; John W. Headley, "The Confederate Secret Service," *The Photographic History of the Civil War*, ed. Francis T. Miller 10 vols. (New York: Thomas Yoseloff, 1911), 7:286–301.

5. Joseph G. Baldwin, *The Flush Times of Alabama and Mississippi* (New York: D. Appleton and Co., 1853), 174.

ered the "new El Dorado," where it was said fortunes could be made in a day—or at least in a month, as in the case of a man who purchased a section of land from an Indian for $1,000 and made a profit of $80,000 on resale one month later.[6]

Robert Gordon, a Scotsman related to the Edmondsons by marriage, is an example of a man who was in the right place at the right time. Gordon was a merchant and lawyer in Cotton Gin Port across the Tombigbee River from the Chickasaw Nation. His partner was John Bell, the surveyor-general of the Chickasaw cession. Before the final treaty was signed, Gordon knew the sites of the best land and the names of the Indians allotted those lands. He acquired great wealth and built a Greek Revival mansion called Lochinvar, which still stands outside Pontotoc.[7]

Belle was the eighth child and fifth daughter born to Mary Ann Howard and Andrew Jackson Edmondson. Her father was a veteran of the War of 1812 and a surveyor of the Indian cession; he remained at Pontotoc as Receiver of Public Monies and Recorder of Deeds at subsequent land sales. Ever the man of honor, Edmondson did not make money during the "flush times." He once told a granddaughter that he could have been a very wealthy man had he chosen to deal unfairly with the Indians. There were many opportunities to do so.[8]

In 1849, Belle's father was elected clerk of the chancery court at Holly Springs, a pretty town in Marshall County known for its fine mansions and excellent schools. The years at Holly Springs seem to have been happy ones for the family. They lived in a home described as "beautiful Blythewood," and the daughters attended Franklin Female College. Belle is described in family correspondence during her early years as "the worst child ever" and "warm-hearted but wild."[9]

Franklin Female College was more a finishing school than a college and was advertised as a place where "strict reference will be had at all times to the manners and habits of the young ladies." Belle's courses may have included Mental and Moral Philosophy, Mathe-

6. W. H. Sparks, *The Memories of Fifty Years* (Philadelphia: Claxton, Remsen & Haffelfinger, 1872), 364; untitled typed manuscript, unsigned, undated, Thompson-Pound Collection, Special Collections, MSUS.

7. Mary Elizabeth Young, *Redskins, Ruffled Shirts and Rednecks* (Norman: University of Oklahoma Press, 1961), 116–17. See also E. T. Winston, *Story of Pontotoc* (Pontotoc: Pontotoc Progress Printing Co., 1931); diary entry, 23 June 1864, BEDNC.

8. Genealogy charts, EFP; U.S. Congress, House, *Expenditures from the Chicksasw Fund*, H.R. 65, 27th Cong., 3rd Sess., 1843, 75, 77; Susan Bray Williams to Josephine, 26 Nov. 1931, EFP.

9. Mary to Mother, 11 Feb. 1851; Mary to Jo, 15 Mar. 1855, EFP.

matical Astronomy, Geology, Chemistry, Drawing, Painting, Voice, Guitar, French and Italian.[10]

Belle's father became a full-time farmer in 1856, when he moved his family to a farm north of Holly Springs. During that time, Belle suffered from a nervous disorder. She was unable to receive or write letters because of a state of "extreme nervous excitement." A letter to Belle from her doctor spoke of her "spells" and advised her to try cupping, a method that forced blood to the surface of the skin through use of a heated cup or glass that created a vacuum. This was a common treatment for headaches, cramps, bruises, and congestion.[11]

Girls who came of age during the decade of the fifties were influenced by the cult of the "genteel female." Marriage and submission to men were highly touted goals to which all women were expected to aspire. Literature of the era, created by women for women, extolled the refining and spiritualizing influence of the female. Literature of this period was of the "Graveyard School," typified by an obsessive emphasis on solitude and a perception of death as an escape from an evil world. Small wonder that a high-strung, susceptible young woman like Belle went into a decline in her late teens. It was the fashionable thing to do.[12]

On the eve of the Civil War, the Edmondsons moved to Elm Ridge, a farm in Shelby County, Tennessee, located eight miles from Memphis. Belle's older brother Jimmie was a merchant in that city, and her cousin Frazor Titus was a cotton factor and one of Memphis's wealthiest men.

Overlooking the Mississippi River and surrounded by rich land east and northeast, Memphis was the economic and cultural center of the interior South. A hamlet of 600 inhabitants when a troupe of

10. William Baskerville Hamilton, "Holly Springs, Mississippi to the Year 1878" (M.A. thesis, University of Mississippi, 1931), 129; advertisement in *Memphis Daily Appeal*, 17 Mar. 1851; *Franklin Female College Catalogue* (Holly Springs: Mississippi Times Cheap Book and Job Print Office, 1854), MDAHJ. See also Hodding Carter, "A Proud Struggle for Grace, Holly Springs, Mississippi," in *A Vanishing America, Twelve Regional Towns*, ed. Thomas C. Wheeler (New York: Holt, Rinehart and Winston, 1964), 56–79.

11. Mary to Eddie, 3 June 1859; Mary to Father, 10 June 1859; R. C. Malone to Miss Belle Edmondson, 25 Oct. 1859, EFP. For a more complete description of dry cupping, see *Black's Medical Dictionary*, 35th ed., 1987, 176.

12. Margaret Sue Chisman, "Literature and Drama in Memphis, Tennessee to 1860" (M.A. thesis, Duke University, 1942), chap. 3 passim. See also Clifton Joseph Furness, *The Genteel Female* (New York: Knopf, 1931); Fred Lewis Pattee, *The Feminine Fifties* (New York: D. Appleton-Century Co., 1940).

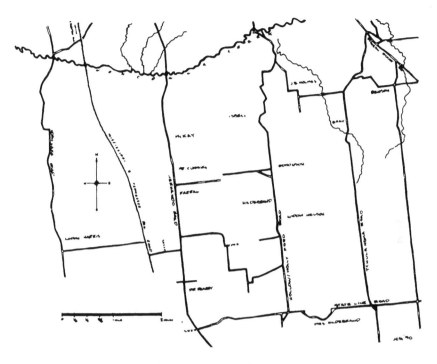

Map of Memphis Environs c. 1863

This map of Memphis and environs, drawn in 1863 by a Federal officer, shows the main roads leading into the city from the south and southeast. The Pigeon Roost Road [now U.S. 78] and the Hernando Road [now U.S. 51] were the main arteries then, as today. The Pigeon Roost Road was the old Chickasaw trail that ran southeast from the Mississippi River. The Hernando Road ran almost due southwards towards Jackson, Mississippi. Other roads were the Tchulahoma Road, the Horn Lake Road, and the Holly [Hollow] Ford Road.

Elm Ridge, the Edmondson home (a story-and-a half log structure), was located on the Holly Ford Road, about three miles from the Mississippi state line and eight miles from the heart of Memphis. Like most of the property in the neighborhood, Elm Ridge was a farm, not a plantation. Today the old house site is occupied by the Memphis International airport.

Federal picket posts were at Nonconnah Creek some three miles from Elm Ridge. The Confederate pickets and "Dixie" were thirty miles away, on the south bank of the Coldwater River. The area in between was a virtual no man's land where both sides skirmished and raided.

strolling players toured there in 1829, it had become by 1860 the sixth largest city in the South. James D. B. DeBow commented in his 1859 *Review* that Memphis was rapidly becoming a center of commerce and intercommunication between North and South. The town's rapid growth over a thirty-year period was the result of its location on the Mississippi River and the presence of railroads. Two important railroads, the Mississippi & Tennessee and the Charleston & Memphis, terminated there. DeBow reported that a trip from Charleston to Memphis took forty-two hours—not on the same rail line.[13]

Much of the city's wealth came from cotton. Within a 100-mile radius of the Memphis cotton markets were some of the most fertile cotton-producing areas in the country. When the Edmondsons moved to the Memphis vicinity, the city had six newspapers, three female seminaries, two medical schools, twenty-one churches and public schools, and a popular theatre.[14]

When Belle was twenty, she met Carlo Patti, a concert violinist and composer who had recently arrived in Memphis. To a young small-town woman like Belle, Patti, who came from a family of renowned opera singers, must have seemed glamorous. Carlo was born between acts of *Norma* in the Theatro Madrid, where his mother, a "fiery soprano," was singing the lead![15]

Before coming to Memphis, Patti had been orchestra leader at the Varieties Theatre in New Orleans and was credited with being the first to popularize the song "Dixie," which he used as a drill number in a burlesque of Indian dramas called *Pocahontas*.

Carlo was twenty years old and divorced when he met Belle. Composer and concert pianist Louis Moreau Gottschalk toured with Patti and described him as a handsome Bohemian type whom young girls greatly admired. Gottschalk called Carlo "Sunshine Patti . . . because of the happy thoughtlessness of his character."

In Memphis, Carlo organized local talent and formed the Mozart

13. Gerald M. Capers, *The Biography of a River Town: Memphis, Its Heroic Age* (Chapel Hill: University of North Carolina Press, 1939), chap. 5 passim; Franklin Solomon Smith, *Theatrical Management in the West and South for Thirty Years* (New York: Harper & Co., 1868), 57; G. H. Steukrath, "Memphis, Tennessee," *De Bow's Review* 27 (Aug. 1859): 235–39.

14. Capers, *Memphis*, 134; James D. B. De Bow, "Editorial Miscellany," *De Bow's Review* 27 (July 1859): 112–18.

15. Obituary of Carlo Patti, *St. Louis Globe*, 18 Mar. 1873; Herman Klein, *The Reign of Patti* (New York: De Capo Press, 1978), 431–32.

Club and the Philharmonic Society; it was probably because of Belle's musical talent that she met him. Because Carlo was famous for his romances, Belle's family and friends were horrified when she became involved with him. The Patti romance ended after the war started. Gossip had it that Carlo left Memphis in order to break his engagement to Belle.[16]

When the cataclysm struck the nation in 1861, Mississippi rushed headlong into the Confederacy, but Tennessee did not. In a referendum held February 9, 1861, voters failed to approve a secession convention. Memphis's large foreign-born population was lukewarm to the idea; by June, however, after the firing on Fort Sumter and Lincoln's call for troops, Tennessee finally seceded.[17]

Belle's brother Jimmie organized the Bluff City Grays, Company B, 154th Tennesseee Regiment. A second brother, Eddie, also joined this unit. The Grays were initially sent to Columbus, Kentucky, and later moved into the campaigns in southeast Missouri.

The war in the Western Confederacy was vital to the final outcome of the conflict. Multiple frontiers and problems of command control made for hard times. Creating military departments did not ease the situation but established another level of bureaucracy. The Confederacy had widespread defensive responsibilities and a large area made vulnerable by multiple waterways.

Tennessee, which stretched from the Appalachian Mountains to the Mississippi River across the middle of the South, was strategically important to both sides. Equally important were the Mississippi Valley and the Nashville-Chattanooga-Atlanta corridor.[18]

16. Several sources cite Patti as the first to popularize "Dixie" but all cite the same authority, Mary C. Owens, *Memories of the Professional and Social Life of John E. Owens* (Baltimore: John Murphy & Co., 1892), 110–11; Louis Moreau Gottschalk, *Notes of a Pianist*, ed. Jeanne Behrend (New York: Alfred A. Knopf, 1964), 61, 128, passim; *Memphis Daily Appeal*, 14 Mar. 1860; John W. Keating, *History of the City of Memphis and Shelby County, Tennessee*, 2 vols. (Syracuse: D. Mason & Co., 1888), 1:445; Emily Perkins to Belle, 26 Feb. 1862, EFP.

17. Capers, *Memphis*, 141.

18. Archer Jones, *Confederate Strategy from Shiloh to Vicksburg* (Baton Rouge: Louisiana State University Press, 1961), 113. See also Thomas Connelly, *Civil War Tennessee, Battles and Leaders* (Knoxville: University of Tennessee Press, 1979); John Berrien Lindsley, *The Military Annals of Tennessee, Confederate* (Nashville: J. M. Lindsley & Co., 1886; repr., Spartanburg: The Reprint Co., 1974), 596; John Hallum, *Reminiscences of the Civil War* (Little Rock: Tunnah & Pittard, 1903), 359–61; John P. Young, *Standard History of Memphis, Tennessee* (Knoxville: H. W. Crews & Co., 1912), 339.

The nearly parallel rivers of Tennessee—the Cumberland and the Tennessee—provided tempting invasion routes. Confederate forces evacuated Nashville in early 1862 after they had suffered defeats at Mill Springs, Kentucky, Fort Henry on the Tennessee, and Fort Donelson on the Cumberland.

In April 1862, Union troops massing near Pittsburg Landing, Tennessee, for an advance on Corinth, Mississippi, were attacked at Shiloh. Both of Belle's brothers were in the battle but escaped injury. Belle nursed the wounded from Shiloh at Overton Hospital in Memphis. There she met Major Adam Nase, U.S.A., who was a prisoner of war. He would later assist her when she had difficulties with Federal authorities.[19]

The Battle of Shiloh delayed the Union advance, but Memphis was compromised. The fall of Corinth and Mississippi River fortifications upstream made Memphis so vulnerable that the river battle for the city on June 6, 1862, was very brief. Occupied Memphis became a Federal staging area and supply depot for the Vicksburg Campaign. The campaign to capture that city, however, took another year.

After Vicksburg fell, Federal forces controlled the Mississippi River, but the Mississippi interior was never completely subjugated. Throughout the rest of the war, the state was the scene of almost constant military activity.

Memphis, with its gateway position, was at the hub of Union offensive operations. Thanks to its abundance of supplies and provisions, Memphis also became a "depot of supplies for the hostile army of the interior," as smuggled contraband flowed southward. Bribery and negligence made it difficult for the Federal forces to control smuggling and other illegal activities.[20]

Security was tight on all roads with access to Memphis. Oaths of loyalty to the Union were required before permits could be obtained or before a pass to leave the city could be approved.

Women were especially adept in the art of smuggling. When Fredrick Law Olmsted visited Memphis, he heard tales about local women who concealed goods in their clothing and were said to be bold and shrewd in their deceit.

Smuggling contraband through the lines was considered treason.

19. Diary entry, 30 Apr. 1863; Major Adam Nase to Major General Hurlbut, 1 May 1863, EFP.

20. M. A. DeWolfe Howe, ed., *Home Letters of General Sherman* (New York: Charles Scribners Sons, 1909), 231.

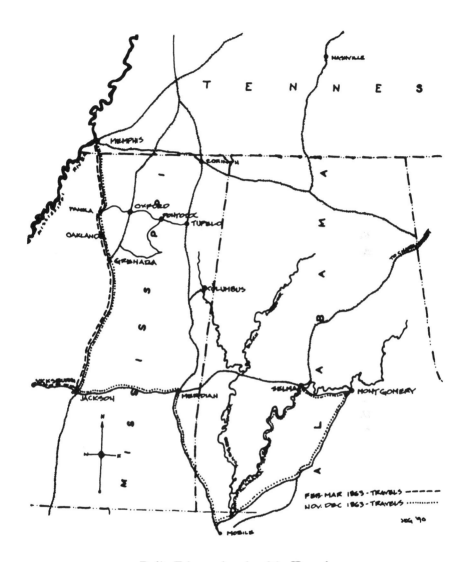

Belle Edmondson's 1863 Travels

In at least one case in 1864, a smuggler was hanged. Spies and informants were everywhere. The dreaded Irving Block Prison, known as the "Bastille," was located in the heart of Memphis and was filled with civilian men and women as well as with Confederate soldiers. The dealings in Memphis were so vice-ridden that one historian noted: "Memphis provided the original scene and design for the corruption of North and South together."[21]

Two published accounts mention Belle's smuggling activities. One was in a book published by a Federal soldier in 1863. According to his account, a "Miss Edmonton" was ordered banished through the lines for waving a Confederate flag at a boatload of prisoners. He related that she smuggled three pairs of fine cavalry boots before being expelled. Belle later presented them to Confederate Generals Sterling Price, Earl Van Dorn, and John Pemberton at Holly Springs. A newspaper clipping describing this incident is among her papers.[22]

The other account was in a Confederate officer's memoirs written long after the war. Although he does not refer to Belle by name, he wrote that a "brave woman" had been able to slip through the lines with medical supplies and enough gray cloth for his wedding suit. The officer, Captain William Clark Kennerly, was mentioned in Belle's 1863 diary and in some of her letters. Belle's father wrote to Belle about Kennerly's suit material in a letter dated November 11, 1862.[23]

It must have been some time after the fall of Memphis that Belle met the Missouri troops she later adopted. She and her friend Hal Rodgers designed a flag for General Price. His note of appreciation and the flag design are among her papers. Belle also received letters from Missouri officers telling her that their troops would hold her name in "sacred honor," and that her self-sacrifice and patriotic de-

21. For a description of Memphis under military rule, see Ernest Walter Hooper, "Memphis, Tennessee, Federal Occupation and Reconstruction 1862–1870" (Ph.D. diss., University of North Carolina, 1957); Joseph H. Parks, "A Confederate Trade Center Under Federal Occupation, Memphis, 1862–1865," *Journal of Southern History* 7 (Aug. 1941): 289–314; Jane Turner Censer, ed., *The Papers of Fredrick Law Olmsted: Defending the Union*, vol. 4 (Baltimore: Johns Hopkins University Press, 1986), 554–55; Jonathan Daniels, *Prince of Carpetbaggers* (Philadelphia: J. B. Lippincott Co., 1956), 60.

22. James Duggan, *History of Hurlbut's Fighting Fourth Division* (Cincinnati: E. Morgan Co., 1863), 165.

23. William Clark Kennerly, *Persimmon Hill, A Narrative of Old St. Louis and the Far West* as told to Elizabeth Russell (Norman: University of Oklahoma Press, 1948), 245.

votion would "make your name a household word to the Army of the West."[24]

In addition to providing supplies, residents of occupied Memphis also furnished information about enemy activities. Scouts and their contacts kept the Confederate commanders informed of the location and movement of Union forces.

Captain Thomas H. Henderson led one detachment of these scouts that operated in the west Tennessee/north Mississippi area. At first glance, Henderson seems a strange choice as leader of a company of scouts. He was a middle-aged man from New Orleans who had been a commission merchant before the war; his roots were in west Tennessee, however, and he was related to General James R. Chalmers of Holly Springs, Mississippi.[25]

Henderson received permission from General Pierre G. T. Beauregard to raise a company of independent scouts less than a month before the Battle of Shiloh. The mission of the detached unit was "to scour the country in the face of the enemy, to arrest the disaffected, to harrass [sic] the enemy, and report his movements."

The men Henderson collected were excellent horsemen from Kentucky, middle and west Tennessee, Alabama, north Mississippi, Arkansas and Louisiana; one man was a "horse-shoer" from Ohio. Scouting was a dangerous occupation. The scouts, "spies if you will," were the eyes and ears of the army. Always between the lines, they often masqueraded as local people, giving out false information and obtaining valuable facts in return. "Those whose nerves could stand it loved the duty and the danger," wrote one ex-scout years after the war.[26]

Perhaps it was the duty and the danger that attracted Belle to the scouts' service. No doubt other women in the South performed similar work, but no records exist. The extent of Belle's service is evident from her papers. Although her work is never in the documents called spying, the family oral tradition holds that she was indeed a spy. Belle was an attractive young woman. She may have obtained

24. General Sterling Price to Belle, 5 Nov. 1863; Major Thomas H. Price to Belle, 24 Nov. 1862; Gratz A. Moses to Belle, 28 Jan. 1863; Major H. W. Tracy to Belle, 16 Mar. 1863, EFP.

25. Obituary of Samuel Henderson [Thomas Henderson's brother], *New Orleans Daily States*, 25 Feb. 1891; W. L. Alexander to C. P. Newton, 24 Mar. 1917, Confederate Collection, TSLAN, cited hereafter as CC.

26. Thomas Henderson and A. J. Tully to General [P.] G. T. Beauregard, 10 Mar. 1862; General Beauregard's endorsement, 20 Mar. 1862, RG 109, NA; J. L. Weaver to Mr. & Mrs. J. A. Clark, 5 Apr. 1917, CC; R. B. Anderson, "Secret Service in the Army of Tennessee," *Confederate Veteran* 21 (1913): 345.

information about movements of troops, as well as supplies and ammunition, by talking to and flirting with young Union soldiers. A
facetious bet she made with a soldier from the 16th Army Corps
about which side would win the war remains among her papers.

In 1863, Belle was engaged to Dr. Gratz Ashe Moses, a friend of
Captain Kennerly. Dr. Moses was a surgeon attached to General
Pemberton's command. The story of the romance's end is recounted
in her 1863 diary, a slim, pocket-sized book, which may have been
intended as a record of trips taken but also recorded her heartbreak.

The letters Belle received in 1863 flesh out the story told in the
diary. A reader of these letters wonders why Belle was jilted by Dr.
Moses. Perhaps he learned of the Carlo Patti romance. The dictum
of the era was, as Mary Chesnut wrote, that "no young girl should
be the heroine of an inexplicable affair."[27]

The risks Belle took in smuggling and gathering information may
have lowered the esteem in which her fiance held her. One Confederate officer stationed in north Mississippi may have had Belle in
mind when he wrote that it demoralized a young woman to be
among the traffickers and smugglers of Memphis. "Some of our best
and most polished girls have been gradually driven from the high
ground of modest demeanor."[28]

Belle was devastated by the rejection and may have been suicidal.
Major Thomas H. Price, one of Dr. Moses's friends, wrote her a
long, strange letter. His prose was so flowery and obtuse that it
seemed to be written in a code—the style of writing Mark Twain
referred to as "Sir Walter Scott's disease." The gist of that letter
appeared to be the following advice: "and I must believe that one
who has exhibited *so much* fortitude, and encountered so many dangers for the good of others & a beloved country in distress, will at
least exercise some of that large store of virtue for self-protection."[29]

Belle's 1864 diary continued the story begun in the previous one.
Feelings of self-pity and isolation from the rest of her family were
constant themes. She feared for her sanity and thought God was
punishing her. The number of letters from her military correspondents decreased.

Belle continued her smuggling, mail transportation, and infor-

27. C. Vann Woodward, ed., *Mary Chesnut's Civil War* (New Haven: Yale University Press, 1981), 556.
28. William M. Cash and Lucy Sommerville Howorth, eds., *My Dear Nellie: The
Civil War Letters of William L. Nugent to Eleanor Smith Nugent* (Jackson: University
Press of Mississippi, 1977), 164.
29. Major Thomas H. Price to Belle, 4 Dec. 1863, EFP.

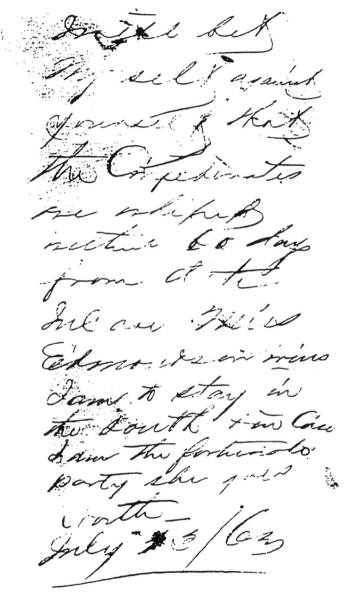

Belle's Bet with Union Sympathizer

"I will bet myself against yourself that the Confederates are whipped within 60 days from date[.] In case Miss Edmondson wins I am to stay in the south in case I am the fortunate party she goes North—July 3/63" [unsigned, written on back of pass through the lines]

mation-gathering activities in and out of Memphis, though on a lesser scale. The authorities were closing in on her. Finally, a warrant was issued for her arrest. With the help of Captain Samuel Woodward, General Benjamin Grierson's handsome adjutant who had an eye for the ladies, she avoided arrest and returned to Elm Ridge. But her days at home were numbered; after an explosive visit from her pro-Union friend and confidante, Miss Em, she was forced to flee south.

Belle reached the safe haven of Waverley on a hot day in July, 1864. It is not known how long she remained there. Her extant writings ended at Waverley on November 21, 1864.

When did Belle's exile end? She was at Waverley in 1865 as an honoree at a ball held there on December 21. No other facts are known.

Belle's postwar years can be partially reconstructed from the meager documents available: three letters from Helen to Belle, dated January 17, 1868, August 23, 1869, and December 25, 1870; an 1872 letter from Jefferson Davis to James Phelan; and the 1873 diary of Belle's cousin Martha Titus.

The tone of the letters indicates that the sisters were close. Belle was unmarried and living at Elm Ridge. Helen lived in Holly Springs, where her husband Brodie Crump was a successful merchant. Helen's letters told of her two small children and their love for Aunt Belle; her servant problems (she wanted to get Laura, Belle's ex-slave, but Laura had a baby); and her yearning for news from home. In the last letter, Helen asked Belle to visit and bring her music while Brodie was on a business trip to New Orleans.

Helen died in 1871. Belle's father died the following year. After their father's death, Belle's brother Eddie and his wife and two children lived at Elm Ridge with the spinster sisters, Belle and Joanna. By then, their widowed sister Mary Anderson (who had lived with during the war) had remarried and lived nearby. Helen's motherless children visited Elm Ridge during the summer of 1872 and were admonished in a letter from their father to obey their "dear good aunts." [30]

The Jefferson Davis letter and Martha Titus's diary offer a glimpse of the last two years of Belle's life. Davis came to Memphis in late 1869 and was followed by his family later. He was president of the Carolina Insurance Company, and Belle's brother Jimmie was general agent. On August 6, 1872, Davis wrote to James Phelan about

30. Brodie Crump to Will Crump, 27 June 1872, EFP.

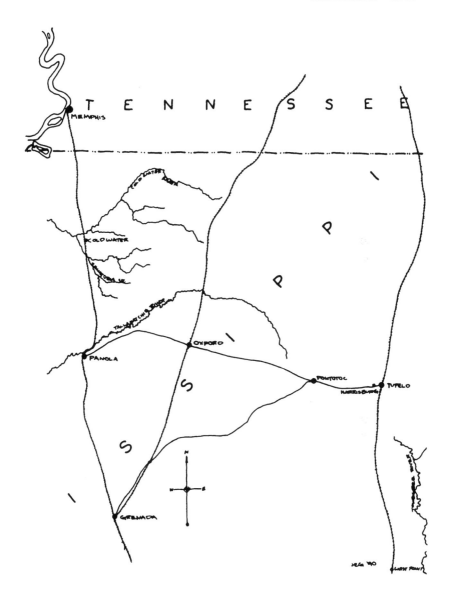

In Refuge, 1864

his son: "Billy went to the country [Elm Ridge] with Miss Belle Edmondson, and notified us that he will come to see us, if he first has a promise that he may return to the country." Young Billy Davis died two months later of diphtheria.[31]

As Belle moved in and out of the pages of Martha Titus's 1873 diary, she seemed to be at the center of some family controversy. On June 1, Martha noted, "Belle E is with us and in a most uncomfortable frame of mind." On June 19, Martha visited Mrs. Davis to discuss "Belle's affairs." Finally, in an entry dated July 1, Martha wrote: "Belle E announced her engagement to Col H today." She gave no clue as to his identity.

Two weeks later, Belle was dead. "Before daylight this morning Jimmy Murrell brought us the tidings of Belle's most unexpected death." She was buried the next day beside her parents at Elmwood Cemetery in Memphis. Her death went unrecorded in the local newspapers. No death certificate was issued.[32]

Jefferson Davis was in the process of being maneuvered out of his job with the Carolina Insurance Company but took time to write his wife in Baltimore: "You have of course heard of the sudden death of Miss Belle Edmondson." That was all. He made no mention of the cause of her death.[33]

One of Belle's nephews (her brother Eddie's son) commented on her death in an interview recorded shortly before his own death. He was born long after his aunt died, but he spoke of what he remembered having heard:

> I'm going to tell you something maybe lots of people don't know. You see, when Aunt Belle died, she was engaged to marry a Yankee officer. And when she died, she died right now. . . . They think she was poisoned. Medicine. It was a prescription they had filled. Whoever filled it didn't know how to fill it or something. Now that's what was said . . . that's what I heard Father tell. . . . She was sick in bed and they had a prescription filled in Memphis. And they'd given her one dose of this medicine and when she took that, she just threw her hands up and hollered "Mother" one time, and she was gone. [Father] said [it was] the only thing they could figure out. She wasn't too bad sick.[34]

31. Jefferson Davis to James Phelan, 6 Aug. 1872, Nannie Mays Crump Collection, LC.

32. Martha Titus diary, Special Collections, MSUM.

33. Jefferson Davis to Varina Davis, 23 July 1873, Special Collections, UAT.

34. Interview with Thomas Ridgely Edmondson, Nov. 1963, taped by a relative, EFP.

There is no evidence to support the nephew's claim that Colonel H was a Yankee. Perhaps this was a tale that grew over the years around this legendary relative.

Although Memphis suffered little during the war compared to other southern cities, the bitterness and animosity that were part of the war's legacy lingered for a long time. Many of the town's prominent citizens were financially ruined. Tensions existed among the four distinct groups in the city: Negroes, Federal troops, merchants from the North, and locals.[35]

Local gravestone inscriptions indicate the depth of feeling. Some of the neighbors mentioned in Belle's diary are buried in the Edmondson Cemetery, named for another family. One gravestone bears this inscription: "I have no flag or country since 1865. An alien in the land my forefathers defended in war since 1624." A stone in another local cemetery reads: "To my . . . noble, gentle, brilliant and brave brother, killed for defending his home against the most envious lot of cut throats that ever accursed the face of the earth."[36]

Two writers who visited Memphis during the postwar period commented on conditions there. Whitelaw Reid thought the men of Memphis seemed "overwhelmed and prostrated under the sudden stroke of calamity"; and Lafcadio Hearn had an impression of "a place that had been stricken by some great misfortune beyond recovery."[37]

Occupied by Federal troops until 1869, Memphis was the site of a race riot. Jefferson Davis's presence was a further reminder of what had been lost.

Some months after Belle's death, Martha Titus wrote in her diary that Colonel Hamilton had come to call, and sister Tate had a picture of this colonel in her photograph album. A history of Memphis contains a biographical sketch of Colonel Hugh A. Hamilton. He was an ex-Confederate officer who became a resident of the city in 1867. Thirty-nine years old when Belle died (she was thirty-three), he did not marry until 1882. "He was highly educated and his taste for literature and science led him to devote most of his leisure time to

35. Capers, *Memphis*, 163.

36. Charlotte Edmondson Elam, Margaret Inabinet Erickson, and Ruth Wyckoff Hunt, *Gravestone Inscriptions from Shelby County, Tennessee Cemeteries* (Memphis: Milestone Press, 1971), 50, 113.

37. Whitelaw Reid, *After the War: A Southern Tour* (New York: Wilstach and Baldwin, 1866), 295; Lafcadio Hearn, *Occidental Gleanings*, ed. Albert Mordell, 2 vols. (New York: Dodd, Meade and Co., 1925), 1:156.

reading and study." He would not have been a bad match for Belle, and it is tempting to think he was her Colonel H.[38]

It is known that there were three epidemics of dreaded diseases in Memphis in 1873, the time of Belle's "most unexpected death." Smallpox appeared in early winter and was followed by a "malignant type of Asiatic cholera" in June and July. In August, yellow fever was beginning to spread and had reached epidemic proportions by September.[39]

Four days before Martha Titus reported Belle's death, she noted that Joanna was very ill and the next day recorded that Belle was quite unwell. It is possible that Belle was the victim of one of that summer's epidemics.

Belle Edmondson was a musician and poet. Her death ended a troubled life. Often at odds with family members and authority figures (especially males), she may have been too liberated for an age that demanded rigid protection of females. Women who grew up in the decade before the war have been called a lost generation. Accustomed to regarding themselves in terms of their relationships to the males in their lives, they were "more conscious of being wives, mothers, daughters, and sisters" than of being independent people. Spinsterhood was not a happy choice for them. As it turned out, Colonel H—regardless of where his loyalties lay—really was Belle's last chance.[40]

After her death, Belle Edmondson was forgotten. The story of her heroic deeds for the "good of others and a beloved country" was lost, unrecorded in area histories of the war. No chapter of the United Daughters of the Confederacy was named in her honor, although one was named for her friend Annie Perdue. Annie was banished from Memphis, while Belle was convinced that she would be sent to Alton Prison if arrested. Of course, Annie married a certified Confederate officer.[41]

The men who caused Belle so much grief also survived the war. Carlo Patti, thirty-two and almost penniless, died in St. Louis the same year Belle did. His obituary described him as erratic in char-

---

38. O. F. Vedder, *History of the City of Memphis and Shelby County, Tennessee,* 2 vols. (Syracuse: D. Mason & Co., 1888), 2:33–34; first volume by John M. Keating.

39. Young, *Memphis,* 157.

40. Marjorie Stratford Mendenhall, "Southern Women of a 'Lost Generation,'" *South Atlantic Quarterly* 33 (1934): 334–36. See also E. Merton Coulter, *Lost Generation* (Tuscaloosa: University of Alabama Press, 1956), and Ann Firor Scott, *The Southern Lady: From Pedestal to Politics 1830–1930* (Chicago: University of Chicago Press, 1970).

41. J. Harvey Mathes, *The Old Guard in Gray* (Memphis: C. S. Toof, 1897), 279.

acter and loose in habits but generous and warm-hearted. His wife was the opera singer Nully Pieris, who gained notoriety as a witness in the Jim Fisk murder trial.[42]

Dr. Moses returned to St. Louis and became a prominent gynecologist. He suffered a fall and was paralyzed the last seventeen years of his life. He lived into the 20th century and was survived by his wife and children.[43]

The lives of Belle, Patti, and Moses, like those of many who survived the Civil War, exemplified what Sherwood Bonner called "the splendid excitement of passionate tragedy."[44]

42. Carlo Patti obituary; W. A. Swanberg, *Jim Fisk: The Career of an Improbable Rascal* (New York: Charles Scribners, 1959), 112.
43. Dr. Moses obituary, Necrology files, MHSSL.
44. Sherwood Bonner, "From '60 to '65," *Lippincott's* 18 (Oct. 1876): 500.

Chronology

1780   Belle's grandfather, Lieutenant Robert Edmondson, Jr., distinguished himself at the Battle of King's Mountain.

1787   The first year of taxes and polls in the area that became Davidson County, Tennessee. The Edmondsons, Buchanans, and Tituses listed as residents. Robert Edmondson, Jr., survived an attack by Indians at Neely's Bend, Tennessee.

1793   Birth of Andrew Jackson Edmondson, Belle's father, named in honor of a neighbor.

1812   Andrew Jackson Edmondson mustered into service as ensign with Thomas Williamson's regiment of Tennessee volunteers.

1814   Edmondson made orderly sergeant in Captain Thomas Jones's regiment of mounted gunmen at Battle of New Orleans.

1818   Andrew Jackson Edmondson married Jane Scott Walton in Maury County, Tennessee.

1819   Death of Jane Scott Walton Edmondson after birth of son, Robert Walton Edmondson.

1822   Edmondson married to Mary Ann Howard, Belle's mother.

1824   Edmondson elected sheriff of Limestone County, Alabama.

1834   Edmondson surveyor in the Chickasaw Cession lands.

1836   Edmondson appointed Receiver of Public Monies and Recorder of Deeds at Pontotoc, Mississippi, during the Indian land sales.

1840   Birth of Isabella Buchanan Edmondson at Pontotoc.

1849   Edmondson elected clerk of chancery court in Holly Springs, Mississippi. Daughters attended Franklin Female College there. Family home was "beautiful Blythewood."

1856   Family moved to farm at North Mount Pleasant in northern Marshall County, Mississippi.

1859   Belle completed education. Had strange illness.

1860   Edmondsons moved to Elm Ridge, a farm in Shelby County, Tennessee. Belle met Carlo Patti, popular concert violinist, composer, and orchestra leader.

1861   Death of Belle's mother. Brothers off to war. Belle engaged to Carlo Patti.

1862   Carlo Patti romance over. Memphis fell to Federals. Belle banished from city for waving a Confederate flag. Belle adopted Missouri troops, began smuggling through the lines.

1863   Belle engaged to Dr. Moses. Began work for Captain Henderson's Independent Scouts. Engagement ended. Made Heroine of Jericho at Christmas.

1864   Warrant issued in Memphis for Belle's arrest. She took refuge at Oxford, Pontotoc, Tupelo, and Columbus. Extended visit at Waverley.

1865   Belle at Waverley for ball in late winter.

1869   Jefferson Davis in Memphis as president of Carolina Insurance Company.

1871   Death of Helen Edmondson Crump.

1872   Death of Belle's father.

1873   Belle engaged again. Sudden death at Elm Ridge two weeks later.

Who's Who in the Documents

THE FAMILY

Father Andrew Jackson Edmondson (1793–1872).

Mother Mary Ann Howard Edmondson (1800–1861).

Brother Robert Walton Edmondson (1819–1876), Belle's half-brother. Married to Amarilla Ragsdale. Their home was near Columbus, Mississippi.

Sister Jane Scott Edmondson Kilpatrick (1824–1863), wife of Judge William Kilpatrick. Their home was at Pontotoc.

Mollie Mary Holmes Edmondson Anderson (1829–1901), widow of John Adair Anderson, sister-in-law of Confederate General James Patton Anderson. Lived at Elm Ridge until she remarried in 1871.

Jimmie James Howard Edmondson (1831–1884), married to his cousin Mary Titus, deceased. Memphis merchant. Organized Bluff City Grays in 1861. Formed Selma Naval Company to outfit and sail the blockade-runner *Charlotte Clark*.

Joanna Joanna Hay Edmondson (1834–1878), never married.

Tate Sarah Rebecca Edmondson Dashiell (1836–1878), renamed herself Elizabeth Tate. Married to Major George Dashiell, "Bro George." Lived at Elm Ridge during the war.

Eddie Edmund Augustus Edmondson (1839–1913), private. Elected lieutenant in Seventh Cavalry for a short time in 1864.

Belle Isabella Buchanan Edmondson (1840–1873).

Helen Helen Louisa Edmondson (1843–1871), married Major Brodie Crump on June 23, 1864.

Jimmie's Child: Frazor Titus Edmondson (1855–1910).

Tate's Children: Robert Moon Dashiell (1859–1919), Mary Howard Dashiell (1862–1918).

Jane's Children: Mary Kilpatrick (1848–1891), Joshuah William Kilpatrick (1854–?), Andrew Edmondson Kilaptrick (?), Sallie Hobson Kilpatrick (1861–?), Francis Kilpatrick (1862–1866).

Robert's Children: Andrew Scott Edmondson (1852–1923), Robert Yakely Edmondson (1854–1903), Jane Katherine Edmondson (1856–1947), Samuel Gholson Edmondson (1858–?), Hugh Clem Edmondson (1860–1919).

THE KIN

Cousin Frazor Frazor Titus (1800–1870), wealthy cotton factor. A refugee from Memphis after June 6, 1862. His stepmother and first wife were Edmondsons. He was Jimmie's father-in-law.

Cousin Sallie Sara Wilson Titus (1822–1873), second wife of Frazor Titus.

Cousin Mat Martha Titus (1832–1899), oldest child of Frazor Titus and his first wife. Raised Frazor Titus Edmondson.

Jim James Titus (1836–1864), captain of a company of dismounted cavalry. Killed in Nashville campaign.

Johnnie John Titus (1841–1873), rank unknown, served in Paymaster Department, Forrest's Cavalry.

Ebb Ebenezer Titus (1845–1876), private, Forrest's Command. Oldest child of Frazor and Sallie.

Will William Sawyer Titus (1847–1912), private, Forrest's Command. Youngest child of Frazor and Sallie.

Miss Em Emily Ester Dashiell Perkins (1822–1895), sister of Major George Dashiell, Tate's husband. Mother of Nannie, Dashiell and Emily Perkins. Friend of General Grant. Widow of Albert Green Perkins.

Cousin Campbell A. Campbell Edmondson [dates unknown], lt. colonel, De Soto Rangers. Distant kin.

Aunt Mary Mary Walton Gordon (1813–1869), Belle's father's sister-in-law (his first marriage), wife of Robert Gordon, wealthy planter in Pontotoc, Mississippi.

Cousin Jimmie James Gordon (1833–1912), colonel, Second Mississippi Regiment, Armstrong's Brigade. On detached service. Went to Europe in 1863 with Jimmie on the *Charlotte Clark*. Only surviving child of Robert and Mary Gordon.

Cousin Ginnie Carolina Virginia Wiley Gordon (1836–1903), wife of Colonel Gordon, daughter of Yancey Wiley of Oxford, Mississippi. Niece of Jacob Thompson.

THE SERVANTS

The Edmondsons owned eighteen slaves at the time of the 1860 census. These are the only ones mentioned in the diaries:

Laura Belle's maid.

Bettie Tate's maid.

Uncle Elam, Margaret, Kate, Peter, Jack, Jane and Dink.

FRIENDS AND NEIGHBORS

Colonel Perkins G. W. Perkins, relative of Miss Em's by marriage. Father of Prior [Pryor] and Anna. Lived at Bullfrog Corners, Mississippi, just over the state line.

Hal Rodgers Belle's girl friend. Lived outside Memphis, probably near Germantown. Took refuge with Belle in 1864.

Shallie Kirk Belle's friend. Refugee from Memphis in summer of 1863.

Annie Perdue Belle's friend. Engaged in smuggling and moving Confederate mail. Owned a dress shop in Memphis.

MILITARY CORRESPONDENTS

Thomas H. Henderson Captain of a company of Independent Scouts. Commission merchant in New Orleans before the war, with family ties in west Tennessee.

Thomas H. Price Major, Ordnance Department. Nephew of General Sterling Price. St. Louis lawyer before the war. Harvard graduate.

Henry W. Tracy Major, Chief Commissary of Subsistence. St. Louis businessman before the war.

Editorial Procedures

Belle's diaries and her correspondents' letters were not written with a view towards future publication. Diary entries and letters were often written in great haste. We have followed certain editorial procedures in order to make the material read more easily.

Faithful transcription of the original material was the first goal. What was written and how it was written were not changed. Spelling and grammar were left as they were. When corrections were necessary, brackets were used. Proper names were corrected in brackets the first time and silently thereafter. Initials in place of names were left standing when the reference was clear. Unclear names were enclosed in brackets.

Belle's inconsistencies in capitalizing common nouns [tea, Tea, etc.] and omitting the period after abbreviations [Dr Mrs Col] were unchanged. Dashes which were intended to end sentences or make a pause were changed into periods and commas, except where a dash seemed appropriate. In the brief entries of the 1863 diary, more dashes were left than in the longer entries in the 1864 diary.

Ampersands were retained. Belle's use of apostrophes before the s in plurals [soldier's] and commas in words like o'clock [o,clock] were corrected.

Abbreviations

ADAHM   Alabama Department of Archives and History, Montgomery, AL

BEDNC   Belle Edmondson, Diary for 1864, University of North Carolina, Chapel Hill, NC

CC   Confederate Collection, Nashville, TN

CHS   Cincinnati Historical Society, Cincinnati, OH

CHHS   Chicago Historical Society, Chicago, IL

EFP   Edmondson Family Papers, privately held

ISHLS   Illinois State Historical Library, Springfield, IL

KHST   Kansas Historical Society, Topeka, KS

LC   Library of Congress, Washington, DC

MDAHJ   Mississippi Department of Archives and History, Jackson, MS

MHSSL   Missouri Historical Society, St. Louis, MO

MSUM   Memphis State University, Memphis, TN

MSUS   Mississippi State University, Starkville, MS

NA   National Archives, Washington, Dc

PFP   Perkins Family Papers, privately held

SHC   Southern Historical Collection, University of North Carolina, Chapel Hill, NC

TSLAN   Tennessee State Library and Archives, Nashville, TN

UAT   University of Alabama, Tuscaloosa, AL

WC   Waverley Collection, Starkville, MS

. . . and I thought how the War had tried to stamp all the women of her generation and class in the South into a type and how it had failed—the suffering, the identical experience . . . was there in the eyes, yet beyond that was the incorrigibly individual woman: . . .

William Faulkner, *The Unvanquished*

I

The Carlo Patti Romance

LETTERS: 1861–1862

From Emily E. Perkins

Friday night 10 O'clock [n.d.]
[ca. Spring 1861]
Jackson [Tennessee]

My dear Belle,

I have been so much engaged as to render it impossible for me to write to any one—or you would not have [been] apparently neglected— Mrs Humble had another child to day—the necessity of remaining up to give her medicine, gives me little time for you. We leave for Murfrees- boro on Tuesday morning next—and I hope it may prove beneficial to her but her lungs are much involved. I deeply sympathize with you in your loneliness, I do hope you find a patient determination to pursue the path of duty is working for your good. All have trials—All nearly think their trials are harder to bear than any one else had to bear—but be assured "the heart removeth its' own bitterness" and many are the bleeding hearts that have no Hope—no Future—in which to lose, as it were, bitter memories by creating for them new Hopes—and more en- during Joys. Yet strive as we may *alone*, we can not be happy until our hearts are chastened and purified by the Savior's love—Oh! t'is so sweet when deeply troubled, when all looks dark—and no star beams on our earthly path to look beyond and see the Star of the Savior's love ready to light us to Him. So sweet is it—when all seem to have forsaken us— to lean upon his bosom and feel the arms of his Mercy encircling us. Dear Belle—this Affliction is sent upon you to draw you to Him—if you resist—and murmur greater still will be the scourge—heavier the blow.

I wrote to Nannie a few days since but suppose she may be at your Fathers. I often think of my pleasant visit to you all, and only wish I may have it in my power to repeat it. With regard to your plan of getting a situation in New Orleans, I would not advise you even to think of it— A great City is not the place for an unprotected woman, especially dear Belle for one so entirely uninitiated into the worlds ways as you are— Men are full of deception—A young pure girl—full of trust must be protected by those who love her. Tis hard enought to be thus circumstanced when years of experience and observation have taught one caution—but I can't conceive a greater Misfortune to an unprotected woman than to be alone in such a place as N. Orleans.

I approve your plan of Teaching if—as it will be a pleasure and profit to you—but seriously I would say to you as to my darling Nannie—go to a smallplace—Oh no! Belle, t'would not do. Have you had *any letters* since I left? I hope you are firm—I heard from a stranger many things concerning P-[Patti] that made [me] feel indignant that *I* had ever received him at all as an acquaintance—

Belle dear—he is very depraved, and the gentleman who mentioned these things to me said Miss N. & Miss K were ruined in the estimation of gentlemen by having received him. I *beseech* you never to *speak* of *him to any one* and do, for your self respect *destroy* every thing you have belonging to him—You did not mention him in your letter—I hope you *know* my mention of him is for your good. Write me what you *feel*—; direct your letter to the Care of Dr. W. H. Lytle—Murfreesboro, Tenn. Emmie sends her love—My love to all, especially Father & Mother— tell the former *I am getting ready to help Lincoln*[1]—Goodbye—

Your aff friend
Emily E Perkins

From Emily E. Perkins

Bolivar [Tennessee] Sept 8th 1861

My dear Belle--

How can I comfort "whom God has not comforted" yet I can sympathize with you. When Nannie's letter came I seized it with eagerness for I had an indefinable dread that I should have bad news, but I

---

1. Emily Dashiell Perkins was "an ardent unionist," according to her son's account of his war experiences. Editors' interview with Kate Pinckney, 4 July 1980; A. H. Dashiell obituary, clipping from unnamed, undated newspaper; A. H. D. Perkins, "Record of Civil War Experiences," ca. 1900, privately held, typescript copy in editors' possession.

thought it would [be] concerning my child, and when I read "our dear Mother is dead"—I can't describe to you the shock at first, and afterwards the acute sorrow the *realization* of the fact brought.[2] She—the fond Mother—devoted Christian & true friend gone—for ever—but only from Earth—in Heaven we may—if we *will* see her again —There she lives, and I fondly trust and believe her Guardian Spirit is permitted to hover around those she loved so fondly upon Earth. So dear one, you may be comforted—tho unseen to mortal vision—yet—trust me, she hovers around you—She will warn and guide you aright. Then too—when your own body must lie down in the dust and your Spirit stand on the edge of the "Dark River" of Death—if its wings are burnished with love to Him—He will bring you in your passage over—and may not *her* Spirit bear you to His feet? This is not an unfounded theory, but borne out by [Reformitive?] teaching. My mind is called to this subject and confirmed in its belief by our Rector's Sermon this morning in which he showed so clearly that every human being has its guardian Angel. Give to God dear Belle—and he will be your Friend. None sorrows for you more than I do—or with your great affliction.

I would like very much to see those letters. Have you even written to him? I do not feel unkindly towards him dear Belle—but I do love you very much; and as I warn Nannie I will talk to and watch over your interest. I cannot think him dead, I heard he was wounded and fear entertained for his life, but I have not heard from him since—Nothing can be known with certainty till the official report of the deaths are given.[3] But he [is] *dead* to you—for he is a *married man*—could God recognize any other marriage is right? Belle I must tell you that he sent Laura his picture and wrote to her and his friend that *she* was *dearer than his own life*—I can't bear to wound you—but I must for your own sake. I will not say aught against him —I know how fondly you love him and will try to ascertain for you if he still lives. Let your mind dwell on him as little as possible—Read—paint—engage in charitable Acts—All these are right and will divert your mind. I wish you could be with me— but the employing a Music Teacher is the promise of the Trustees and they retain one they have had for 2 years past. And the hard times do not admit a Teacher for Drawing, Painting &c.

I arrived here on the 30th of Aug. I spent a delightful summer among my friends, notwithstanding Mrs Humble's constant sickness and the

2. Mary Ann Howard died 3 August 1861. Genealogy charts, EFP.

3. Carlo Patti enlisted in the Maury Grays and served in Virginia in 1861. He was reported "killed and resuscitated in several official bulletins." *Memphis Daily Appeal*, 20 June 1861; Klein, *Reign of Patti*, 431.

consequent confinement to myself. I formed some pleasant acquaintances and one firm friendship with a gentleman whom the world calls A
Maniac—he is a Neuromaniac—but, I think I can cure him. Do not
smile at my taste—for I know *you* would love him—handsome—
gentle—highly intelligent—profoundly scientific—in all the ordinary
affairs of life as rational as any one—yet on one subject—you will see
his cheek blanch—his lip grim—and whole countenance change. Driving out with my brother-in-law I met him—and in the momentary
glance of his eye I was fascinated. He too seemed to feel that I sympathized with him—(all in a minute)—He called again & again. And during a severe sickness I had he was one of my Physicians. He told me his
whole habit changed when with me—And my leaving seemed like taking away the spring of life—And why? Simply because I had understood
his Nature—and when with me he could forget his Mania. No don't
think this an attachment of the heart—it is not, only so far as friendship
goes—but I doubt not he will be in the future a happier man—I doubt
not the [illegible] this being foolish —And would suggest the Asylum
for him. When I see you I will tell you all the circumstances. He is a
divorced man—his wife left him because she was afraid of him—poor
woman —she is doubtless an excellent woman—but could no more
understand him than any other impossibility should occur.

I regret so much and sympathize deeply in [illegible] afflictions—
poor Mother! Your heart bleeds, but the Angel baby is happy—that
should comfort you! Yet "Jesus wept" and He will not chide when our
hearts pour out overflowing waters. The bell is tolling now—A young
man is cut off in the Morning of life—poor fellow—he died of Mania
potu.[4] I must stop for the present to attend the service.

Monday morning. I attended the funeral service—so beautiful as it is
in our Prayer book. Poor young wife and children left in poverty.

Emmie sends her love to you, and says you must give her love to all
and kiss all of them for her—"and a kiss for you too." It is near school
time, I intended filling the page—but I must close as I am anxious this
should go this Mail. I will enclose a few lines to Tate. My love to all.
Write soon I will answer promptly. Tell Mollie Ann I will write to her
next.

Your aff friend

Emily E Perkins

Try to be cheerful, 'tis a Christian duty—

---

4. Mania apotu, delerium tremens, *Dorlund's Illustrated Medical Dictionary*, 26 ed.,
1951, 774.

From Emily E. Perkins

Bolivar—Jan 30th, 1862

My dear Belle—

Nannie tells me you are going to Iuka to teach—do you know what you are undertaking? A life of self denial and pain—for you must be—not what you have been the happy girl unrestrained by this or that—but you will have to consider and mark every word before spoken—Oh 'tis a miserable life for a young girl—but for you—t'will be at least an antidote for care. In all my troubles dear Belle I have felt thankful I was compelled to be employed *mentally*. (My pen is so bad I can scarcely write at all—) And you will find in the constant employment a cure of ennuyi [sic]—but do not out of school hours when your body will lassitude [sic] give way to gloomy thoughts—but rather employ yourself in *judicious* reading—Avoid as you would a *Cobra* all exciting reading—t'will produce or rather incur the feverish state into which you have already fallen.

In reference to the package you sent me[5]—You *know* dear Belle all I can say about that matter, but *I know* too, how the heart will yearn for communion with one it loves—and I can sympathize with and pity with my whole soul. The letters to a stranger seem full of affection—do you not know Belle that we can *write* any thing. Did he when with you, and tempted by another evince the same affection? Search the past and answer me! The Italian character is passionate, vindictive—*forgetful*—you think now he can't forget you—My dear child, it gives me much pain to probe your heart thus, but I fear for you—In pique—he broke the miniature—and in remorse he turns to you—he cannot but feel grateful for his untiring affection and thought for his comfort and for your sake I would like to feel sure it is the love that would endure the chances and changes of this life—so full of variations—so trying to the heart's best affections! He is a boy almost—his associations among women—excluded as he has been by the ban of society from her virtues and pure generally—has been such as to accustom him to look lightly upon women and their affections—he is like a child in playful friendship—and like one too in being charmed with every new face. Belle how can, why must I reiterate to you that he left Memphis more than aught else to *rid himself* of his engagement to you! He went—never expecting to return—nor intending to do so.

In my last conversation with your Mother you were the burden of our

---

5. Carlo Patti's letters to Belle were extant until a few years ago but have since disappeared. Interview with Betty Lou Stidham, Mar. 1981.

thoughts and conversation—and her last words almost prophetic they seem to me—were "Oh! Take care of my child—my Belle—" And frequently she would say during our drive—"Oh! keep her from marrying him I fear she will be a deserted wife"—Belle, Belle my child, I am not a stern judge I know how bitter the anguish of casting him off—but how *infinitely* more bitter to be a deserted wife—all hopes of happiness from *any* source cut off & denied you. There is no hope of happiness save in pursuing the path of duty. God has already severely afflicted you in taking from you your Mother—He may the more afflict—allow you to follow your own course and marry him—I hope not for your sake and your Father's gray hair and *Mothers memory*. You asked me to write to you freely as your Mother would—I have written *more* freely—for she told me she feared to say *all* she felt to you you were so unhappy. I think this was unwise—Belle you are a *woman*. You have more than ordinary mind—You *can* endure—you can show an amount of perservence and energy few girls are capable of—why then in this—tho a trial—not show yourself equal to it—My child be firm—*do not* I pray barter your happiness for a bauble—a chimera.

Forgive me Belle for talking plainly to you. But if you could only hear how *all* speak of him—who know his private life you would avoid him. I like him as far as I *know* him personaly—but I like not his want of honor and independence. You did very wrong Dear Belle to let him have your diguereotype [sic]—Suppose he was killed or wounded—and your likeness found in his possession—what a blot upon your fair fame and name. You may said Eddie has Nannie's—but his *name* is honorable. Don't feel angry—all I say to you is because I love you—And because that Angel Mother's last words are ever ringing in my ear when I think of you. I can't help—except by my sympathy—look to Him who alone has power to *know* all hearts.

With regard to your new home I am told 'tis very pleasant—And in the summer quite beautiful—I have a friend who is there occasionaly—Mr Severson of Miss. If you meet him—you will find him pleasant. What will you teach—the ornamental branches? Write to me frequently and tell me all you feel and think—this is the last time I will raise an objection—And I have done this because you asked me to advise you—As did *she.* I hoped very much to see you—but we will hardly meet before summer. I want—if possible—to go to Memphis before I go up the country this summer—When will your school close? I beseech you not to send your *money to those who will spend it on sensual pleasure.* If you have to give [it] away bestow it upon the destitute widows and orphans this war has made. Did your Father consent to your teaching? Oh

I want so much Belle to *tell* you all this—I fear that on paper t'will seem cold & hard & stern—but 'tis not—and while I write I yearn to put my arms around you and banish the throb of pain t'will occasion. I will preserve your package safe—no one will see it. Tell me what you are going to do in the matter—I will love you none the less—only pray that God will avert evil from you. Goodbye. I have been too sad to write before this.

Your aff friend
Emily E. Perkins
Love to all.

From Emily E. Perkins

Bolivar, Tenn. Feb 26th 1862

My dear Belle—

The multiplicity of cares with which I have been burdened since the receipt of your letter has tended to prevent my replying, but aside from this, I scarce know how to reply—how to write the letter you wished—whether to let him know your determination was the result of the family opposition or your own sense of right—and in what terms to express it—whether to convey to him the sense of your determination being irrevocable or not—while thus waiting and pondering. I hear Patti is in Memphis[6]—could I afford it I would go to Memphis on Friday morning ('tis fast day, no school) and see him for you. I suppose you have seen him, and I fear have let him see tis no work of yours the breaking the engagement, if you have had the strength to break it at all. I feel deeply for you and would like of all things to be with you. Be firm, and whatever you do—*be firm*—you have given your promise to Jimmie—he knows what is best—do as he wishes. You can't tell Patti you *do not love him*—I don't ask it—but don't encourage him by telling him again how deeply you are attached to him. I fear you will attend his Concert if he gives one. Your mourning will be an excuse not to—yet if you have *strength* not to betray yourself—go. Many curious eyes will watch you—be *very* guarded—Let none know how deeply you feel. Don't I pray of you meet him clandestinely—'twill blast your reputation—If you see him—present my regards—but if you must see him get Tate to let you invite him to her house—And let there be an end to the engagement. I

6. Carlo Patti was back in Memphis giving a concert at the Odd Fellow's hall and ready to reenlist. *Memphis Daily Appeal*, 25 Feb. 1862.

am very glad you did not go to Iuka—since the Army have so nearly approached us, 'twould be very unsafe for you. I glean from what a lady of Memphis said here that you are associated somewhat with Patti[7] —so be very careful—A young girl can't be too particular. Nannie has had her hair cut off—I don't think it any improvement to her, but many do. I have fallen heir to her braid which is a decided improvement to me. Oh how much I wish it were in my power to go to Memphis. I go to Jackson tomorrow—I learn there is much excitement there. Tell Tate Mary Ormand Butler is packed up ready to run. But I must close—I am worn out—and as I go tomorrow have some preparation to make. Goodbye dear Belle—may God defend and strengthen you.

Your aff friend
Emily E. Perkins

Write me all that passes between you, I will not blame only counsel.

From James Howard Edmondson

Columbus [Kentucky] Feby 28 [1862]

Dear Bell

I write this note in great haste & shall be forced to be brief—I have just learned that Mr Patti was in Memphis and that you were receiving his attentions as formerly, which Bell I must say very much surprised me even to hear it—my authority is reliable but you do not nor never will know it is someone whom you do not nor will not ever suspect. Bell I thought you promised me you would drop this matter—if you did not, I am forced from what I know to make it a *Sine Qua non* to our agreement and I might almost say to my brotherly love—You cannot imagine Bell the mortification it gives me to think that my Sister will receive the attentions of a man of whom I know so much, that is devoid of honor, and that too—after she has been told of all this by a brother who loves her and in doing so considers only her own good—I cannot now believe but that you have been guilty of this great indiscretion without giving the facts a full consideration—and that after you look at the matter again you will do as I wish you—Everything is upside down here from excitement and I cannot write more. I expect you however or ask you

---

7. Carlo was associated with the Mozart Club and the Philharmonic Society in Memphis. Belle may have belonged to either or both organizations. Ibid., 14 Dec. 1860, 20 Dec. 1860.

that while that man remains in our city that you go out home at once and remain there until he leaves Memphis—

Your affectionate Bro
J. H. Edmondson

To Mr Patti From Belle In Emily Perkins Handwriting
Mr Patti—

Your last letter from Columbia was received only yesterday the previous one, a day or two before. You may be momentarily surprised at the tenor of this—so unlike my former letters—but calm reflection—the advice of my friends, and more than all, my own self respect demand that I should take this step—I wish our engagement to be cancelled from this moment. I have no wish to *share* a heart. In friendship—there is room for all who are worthy —but in Love I must be—as I thought I was, alone. Facts which have come to my knowledge, Mr. Patti, respecting your feelings for—and care towards another, have eradicated from my heart every desire to be more to you than an Acquaintance & Friend—I do not say the pure heart worship I have poured out on the Altar of Love can be directly forgotten—but time and justice to myself will enable me to conquer. My brothers are bitterly incensed against you—should they meet you I could not but fear the consequences.

I am convinced from hearing it from an indisputable *source* that only for a very little while did you even imagine you loved me, and so since as I am thus convinced I request all communication from you to cease. The money was enclosed ready to be forwarded to you. Of course I will not insult you by sending it.

Yr friend
Belle.

From Carlo Patti To Henry Farmer

Head-quarters. Signal Corp's
Tupelo Miss July 8th/62

Dear Brother,

It is a long time since I heard from you, I wrote three or four times but in vain, Henry you write to me.

I have talk to Capt Cummins about you & he told me that immediately he hears from you he will have you detail, so write to me immediately & you shall come with us.

At last when cut off from our homes, friends, & everything. Miss

Laura she is taken from me by that *Scoundrel* of *Union Son of a Dog.*
Breth, may *hell* take him to the devil. Henry I love her yet.

   I am very busy & must close this letter write to me immediately
   Good-by forget never your brother

> Carlo Patti[8]
> Signal Corp's
> Care of Capt Cummins
> Tupelo Miss.

[Note on envelope]

My dear friend *Carlo is already* a *married* man.

Mrs Tannelhill is personaly acquainted with her

> Your brother
> Henry

8. Carlo was a prisoner of war at Camp Douglas near Lake Michigan after the Battle of Shiloh. His sister Carlotta, a well-known opera singer, appealed to the Archbishop of Chicago and Carlo was paroled. By 18 July 1862, Carlo was on detached service with the Signal Corps. Some months later he was listed as a deserter giving concerts in the East. *Memphis Daily Appeal*, 8 March 1862; Gottschalk, *Notes*, 61; Muster rolls: May 1861-Dec. 1863, RG 109, NA.

2

Travels in Dixie

1863 DIARY

February

MONDAY 9 Left Home for Dixie, roads terible—only 10 miles—staid at Mrs Johnson five miles from Hernando.

TUESDAY 10 Traveled to within two miles of Senatobia broke the tongue from the Ambulance. Staid at Mrs Ranes [Raines?]—Raining.

WEDNESDAY 11 Did not get off until one OC—went five miles broke down, staid with Col Bedford.

THURSDAY 12 Started two OC—traveled twelve miles, staid four miles from Panola at Mr Perris—Raining.[1]

FRIDAY 13 Left early, traveled to Oakland three miles from the Cars,[2] and twenty five miles above Grenada. Staid at Hotel—Raining.

SATURDAY 14 Arrived at the Train, at 10 OC—after waiting three hours. (Oh! for patience). Started for Grenada[3]—arrived at that

1. The road Belle traveled after she left Elm Ridge roughly followed the Mississippi and Tennessee Railroad. The towns she passed—Hernando, Senatobia and Panola, Mississippi—were stations on that line. From Memphis it was approximately twenty-two miles to Hernando, thirty-six miles to Senatobia, and fifty-eight miles to Panola. Panola, on the south side of the Tallahatchie River, was the headquarters of Brigadier General Ronald Chalmers, who commanded the Fifth Military District, Department of Mississippi and East Louisiana. Map of the Gulf (West); General Orders No. 1, 10 Mar. 1863, *OR*, 24, pt. 3, 661.

2. Oakland was sixteen miles from Panola. After 1862, the Mississippi and Tennessee line was out of commission between Memphis and Oakland. By 1863, train service was sporadic from Oakland to Grenada. Thomas D. Clark, *A Pioneer Southern Railroad: From New Orleans to Cairo* (Chapel Hill: University of North Carolina Press, 1936), 118; Carlton J. Corliss, *Main Line of Mid-America: The Story of the Illinois Central* (New York: Creative Press, 1950), 196–97.

3. Grenada, one hundred miles south of Memphis, was the headquarters of Major General W. W. Loring, who commanded the First Division. The M & T Railroad

place three OC—at Collins House. Col [Clay] Taylor came round. I went to Mrs Moors [Moore's] private boarding [house] where Mrs Taylor was.[4]

SUNDAY 15 Left for Jackson 8 OC—in company with Col Taylor & Lady—arrived at three—went to Bowman House[5]—a miserable place, but spent a delightful evening. Capt Kennerly came round, with his friend Dr Moses.

MONDAY 16 Col Taylor succeeded in getting a private boarding house—Maj Hunt's which we are very much pleased with.

MONDAY 23 Gen Price came back from Richmond to day, leaves for Arkansas in two weeks.[6]

March

MONDAY 2 Left Jackson for Vicksburg at daylight—on a pleasure trip—in company with, Gen Price and Staff. Mrs Taylor, Mrs and Miss Martin, Mrs and Miss Freeman, Miss Lucy Gwinn and Miss Waugh. Spent a delightful evening at the Castle dancing.[7]

---

joined the Mississippi Central at this town. General Orders No. 5, Organization of the Army, Department of Mississippi and Eastern Louisiana, 21 Jan. 1863, *OR*, 24, pt. 3, 592; Corliss, *Main Line*, 194–95.

4. Colonel H. Clay Taylor, veteran of the Mexican War, was aide to Major General Sterling Price. His wife was Louise Pratte Taylor, daughter of General Bernard Pratte of St. Louis. Necrology Scrapbook, MHSSL; Kennerly, *Persimmon Hill*, 185; M. M. Quaife, ed., *Absalom Grimes: Confederate Mail Runner* (New Haven: Yale University Press, 1926), 111.

5. The Bowman House was the principal hotel in Jackson, Mississippi. Other travelers during the Civil War found it lacking. Sylvanus Cadwallader, *Three Years with Grant* (New York: Knopf, 1955), 74; Albert Deane Richardson, *Secret Service: The Field, the Dungeon, and the Escape* (Hartford, Conn.: Jones-American, 1865), 80.

6. Major General Sterling Price (1809–1867), Governor of Missouri before the war, received his orders for transfer west of the Mississippi River 27 Feb. 1863. Special Orders No. 58, *OR*, 24, pt. 3, 646. For an account of General Price's relations with Jefferson Davis and his efforts to return to the Trans-Mississippi Department, see Albert Castel, *General Sterling Price and the Civil War in the West* (Baton Rouge: Louisiana State University Press, 1968).

7. Castle Hill was a mansion with surrounding moat. It was built in the 1850s for banker Thomas Robbins. In 1865, it was destroyed by the Federal Army. Articles in *The Vicksburg Daily Whig* the first week of March 1863 complained of the dancing parties going on all week long. Samuel Carter, *The Final Fortress: The Campaign for Vicksburg 1862–1863* (New York: St. Martin's Press, 1980), 15, 310; Peter F. Walker, *Vicksburg: A People at War* (Chapel Hill: University of North Carolina Press, 1960), 50.

TUESDAY 3 Gen [Stephen D.] Lee[8] gave Gen Price a Ball at his Hd. Qts. Mrs Willis's Residence. We visited all of our Fortifications around the City, and also the battle ground seven miles above.[9] We have a splendid view of the Yankee fleet oposite the City.

WEDNESDAY 4 Danced at the Castle, on the Green until one OC. Left Vicksburg at three, arrived at Big Black [River] after dark. Walked the Trestle, met another train, proceeded one mile ran off the track, where we went up to Landis's Batery[10] and had a splendid cup of Coffee in honor of Gen Price's visit.

THURSDAY 5 Traveled all night—arrived at Jackson at six OC, this morning.

SATURDAY 7 Mrs Freeman gave Gen Price a Party, went with Maj Maclean spent a delightful evening.[11]

MONDAY 9 Gen Price and Staff left for Arkansas to day. Lucy Gwin, Miss Freeman, Mrs and Miss Martin, Mrs Taylor and myself went as far as Hazelhurst[12] with them. There we bid them a long farewell.

TUESDAY 10 Col Taylor and Lady, Maj Price & Lady left on the six OC train for Mobile. I am all alone to night.

WEDNESDAY 11 Mrs Bredell[13] and I left Jackson six OC this morn-

8. Brigadier General Stephen D. Lee (1833–1908) commanded a brigade, Maury's Division, at Vicksburg. He was in command at Chickasaw Bluffs during the Federal assault there 29 Dec. 1862. After the fall of Vicksburg, Lee was exchanged, promoted to Major General and assigned to command all cavalry in Mississippi. List of Generals under Johnston's Command, 27 Nov. 1862, *OR*, 17, pt. 2, 765; Brigadier General George W. Morgan, "The Assault on Chickasaw Bluffs," *Battles and Leaders of the Civil War*, 4 vols. (New York: The Century Co., 1884), 3:463; S. Cooper to General S. D. Lee, 7 Aug. 1863, *OR*, 24, pt. 3, 1048.

9. The battle of Chickasaw Bluffs was part of the first Vicksburg Campaign, 27 Dec. 1862–3 Jan. 1863. The Union forces under General Sherman suffered great loss of life. Morgan, "The Assault," 465; Lloyd Lewis, *Sherman, Fighting Prophet* (New York: Harcourt Brace & Co., 1958), 256.

10. Captain J. C. Landis and his battery were stationed at Winkler's Bluff on the Big Black River to guard that stream and keep enemy vessels from passing into the Mississippi. R. Hutchinson to Col. Wirt Adams, 10 March 1863, *OR*, 24, pt. 3, 674–75.

11. Probably Major Lauchlan A. Maclean, General Price's A.A.G. General Orders No. 1, 21 July 1862, *OR*, 17, pt. 2, 654.

12. Hazelhurst was a town on the New Orleans, Jackson and Great Northern Railroad. General Price, accompanied only by his staff and a small bodyguard, crossed the Mississippi River 18 March 1863. Clark, *Pioneer Railroad*, map, frontispiece; Castel, *Price*, 139.

13. Angelina Bredell, wife of Edward Bredell, a St. Louis merchant, and mother of Captain Edward Bredell of General Bowen's staff, was known to the Federal au-

ing, arrived in Grenada at three. Went to Hotel, but left very soon for Mrs Frelighs [Freleigh]—Dr Moses and Dr Hanes called and I feel teribly fatigued they staid until twelve OC.

FRIDAY 13 Battle at Greenwood,[14] had a long walk with Dr Moses to listen to the echoes of the distant cannons. Fate—how strange, and yet how blessed and happy. "Oh! who, in the course of his life, has not felt some joy without security and without the certainty of a morrow"—[15]

SUNDAY 15 Attended the Presbyterian Church, with Dr Hanes. Dr Moses came down and spent the evening. Oh! ever memorable, and happy moments—how quickly they pass away. After tea our Sad farewell. "Time hath power over hours, none over the Soule"—

MONDAY 16 We were disapointed in getting off this morning. Dr Moses left for Yazoo with Gen Tilghman.[16] Mrs Hodges [Hodgen] and myself had a lovely ride. Dr Hanes Sister came. We all spent the evening together yet with me there was a void—this is my first trial these are terible times for young Affections.

TUESDAY 17 Mrs Bredell and myself left Grenada on the 7 OC train—arrived at Yockney[17] at 12 OC—got an Ambulance reached

---

thorities at St. Louis as one of the disloyal rebel women who "have been actively concerned in both secret correspondence and in carrying on the business of collecting and distributing rebel letters." Her son was later killed in the Nashville Campaign in the fall of 1864. He was buried in the family garden at St. Louis. Necrology file, MHSSL; F. A. Dick, Provost Marshall General to Col. Hoffman, 5 March 1863, *OR*, II, 5, 319–321.

14. The attack on Fort Pemberton, 11 March–5 April 1863, was part of the unsuccessful Yazoo Pass Expedition. Edwin C. Bearss, *Decision in Mississippi* (Jackson, Mississippi: Mississippi Commission on the War between the States, 1962), chap. 4 passim.

15. In her 1864 Diary, Belle noted that this quote was from Raphael. It was probably from *Raphael's Prophetic Almanac*. Diary entry for Sunday, 14 March 1864, BEDNC, copy of original in editors' possession; *Raphael's Prophetic Almanac* (London: W. Foulsham Publishers, 1863).

16. Brigadier General Lloyd Tilghman (1816–1863) commanded a brigade, First Division, under Major General Loring. He was killed almost two months later at the Battle of Champion's Hill. James Spencer, comp., *Civil War Generals* (New York: Greenwood Press, 1986), 293; General Orders No. 5, 21 Jan. 1863, *OR*, 24, pt. 3, 592.

17. The Yoknapatawpha River [now called the Yocona] shows up on various maps with similar spellings. A Federal officer referred to it as the "Yacona Pataffa" and wrote that the name came from an Indian word meaning oak fruit. Belle's spelling probably comes close to the pronunciation of her day. William Faulkner used this spelling to name his mythical county. Map of the Gulf (West); Colonel William Camm, "War Diary, 1861–1865," Fritz Haskell, comp., *Journal of the Illinois State Historical Society*, 18: 926; Calvin D. Cowles, comp., *The Official Military Atlas of the Civil War* (Washington: Government Printing Office, 1891–1895), plate 154, sheet 19.

Panola at dark. Miserable Hotel. Gen Chalmers, Capt [Thomas] Henderson and several others called after tea. We were bivouaced in the bar room—all visitors recived in the same room.

WEDNESDAY 18 Left Panola early—a weary days travel. Waited three hours at the Ferry—on this side met several Memphians— Celia Carroll on her way to Matrimony. Arrived at Senatobia 10 OC—having walked five miles—the Ambulance being broken. Eat dinner at Sardis. Bivouaced very comfortably to night Hotel de S.

THURSDAY 19 Left Senatobia very late, having to wait for the Ambulance. Arrived at Hernando at 3 OC—passed all of our Cavalry on retreat, at Cold Water Ferry.[18] Bivouaced for the night at Mr Christophers ten miles from Hernando. Mrs B. and I have been quite buisy making preparations to enter the Federal lines to morrow.

FRIDAY 20 Left at daylight, arrived at my Fathers about ten OC. Mrs B. and I staid, the rest went on to Memphis. She will remain several days—until the talk of our arrival has died away. I am happy to reach home yet tis terible to live under Yankee Tyranny—found all well, and everything unchanged at home.

WEDNESDAY 25 Mrs B. left us to day for Memphis—will take the first Boat for St. Louis.

FRIDAY 27 I came in this morning to spend a few days with Shallie [Kirk] & Florence [Molloy], although in the Federal lines. We all attended prayer meeting, and observed our President's fast day. Mrs. B. has not gone yet, met her at prayers.

SATURDAY 28 Shallie and I went on board the Mary Forsyth to bid Mrs B. farewell. I carried all of the letters brought from Dixie, on board and gave them to Mrs MacLean, who is a St. Louis'n and will see them all properly mailed and delivered.

April

WEDNESDAY 29 Tate [Dashiell], Florence, Nannie & myself came to Memphis this noon. I was arrested and taken to Gen Aubrand's [Lauman?] Hd Qts[19] sent back to get a permit. May God forgive me

18. This area, from the Coldwater River to Nonconnah Creek, three miles from the Edmondson home, was a virtual no man's land where cavalry from both sides skirmished and raided. Chalmers's report of 18 March 1863 tells of a series of skirmishes with the enemy, *OR*, 24, pt. 1, 468.

19. No general with this name was found in the list of Union Civil War generals. Belle often spelled names the way she heard them pronounced. Brigadier General Jacob G. Lauman's men were responsible for manning picket posts facing south at the Hernando Road. His name is on the permit she eventually obtained. Belle prob-

if there be sin in hating the Yankees—remained with Florence all night.

THURSDAY 30 Shallie & I went to Maj Nace [Nase], 15*th* Ill whom I nursed while a prisoner in our Hospital[20]—he recovered my things, and kindly gave me a permit, but being old Abe's fast day, I came home without them and will return tomorrow.

May

TUESDAY 19 Shallie Kirk & Mr Geo Atchison[21] came with me Home this evening, no trouble with the Pickets. Mr Atchison leaves in a day or two for the Southern Army—and we were fortunate enough to get every thing through which he will need.

WEDNESDAY 20 Geo Atchison will remain with us a day or two. I love him poor low one—he seems lost. I am very uneasy about him and will prepare his things to night and influence him to leave in the morning.

THURSDAY 21 I found my little friend George easily influenced, and willing to leave this morn if I said so. I am restless I cant account for, he started early. Shallie and I went back to Memphis. God bless Geo, and grant him a safe & speedy trip to dear Gratz.

FRIDAY 22 I returned home this morn. My friend Mrs Clay Taylor and friend Mrs Patton arrived from Dixie. No late news.

SATURDAY 23 Poor Dashiell was taken prisoner first thing this morning—two Regts of Yanks in front of the gate, before we knew anything of it.[22] My uneasiness about Geo is now solved, they took also, three Negros Elam, Lee, and Ben, horses for cash.

---

ably used various roads to enter and exit through the Federal lines. In June she was stopped by General James C. Veatch's pickets at the Pigeon Roost Road post. See General orders No. 61 and 62, announcing the roads to be guarded by the various commands, *OR*, 17, pt. 2, 117–19; endorsement by General J. G. Lauman on back of Major Nase's request for return of Belle's property, 1 May 1863, EFP; endorsement by General Veatch on back of request for return of property taken by pickets 11 June 1863, RG 109, NA.

20. Major Adam Nase was exchanged for Captain Marshall Tate Polk. Thomas Jordan to Colonel P. B. Starke, 30 June 1862, *OR*, Ser. 4, Vol. 2, 794.

21. George Atchison was the young stepbrother of Dr. Moses. Atchison's mother, the widow of a St. Louis builder of steamboats, was a member of the prominent Papin-Chouteau families. Necrology file, MHSSL; Scharf, *St. Louis*, 2: 1531.

22. Dashiell's capture is recorded in the *OR* Report of Colonel Thomas Stephens, 25 May 1863, *OR*, 24, pt. 2, 429–31. Dashiell wrote of his capture at Elm Ridge long after the war: "While sitting on the front porch, deeply interested in *Harper's Weekly* a regt of Yankee Calvalry got to the front gate before I knew it. Taking in the situation at a glance, I ran back through the house to the back gate only to find my horse not

SUNDAY 24 The raide passed in to Memphis this evening. Col Strunk's company allowed our Negros to come home—the horses & Dashiell taken in. Mr Seymour sent for Mrs Taylor and Patton, they went over to Mrs Duke's preparatory to going up River.

July

SATURDAY 4 Vicksburgh, surrendered this morning[23] and an exulting foe, madened by success, imagines the Rebellion crushed—poor deluded fools—tis just begun. Tis God's will you should prosper, and devastate our lovely land so far, and it may be even more than this, yet our faith is perfect. God will bless us. No matter how dim the Star of Liberty may grow, even in Months to come. We are content my Savior, thy will, not ours, be done. "Blessed is the man, whose trust is in thee.["] God is our Sun and Shield, and we will yet come out victoriously free. My poor, poor Gratz where is he—what has he to brighten his hopes. Oh! my Savior, in thy mercy shield him, guide him from all temptation, protect him from disease and harm. And oh! my Father hasten the day which will make us twain. Do not permit me to make him an Idol. I can but tremble even now, with fear, for my deep and holy love. Oh! Gratz, Idol of my heart.

September

SATURDAY 19 Tate, Robert and myself arrived in Panola 12 O clock to day.

SUNDAY 20 Left Panola 1 OC arrived at Grenada 4 OC.

TUESDAY 22 Left Grenada for Panola on train at 8 o-clock A.M. Cars ran off the track & *murdered* a [illegible] No one else hurt but all

---

there. Thinking I could get over the fence, and to the woods before they could pull them down and catch me, I jumped over the fences and into the orchard only to find they had broken down the fences and were right on me and shooting as tho they intended to kill me whether or not . . . I turned and commenced firing at them, and hit a Dutchman in the arm. This seemed to infuriate them to that extent that they could not shoot at all, but while they were at it, Miss Joanna Edmondson, my Southern Mother, ran up and threw herself on me. I don't know whether she knocked me down, or the Yankees, but there we lay, she on top of me and they shooting like the blazes, when a young officer ran up, and knocking their pistols up, ordered them to quit. I was then taken. . . .

23. This entry was obviously written at a later date. The telegraph was down at Memphis and news of the fall of Vicksburg did not reach the city for several days. Captain Henderson had heard rumors but did not hear the news until three days later while he was writing to Belle. See Henderson to Belle, 7 July 1863; Bearss, *Decision*, 445.

badly scared. Reached Panola at 1 o-clock P.M. & found Capt H. & Company anxiously awaiting our arrival.

WEDNESDAY 23 Stayed last night with Mrs Moore. Rose early & had the *blues* all day. Have been troubled with some of Capt H's Scouts all day amongst whom were Lt *McConnell* & S.B. Wilson. Capt H. & Bro [Sam] called on me after Tea. Had quite a nice time but he is so horrid ugly & looks old & is lame besides.[24]

October

SUNDAY 11 "The melancholy days are come the saddest of the year"—[25] How sad, how drear; beautiful, fading Autumn. Each tree from its gorgeous foliage seems crowned king of the forest—How like our hopes and their decay—faded, forgotten.

SATURDAY 17 Went to Memphis this morning—bought for Eddie a beautiful black horse which he named for me. Two or three arrivals from Dixie—Mr Kirk among them. Cousin Sallie [Titus], Sister Mary & I caught in a hard storm, Mr Williams rode Eddie's horse.

SUNDAY 18 Eddie, Ebb [Titus], Mr Imes & Rawlings all left for their command, Forrests Division. They are all fixed for this winter's Campaign.[26]

November

MONDAY 2 Mr Williams and I left home at 8 OC—arrive in Panola 10 OC this evening—no accident. Have not found Mrs Clayton yet. Staid with Mrs Moores.

---

24. Belle is referring to Captain Thomas Henderson, not his brother Sam. Thomas was crippled from a wound received earlier in the year. He was probably in his forties when Belle knew him. An English officer touring the South in the spring of 1863 left this picture of Captain Sam and some of his scouts: "They are a fine looking lot of men, wild and very picturesque in appearance." James Dinkins, *Personal Reminiscences and Experiences in the Confederate Army* (Cincinnati: Robert Clark Co., 1897, reprint ed., Dayton: Press of Morningside Bookshop, 1975), 119; Walter Lord, ed., *The Fremantle Diary—Being the Journal of Lieutenant Colonel James Arthur Lyon Fremantle, Coldstream Guards, on His Three Months in the Southern States* (Boston: Little Brown and Co., 1954), 94, 98.

25. The melancholy days are come, the saddest of the year
    Of wailing winds and naked woods, and meadows brown and sere.
"The Death of the Flowers," by William Cullen Bryant, first published in *New York Review and Atheneum Magazine* Vol. 1 (1832): 485–86.

26. Brother Eddie had been on furlough for sixty days. He probably missed the Battle of Chickamauga, 20 Sept. 1863. Request for furlough with endorsement, E. A. Edmondson to Captain Kinloch Falconer, 16 July 1863, EFP.

T U E S D A Y 3 Left Panola 1 OC—arrived at Grenada at 5 OC. Put up at the DELIGHTFUL COLLINS HOUSE. Decatur [Doyle] and I went round to Mrs Freleighs. We all went round to Mr Bruce and had rather a dull game at cards, arrived back at Collins House 11 OC.

W E D N E S D A Y 4 Brother Jimmie and Mr Rodgers[27] came on the Canton train, did not see much of him, very buisy writing letters all eve. Played cards at Mrs Freleighs had a nice time. Col Case of Mo came home with me.

T H U R S D A Y 5 Left Grenada 11 OC arrived at Canton 5 OC—a miserable time in getting quarters, a room but nothing to eat. Jimmie & Decatur left for up the country. Mrs Warren found our party at Grenada. This is the day of agreement between Capt Ruffin, Rodgers & I.[28]

F R I D A Y 6 Spent the day in Canton on half rations—met with all my friends. Mr Noe's Brother came[29]—Capt Mc and indeed all my friends—had a lively time with Mr Rodgers & Capt Ruffin. Spent a delightful eve. Music &c. A splendid serenade—oh! I am happy once more in Dixie.

S A T U R D A Y 7 Left Canton in Ambulance, a miserable trip. I was delighted to meet Dr Hanes, although it was only for a moment—found all trains crowded, Gen Forrests Division reinforce Bragg. Gen Jackson[30] called to see me, we have a miserable Hotel.

27. Probably Captain Ferdinand Rodgers, McDonald's Battalion, Forrest's Old Regiment. Thomas Jordan and J. P. Pryor, *The Campaigns of Lt. General N. B. Forrest and of Forrest's Cavalry* (New York and New Orleans: Blelock and Co., 1868; reprint ed., Dayton: Press of Morningside Bookshop, 1973), 695. Brother Jimmie formed the Selma Naval Company to purchase and outfit the blockade-runner *Charlotte Clark*. Decatur Doyle, a family friend, was one of the witnesses on James Howard Edmondson's application for a letter of marque and reprisal. Account sheet of Selma Naval Company, privately held, copy of original in editors' possession; application of J. H. Edmondson to J. P. Benjamin, 6 August 1863, United States War Department, *Official Records of the Union and Confederate Navies in the War of the Rebellion* (Washington: Government Printing Office, 1921), Ser. II, 1, 328.

28. Probably Captain James Ruffin, Provost Guard, Co. D, Fourth Mississippi Cavalry, whose headquarters was at Canton, Mississippi. Organization Chart, Jackson's Division, *OR*, 30, pt. 4, 517, 656.

29. A Confederate soldier named Noe was wounded the day after the Battle of Shiloh. Belle nursed him until his death. He was buried at Elm Ridge. His brother may have been Captain James Noe, Assistant Quartermaster, Brandon, Mississippi. *OR*, 39, pt. 2, 708. See diary entry 8 Apr.1864, BEDNC.

30. Brigadier General William Hicks Jackson (1828–1866) commanded a cavalry brigade under Major General Stephen D. Lee after he was exchanged at Vicksburg. Organization Charts, Department of Mississippi and Eastern Louisiana, 20 Aug. 1863, *OR*, 30, pt. 4, 515.

SUNDAY 8 Spent the day in Brandon, took the train for Meridian 3 OC—an awful trip.[31] Did not arrive in Meridian until 4 OC. No sleep, and bored to death by Capt Ruffin's foolishness. Met with Mr Woodson, and heard direct from St. Louis. Mr Elliott I like so much—he is so dignified and gentlemanly.

MONDAY 9 Arrived at Meridian 4 OC this morning. Left 7 o-clock for Mobile a miserable trip did not reach the City until 11 OC at Night. No Cab or any conveyance. After much trouble reached the Battle House where I shall rest until the Ladies return from Bragg's Army.

TUESDAY 10 Took breakfast in our rooms, did not recive baggage until 9 o clock. Dr Moses called at 11 OC—Capt Holland, Dr Nidelet[32] called after dinner, Dr Moses called with them. I am once again happy—have spent a delightful day I have but one trouble, that is having to return to the Yankees.

WEDNESDAY 11 Capt Holland & Dr. Moses gave me a real treat this eve—a delightful ride on Shell Road—also all of our fortifications, and I am confident the Yankees will never take this place. Madam Le Vert & Daughter called.[33] Also made the acquaintance of Gen Polk.[34]

31. Colonel Fremantle rode the railroad from Brandon to Meridian in the spring of 1863. "This piece of railroad was in a most dangerous state, and enjoys the reputation of being the worst of all the bad railroads in the South." Grierson's men destroyed part of this line on their famous raid. Lord, *Fremantle*, 100; Stephen A. Forbes, "Grierson's Cavalry Raid," Illinois State Historical Society, *Transactions*, (1901): 106.

32. Captain Dick Holland was aide to Major General Dabney H. Maury, Department of the Gulf. Dr. Sylvester Nidelet was chief surgeon, Maury's command. Nidelet who was from St. Louis, was a friend of Dr. Moses. Belle smuggled medicines and amputation tools through the lines for him. One of Dr. Nidelist's list requested the following: chlorate of potassium, pulv opium, blistering ointment, morphine, paregoric, laudanum, mercury and chalk, blue mass, mercurial ointment, quinine,and amputating instruments. Special Orders No. 269, Mobile, 25 Sept. 1863, *OR*, 39, pt. 2, 873; List of Hospitals in the Gulf District, *OR*, 45, pt. 2, 718; Nidelet's list, EFP.

33. Octavia Walton LeVert (1810-1877), wife of Dr. Henry LeVert and author of *Souvenirs of Travel* (1857), was a well- known socialite, famous for her parties. When Mobile fell to the Federal forces, she entertained the Union officers as lavishly as she had the Confederates. She was branded a turncoat and ostracized. "Toasting the Town," by Mike Envoy, 9 June 1955, clipping from unnamed newspaper, vertical files, Mobile Public Library; John Kent Folmar, ed., *From That Terrible Field: Civil War Letters of James M. Williams* (Tuscaloosa: University of Alabama Press, 1981), 165, 175; Carl Holliday, *A History of Southern Literature* (Port Washington: Kennikat Press, 1906), 253.

34. General Polk refused to serve under Bragg after the Battle of Chickamauga and was transferred to Mississippi. He spent a few days in Mobile sometime between November 7 and 13. Joseph H. Parks, *General Leonidas Polk, CSA* (Baton Rouge: Louisiana State University Press, 1963), 353-55.

THURSDAY 12 Mrs Clayton & friend left for the Army, I remain in Mobile until they return—Mrs Fackler, Sallie & Sam Elder and others arrived from Memphis this eve. Dr Moses called around and staid until they came.

FRIDAY 13 Dr Nidelet called early, we all went round to Snow's Music Store and had a real treat of Music Violin & Piano. Very unexpectedly I left Mobile with the Memphis crowd—we had a nice trip. Gen Cheatham[35] came up and fortunately we had a car to ourselves.

SATURDAY 14 Mrs Fackler & Ladies left for La Grange [Georgia]. I spent the day at Montgomery. Hal took passage on Jeff Davis for Selma having heard Shallie was there. My Brother will also be there. Passed the day very well reading Romances of a poor young man— Dr Moses recommended.

SUNDAY 15 When waking found the boat 43 miles above Selma—on account of fog, did not reach Selma until 11 o-clock—found Shallie at Church. Several Memphians are here—boarding in the Bank. Oh! I was so happy to meet Shallie—Maj Price is here also. Shallie wrote to Dr Moses, I to his Brother [George Atchison].

MONDAY 16 Spent the day drearily enough. Shallie and I together. Mrs Woodson and Mrs Hendricks called. Jimmie came on the Train I did not see him to Night.

TUESDAY 17 Jimmie and Mr Moon[36] came round. Shallie recived a letter from Dr Moses. Oh! I am so unhappy—miserable how desolate, how drear the future is to me. Spent the evening at Dr Hendricks.

WEDNESDAY 18 Shallie and I are on board St Charles bound for Mobile under care of Mr. Vance. Misery—misery—misery. Little Jimmie Cameron, what a beautiful child. I would give any thing if he was mine.

THURSDAY 19 Spent the day passably well—formed the acquaintance of a sweet Ladie from Mobile Miss Garro—finished my book, played cards &c—had a dance on the boat. I played—in a manner— they danced the Lancers.

FRIDAY 20 Reached Mobile 10 o-clock—found Jimmie here, by R.R., Mrs Linnser and several friends. Shallie, Jimmie, Mr Vance

35. Major General Benjamin F. Cheatham (1820–1886) commanded a division of infantry, Hardee's Corps, Army of Tennessee, Army of Tennessee's effective strength 3 Dec. 1863, *OR* 31, pt. 3, 783.

36. Robert A. Moon (1824–1869), Memphis commission merchant before the war, was involved with Brother Jimmie in the Selma Naval Company and the *Charlotte Clark*. Joseph Lenow, *Elmwood* [Cemetery] (Memphis: Boyle and Chapman, 1874), 135; List of stockholders, Selma Naval Company, privately held, copy in editors' possession.

and I went to the Theatre, miserable affair, Wreck Ashore.[37] We had a nice treat of Oysters—which Jimmie sent to our room after we returned. Nothing of my friend to day.

SATURDAY 21 Spent the day very pleasantly with friends. Gen Quarles[38] called Capt Holland and Dr Moses also. Oh! God what can be wrong. I dread it yet it must come. My dear, dear Brother — how can I give him up.

SUNDAY 22 Went to the Cathedral—heard splendid Music, but nothing of a sermon. Spent the day at Capt Hoinsteins [Hohenstine's].[39] Capt Holland came after Tea, did not see any of our other friends.

MONDAY 23 Spent a delightful day. Madame LeVert called, we spent the eve at her reception, which was rather dull. Dr Moses, Dr Nidelet and Maj Deveroux called. Miss Garro, Miss Hamilton & Mrs Smith—Capt Holland and I called on Beulah,[40] I was charmed with her. Dr Moses staid with Shallie.

TUESDAY 24 Tom Kirtland, Dr Nidelet, Shallie & I went down on Gunboats Nashville & Tennessee, they are superior to any I have ever seen. Dr Moses called after Tea—was introduced to Gen Buckner & Ladie.[41]

WEDNESDAY 25 This day, oh! God what has it been to me. My darling Bro I have parted with for a long time—he goes privateering. Gratz Oh! Gratz, idol of my heart, yet he loves me no more and it must be, tis his happiness tis my eternal misery. O Hope—

THURSDAY 26 Shallie, Capt Holland, Mr Kirtland, Dr Nidelet & I

---

37. John Baldwin Buckstone, *Wreck Ashore, A Drama in Two Acts* (Boston: Spencer, 1856).

38. Brigadier General William Andrew Quarles (1825–1893), a lawyer and judge before the war, commanded a brigade in the Department of the Gulf. His orders for transfer to General Bragg's Command were dated 21 Nov. 1863. General Maury to Colonel B. S. Ewell, *OR*, 31, pt. 3, 729.

39. Probably the same Captain Hohenstine who was a commission merchant in Mobile. General Maury to General Cooper, 28 Aug. 1863, *OR*, 52, pt. 2, 519, 531.

40. Perhaps a reference to the popular Mobile author, Augusta Jane Evans Wilson (1835–1909). Her second novel, *Beulah* (New York: Derby S. Jackson, 1859), attracted national attention. Mary Elizabeth Massey, *Bonnet Brigades* (New York: Knopf, 1966), 15. See also William Perry Fidler, *Augusta Evans Wilson* (University, Alabama: University of Alabama Press, 1951).

41. General Simon Bolivar Buckner (1823–1914), a West Point graduate, was one of Bragg's senior generals who disagreed with his conduct after Chickamauga. Buckner was still in command of a division in East Tennessee and in December joined up with Longstreet at Knoxville. For more information on his dispute with Bragg, see *OR*, 31, pts. 1, 2, and 3.

went to Fort Morgan[42]—gone all day, had a nice time yet there is no more pleasure for me. God of mercy guide me—and protect me.

FRIDAY 27 This is our last day in Mobile. Shallie and I spent it returning calls. Gen Buckner had a review this eve—Dr Moses, Capt Holland, Shallie and I spent the eve with Mrs Smith—oh God how I suffer yet he was near me. I worship, I adore him—yet I know he hates me.

SATURDAY 28 Sallie and Lu Elder, now Mrs Thomas & Mrs Scott arrived at Battle House this morn—how happy they are, oh my heart will break, great God why is it I must suffer. On board St Charles bound for Selma. I dont know what for. What is to become of me—God have mercy, yet he is going.

SUNDAY 29 Spent the day on St Charles—I like Dr Moses cousin so much she is a sweet Ladie. To say I love him would not express one moiety of the deep holy love that is wasting my heart—Oh! Gratz, great God have mercy on me. Why is it I worship him, misery, despair, destruction.

MONDAY 30 Arrived in Selma 11 o-clock, met my Brother, received telegram from Capt Holland, leave for LaGrange to see Tate to morrow, was with him all day, have mercy on me my dear redeemer. Mr Kirtland left us this eve.

December

TUESDAY 1, 1863 Shallie left for Columbiana [Alabama], Dr Moses and cousin left for Demopolis—he has left, and my heart, what is it—Jimmie leaves for Mobile, I leave for LaGrange, under care of Maj Strong and Ladie. (Maj Dickson on board Steamer Comdr Farland.[)]

WEDNESDAY 2 Arrived in Montgomery 8 o-clock. Left at 10 for LaGrange, arrived at 9 P.M. found Tate, Nannie [Perkins] and Bro George [Dashiell]—nothing of importance. The day passed as usual. Maj Strong & Ladie very kind to me.

THURSDAY 3 Met a great many Memphis friends. Nannie & Maria came round. Spent the day at Maj Hunts.[43] Met with Lt Lightner, so many refugees from Memphis in Hotel. Nannie, Tate & I set up until 1 o-clock. Spent eve in Parlor with friends very pleasantly.

42. Fort Morgan was one of a series of forts that guarded the entrance to Mobile Bay. Captain Denicke to Major Marston, 12 Aug. 1864, *OR*, 52, pt. 1, 574.

43. William R. Hunt, Memphis businessman before the war and friend of Brother Jimmie, was in charge of the iron and mining service for Alabama, Georgia, and South Carolina. Lenow, *Elmwood*, 111.

FRIDAY 4 Arrived in Montgomery 11 O.C. Left on two O.C. train for Mobile, have had a memorable trip all way from LaGrange. Met Lu & Capt Scott at Montgomery, Mr Elliott & Lt Parker added to our party. Oh! tis so cold and miserable on the Cars to night, poor Mr Elliott suffers so much.

SATURDAY 5 Arrived at boat day light, crossed bay reached Mobile 8 O-C. Met my dear Bro Jimmie. I was delighted to meet Gen Buckner & Ladie again, had a nice ride down Bay road this eve. Oh! tis so delightful in Dixie—think I must go home and be with those wicked wretches.

SUNDAY 6 Jimmie left to day. Mr Kirtland, Tate and I went to the Cathedral. We met many friends here in Battle House—every one is cheerful & gay, yet my poor, wounded, broken heart—God shield it from utter despair, bless him and make his life happy.

MONDAY 7 The day has been spent as usual—Lt Parker, Col Polk,[44] Nannie, Tate & I took breakfast with Mr Hartsford. Oh! God what is to become of me. I am surrounded by friends, yet I am dying. My heart is fading, and will soon be hushed and forgotten.

TUESDAY 8 Breakfast with Gen Taylor,[45] we had a nice time with friends, left Mobile 5 O-C a gay crowd. Maj Valentine, Capt Carroll, Bullock, Williams. Gen Buckner & Gen Taylor came to the Depot with us. Met Maj Williams & Dr Nidelet at Enterprise.[46] I have missed Theresa [Blennerhasset].[47] Spent the night as well as could be between waking and sleeping.

44. Marshall Tate Polk, Chief of Artillery, Department of the Gulf. Troops in the Department, 20 Jan. 1864, *OR*, 32, pt. 2, 582.

45. Major General Richard Taylor (1826–1879) commanded troops in the Red River Campaign. He was in Mobile at this time to arrange a system of couriers and a signal corps. He was almost captured when he recrossed the Mississippi River in a small boat to rejoin his troops. Admiral David Porter to U. S. Grant, 26 Dec. 1863, John Y. Simon, ed., *The Papers of Ulysses S. Grant*, 14 vols. (Carbondale: Southern Illinois University Press, 1967-), 9: 538–39.

46. Enterprise, Mississippi, a town just south of Meridian on the Mobile and Ohio Railroad, was headquarters of General Polk, where the defeated army from Vicksburg gathered. Parks, *Polk*, 353.

47. Theresa Blennerhasset, an exile from St. Louis, was the daughter of Richard Blennerhasset, a distant relative of Harmon Blennerhasset. She was expelled from the city for refusing to take the loyalty oath. After the war she married John C. Adams of New York and was prominent in society. Under the pseudonym Debra Isaacs, she wrote articles for a St. Louis newspaper about ante-bellum days. Unfortunately, she made no mention of the war, her exile in Mississippi, or her association with Belle. Theresa's father, a criminal lawyer, was prominent in legal circles. Her mother was Theresa Ryan, great-granddaughter of Jean Jacques Rousseau. Scharf, *St. Louis*, 2:1477; Necrology file, MHSSL; Theresa Blennerhasset to Belle, 27 Nov. 1863, EFP.

WEDNESDAY 9 Arrived at Meridian 3 o-c. Met Capt Kennerly at Depot. Staid until 7 o.c., traveled all day reached Brandon 4 o.c. found Maj Adams Ambulance waiting—have a very nice place to stay but I do think men are such fools, now our trunks have been sent to Jackson and we on our way to Canton.

THURSDAY 10 Arrived in Canton 2 o.c. found very nice quarter at Mrs Bass's. Had some nice Music after Tea but of all things we have every prospect for a delightful nights rest. Nannie and I sit up rather late. The old ladies, Mrs Pratte[48] & Dashiell retire.

FRIDAY 11 Awakened at 4 o.c. preparing for 7 o.c. train. Met with terible accident, after several skirmishes with a [illegible] succeeded in capturing it, and burning it alive —found Lt Mc[Connell] waiting to escort us to train. No news from Mr Simmons. Left 7, ar[rived] at 2 o.c. In Grenada. At Mrs Freleighs.

SATURDAY 12 Gen [Stephen D.] Lee and Staff called last eve. I was delighted with the Gen, gave each of us a pass without any trouble— left Grenada 7 o.c. this morn arrived in Panola 1 o.c. Met an Ambulance came to Col Bedfords for the Night, right rough trip, but I expect we will see more.

SUNDAY 13 Raining in torrents this morn—yet we started—swam two slews [sloughs] in Hicky-haly [Hickahala Creek]—not much trouble through Cold Water [River]—reached Hernando very late. Stopped with Mrs Gen Chalmers. We have had a miserable day. I am inclined to think woman, can drink to the dregs any cup of trouble which is given her.

MONDAY 14 Had a very late start, but reached home at 2 o.c. Nothing of interest to day—except our endeavors to keep protected from the bitter cold. Lt McConnell, Mr Harbut [Harbert], & Wilson[49] came after tea. Oh! I am so glad to get back home again.

TUESDAY 15 Poor Mrs Pratte she is almost crazy for fear she will not reach home before Christmas. Nonconnah is swimming—no communication with Memphis for several days. Lt McConnell left this morning.

WEDNESDAY 16 Rain, rain, rain—with no prospects of Nonconnah falling for several days. Mrs Pratte very restless. Mr Harbert and

---

48. Mrs. Betty Pratte, wife of Captain Bernard Pratte, sister-in-law of Mrs. Clay Taylor, and niece of Zachary Taylor. General Johnston from Alexander Stephens, 15 Nov. 1863, EFP.

49. Lieutenant William McConnell, B. T. Harbert and S. B. Wilson were all Henderson's Scouts. They probably constituted the Memphis Scouts. References to them are scattered throughout the *OR*. List of Henderson's Scouts Paroled at Gainesville, Alabama, May 1865, CC.

28

Wilson brought late papers, no news. I wrote to Mrs Moses and Gen Lee to day—nothing of interest to day.

THURSDAY 17 Nonconnah still rising—Poor Pratte, I pray she may get home by Christmas. Ebb [Titus] reached home to day just from Forrests Hd. qts[50]—Eddie was well.

FRIDAY 18 Mr Seymour did not come. Nonconnah oh! Nonconnah when can you be forded. I wrote Mrs Moses to day, gracious only knows when we can have any communication with Memphis. Two of 2 Mo—Mr Edmondson & Davis came to night.

SATURDAY 19 Another day and still Nonconnah swimming. 23 Confederates ate dinner with us to day. Ebb, Mr Harbert & Wilson have gone to Mrs Duke's for late Papers &c. Pratte and I have spent the eve writing letters.

SUNDAY 20 Mr. Seymour came this morn after Mrs Pratte, Tate and I went in the buggy with them over to Mrs Clayton's. Mr Simmons came to day our trunks are in Panola and will be sent as soon as the Waters are down.

MONDAY 21 Tate went to Memphis with Dink, Pratte and Mr Seymour—how I miss her, dear friend of my heart. I came from Mrs Claytons house alone. I feel desparate, but my saviour is near, and I do not fear. I am miserable—oh! God have mercy.

TUESDAY 22 Capt Hohenstine and friend Mr Hurst arrived to day. Mrs Pratte got off all safe last night. Cousin Sallie [Titus] came out to see Ebb. Father has given his consent for Helen to go to Dixie, but I am afraid he will not let me go to Europe.

WEDNESDAY 23 Capt Hohenstine and I went to see Mr Seymour, and he with his usual kind heart, will attend to all my friend's wish in passing up the River. I carried 142,000$ in Confed for Capt H. Met our Conscript officers with their prisoners. Capt Hohenstine gave me a beautiful Diamond button.

THURSDAY 24 Capt H. and friend left on foot for Mr Seymour's. Jim Titus & Mr Ferguson arrived to day. I am convinced to day of an enemy, who I thought was a friend. Oh! Shallie—Shallie—why have you deceived me. Christmas eve our house full of Rebels—God bless them.

---

50. Forrest asked for and received a transfer from Bragg's Army after the Battle of Chickamauga. He was assigned to the command of West Tennessee, "an area then wholly and to all outward appearances completely within the Union lines." Robert Selph Henry, *"First with the Most" Forrest* (Jackson, Tennessee: McCowat-Mercer Press, Inc., 1944), 202; Summary of Events, *OR*, 31, pt. 1, 2.

FRIDAY 25 A merry Christmas for old Elmridge—our house crowded. I had conferred on me the heroine of Jericho.[51] Tate & Joanna also. We had Six Soldiers—(Confed), and a nice Champaign Supper. My poor Bros if they could only be at home. Mollie, Laura, Beulah, Tip and I room together Christmas night.

SATURDAY 26 Mrs Ferguson and Mrs Worsham came out to meet Mr F. Cousin Mat [Martha Titus] and Frazor [Edmondson] and Mammy came out to Night. Father told me a secret to day as a heroine of Jericho. Henry, U.S.A.—Mr Juth's friend came also. My Redeemer guide me I feel thy protection and care more each hour I live.

SUNDAY 27 I have had a great disapointment. Mr Roberts tells me he can not get any thing through the lines for me. No Yanks house full of Rebels—all quiet. Nannie Fletcher, Cousin S[allie] came Non-connah swimming. Mr Harbert & Ebb went over creek. Confederate Gen Lee's command crossed late in the 25, God grant us a glorious victory.

MONDAY 28 As usual we have spent the day with our house full of Rebels—the Yanks passed in sight of us but did not call. I have been sick all day, heard nothing more from the late movement. God shield me from temptation.

TUESDAY 29 Mr Armstrong came out to see the Rebs.[52] Mr Owen & Mr Dunscomb arrived from Dixie. Unfortunately I was compelled to give up my room. Helen & I slept in Parlor. Mr Ferguson went over creek & got back safely.

WEDNESDAY 30 Mr Dunscomb went town with Cousin Sallie & Mat. Mr Owen with his wife went South. Mr Litsum & friend came out to meet Rebs. Eddie & Lt Spotswood arrived to Night from Forrests command,[53] Hendersons Scouts went over creek to Night.

THURSDAY 31 This day will close my happiest year. Yes my happiest and yet my saddest. May God in his majestic wisdom and mercy bless every desire of his heart—crown his future with happiness. I forgive him, oh! my Savior and bless him—teach him to think kindly of

51. Heroine of Jericho, an honorary title conferred on the wives and daughters of Royal Arch Masons. Stephen A. Brown Autobiography, typescript copy, Stephen A. Brown Collection, Special Collections, Mitchell Memorial Library, MSUS.

52. Probably John W. Armstrong, a partner in the Memphis firm of Edmondson [Jimmie] and Armstrong. Williams' Memphis Directory and Business Mirror, 1860 (Memphis: Cleaves and Vaden, 1860), 153.

53. Lieutenant Edwin A. Spotswood, adjutant, Tenth Tennessee Cavalry, was detailed to enter the Memphis lines and seek recruits. Mathes, Old Guard, 195.

me—oh! God have mercy. My heart will break yet bless him. I worship, I adore him. Snowing how cold. Eddie and several Rebels spent the day with us. I am alone at Night in my little room—Laura, Beulah & Tippie Dora.[54] Gratz may God forgive you—I do, and bless you.

[*Poem in back of Diary*]

[How?] like love is yonder rose
Heavenly fragrance round it glows
Yet in the midst of briars it grows
Just like love—

Called to bloom upon the breast
Though rude thorns the stem invest
They must be gathered with the rest
Just like love—

[And?] when rude storms the twain buds sever
They die and they shall blossom never
Yet the thorns be sharp as ever
Just like love—

---

54. Her servant, her dog, and her cat.

3

The Vicksburg Campaign

1863 LETTERS: JANUARY 24–JULY 7

From Ham Patton

Head Quarters Blythes Cavy
Jay 24*th* 1863

Miss Edmondson

We were to stop at your House last night but on account of accidents we could not come.

We started from the city late and our Buggy broke and we stopped at Mr Averys[1] for the night and came on early this morning before they had placed out Pickets, left Miss Noble and the other lady at Mr. Averys—they requested us to write a note to inform them if we got through safe and I concluded one to you would do, as you could inform them, we missed the road to your House and regret very much we could not come by as we promised you to come with the Ladies.

Col Blythe is expecting a small skirmish.[2]

We are certainly under many obligations to our fair friends of Memphis, for their kind assistance, and only hope that we may be able to repay them, by doing our duty to our Country—which is theirs also—

I am now in Dixie and feel some what relieved,—you will no doubt be some what surprised at receiving a letter from one whom you have

---

1. Probably William T. Avery (1819–1880), Memphis lawyer, Democratic congressman (1857–1861) and Confederate officer. Leroy P. Graf and Ralph W. Haskins, *The Papers of Andrew Johnson*, 7 vols. (Knoxville: University of Tennessee Press, 1967-), 3:457n.

2. Colonel Green L. Blythe organized a cavalry unit for the defense of Mississippi and the area south of Memphis. In the month of January he was operating on the Hernando Road within fourteen miles of Memphis. Simon, *Grant Papers*, 7:172.

no acquaintance with and whom you never saw but once but please be
not, for indeed I feel as if all the Ladies in the Confederacy were my
sisters, so far as this is concerned—Mr Wagner wishes to be remembered to the Ladies, and of course I do,—cherishing the fond hope that
all may yet be well, I have the honor to subscribe myself yours

H. Patton

Daniel R. Wagner
Ham H. Patton
Co "F" 15th Miss Regt

From Dr. Moses

Grenada 26 Jay 63

My dear Friend Your letters and one by L also I got on my return
from Mobile. I find every thing in motion our places are being supplied
by fresh troops while we veterans are ordered off to strengthen Vicksburg already strong enough to repel any advance & presume we shall be
just onlookers but if it becomes requested we can give some items to
history by swelling the Enemies list of killed and wounded. Your friends
will all be down there so come soon There will be work for you bring
Hal and F.

You know not how much you are loved. I can hear of your good deeds
Every where they will live while our Country Stands.

The roads are awful now—but our friends who left you last week got
safely through and are here now. I sent you a long letter the other day
directed as this. Give my love to Hal I saw B with her likeness the other
day—with much love your own

M.

Let them come on we are ready—the more you send down the more
will strike from the rolls—

M.

From Dr. Moses

Jackson Miss
10 Feby 63

My dear Child For the last two weeks I have been looking for and
would have written but expected to see you "face to face" Every day &
from every source I hear of your good deeds and kindness. You have
many very warm friends and to few can the present brightening of our
prospects be more agreeable. *They cannot take Vicksburg.* They hesitate
to attack it for they well know they only march to their graves. Their

army is breaking up—desertions are frequent and numerous—while on the other hand our army is increasing and feels sure of victory. We have one of the finest armys that the west has seen under our flag—The white cross was hoisted for the first time the day that Pres. Davis reviewed our troops.[3] All the Mo Regiments have them now.

We look for Miss Maria Walker and party soon—I should think that the roads were better now.

I. (the bearer of this) tells me that you have a hat for me but would not send it because I did not write. Now my dear child you ought to have known me better. I have written three letters two lengthy and one short one—and regret your not getting them. They were sent to Orgill & Bros.[4] I had a fine full length likeness for you taken in Mobile but got those I had ruined by the rain coming down. I have sent down for more and will have one for you & Miss Hal to whom give a *kiss* for me and I think there is another who would send one did he know I was writing. God bless you both—and protect you from the hands of our enemies is the wish of

M.

I am just starting to Vicksburg but will be back—

From E. A. Edmondson

Tullahoma Tennessee
Friday Feby 20th 1863

Dear Sister

I received your dear letter a few days ago by George Iams, accompanying some nice things for which I am under many obligations, and must ask you to thank Laura for her kindness in sending the jacket &c.—I wrote to Helen two or three days ago & sent it to Grenada through the mail Care N. S. Bruce and requested him to forward it by hand, but he may not do it, so you can send there for it if you see any one going there, that is one reason that I dont write home oftener, is that I dont know where to write that you might get it. I want to write home as anxious as you all are, possibly, to hear from me, & to hear

---

3. President Davis reviewed the Missouri troops at Vicksburg and at Grenada during the Christmas holidays, 1862. The flag may be the one Belle and Hal made for General Price. Robert S. Bevier, *History of the First and Second Missouri Confederate Brigades* (St. Louis: Bryan, Brand and Co, 1879), 166; Ephraim Anderson, *Memoirs: Historical and Personal, Including Campaigns of the First Missouri Confederate Brigade* (St. Louis: Times Printing Co., 1868), 257.

4. Belle's mail was directed to Orgill & Bros., a wholesale hardware company in Memphis. *Memphis Directory, 1860,* 190.

from home, and all that is transpiring at and around there, it is my thoughts "by day" & very often in my dreams.

I am writing this letter to send by George Dashiell and have just written on his application, a "leave of absence" for thirty days, if I had known a few days ago that he intended to go so soon I might have gone with him, but now one of the boys has gone to North Carolina on furlough, and I will have to wait his return on the 12th or 15th March next, and then if the "Coast is clear" I may avail myself of the opportunity, and visit home, but they wont give transportation to me & I fear I have not the where with to carry me, but then if there is not much danger of being captured I may attempt it.

Jimmie has succeeded in getting the "Bluffs" [Bluff City Grays] transferred to Forrests Cavalry,[5] and they are now in his Regt, he calls them his children—and was very much pleased when the order was issued—

I suppose Mrs Bulkley & Ire have reached home ere this as they have been on the journey some 8 or 10 days now.

I hope they had a nice time. I received Mrs. Bulkleys dispatch from Montgomery Ala. but Col Beard had not returned then but did so in a day or two. I immediately called on him & told him my business, he was very busy but led me to believe that it was all right—hope that it may prove so. I suppose that you will hear ere you get this that Jimmie was in the Donelson fight, on Forrest staff that day, and he says that Forrest goes in some mighty dangerous places, for a General to go, but we all know that[6]—I wrote Helen about all the news that I had. Much Love to All Write Soon—to your—

Affectionate Brother
E. A. Edmondson

From Tate Edmondson Dashiell

Elm Ridge
March 1st/63

Dear Belle,

Father received your note a day or two ago and was glad to hear you had got safely to your journeys end. We are all well at home and getting on finely. Nannie is with us—as hot a secesh as ever heard though she dont say much. Her Mama made her promise her she would not have anything to say on the subject—one way or the other if she could not

---

5. The Bluff City Grays were one of the detached companies that were combined to form the Eleventh Tennessee Cavalry. Henry, *Forrest*, 127.

6. Not the 1862 fight at Fort Donelson on the Cumberland River but the unsuccessful attack 3 Feb. 1863. Ibid., 123–26.

speak for the Union not to talk at all—and she dont say anything. Sister Em has gone to Illinois to live sure enough, and poor Nannie has to go too very soon I feel mighty sorry for her and have written to sister Em begging her to let her stay with us as she is so anxious to stay too and go to Dixie. I must tell you though of Dashiell Perkins. He left sister Em last May and joined Jacksons cavalry. I wish you would look him up cant you? He is in the Hardaman rangers I think.[7] I could not get sister Em to say anything about him. I feel so proud of him and I know you or anybody would like him. Dont say anything about his Mother to him. I have w.. 'en to Will Taylor[8] asking him to please see if there is anything he needs and what it is for he shall never want for anything as long as I have anything to share. I hope you will have as pleasant a time as possible under these circumstances.

The children are very well behaved and sweet as ever. Mary has grown much and can crawl every where—Robert strengthens in his rebellion every day. I do wish I could go South. I dont know but what I shall make an attempt to go to see George this summer or rather spring.

The Yankees are deserting by the wholesale—we have two with us tonight—we have formed a very pleasant acquaintance with a little Yankee Lieut. who has resigned and joined Capt Leaks. He is a cousin of the Billings and a mighty nice little fellow. I cut out a gray jacket for him am sewing it today. If you see Will tell him I have written to him and directed to Grenada also to Mr. Barbour.

Give my very best love to all my friends. Write to me when you can. Give my love to Perry and Maj Samuels and every body in Dixie.

Your affectionate sister
Tate Dash

From Major Thomas Price*

Jackson, Mississippi
March 8, 1863

Miss Belle Edmondson;

As the sweet notes of the warbling songsters of the wood are welcomed by the worn traveler when the darknes. of the storm is passing away, so thy memory will be to the Missourians in the Confederate

---

* this letter was pasted in Belle's scrapbook.

7. Dashiell Perkins enlisted in the Southern Guards, a company in the 154th Tennessee Infantry Regiment, according to his account of his Civil War Experiences. Perkins, "Record," 1, PFP.

8. Colonel William F. Taylor, Company A, Seventh Tennessee Cavalry, was a Memphis businessman before the war. Young, *Memphis*, 234, 306.

Army who survive the horrible conflict through which we are passing.

God speed you in your angelic mission of imparting comfort and happiness to the soldiers of the South and especially to the Missourians with whom the name Belle Edmondson will ever be a household word. You merit our gratitude; you have it, and I beg to assure you that whatever may befall us in the doubtful future before us, your memory will ever be cherished in the heart of Missourians and will find a place among the best friends of your most obedient servant,

Thomas H. Price

From Dr. Moses to his Stepmother

Mch 14.

I will send you my darlings only a line to ask you Ma to purchase a handsome, heavy plain gold ring, have inscribed in it "G to B.—Mch 12th '63"—"Hope"—send it to <u>Miss Edmondson</u>[marked out] Orgill & Bros Memphis Tenn—it would be best to send it by hand—or express. But please Ma send it soon & Miss E will see that it is properly delivered—I am as usual right well & happy as possible. Yearning & praying to see you all again—Kiss Lou & her little ones for me—Bessie, Mary & love to the boys—Tell my dear Father that even though these years are so many lost ones, I'll improve in surgery and love of home if nothing else—Remember me to Drs. Gregory & Pope—& to all friends—Good night—Devotedly your

own boy
M

Do not address any letters you send me to care of Miss Edmondson—but directly to Messers Orgill & Bros—inside to Miss Edmondson—Tell Tracy's sister to write in same way.

From Major Tracy

Grenada Miss
March 16/63

Miss Belle,

I send by the bearer the promised photograph of one of the greatest men and certainly the best of our Southern Generals.

The representative of a state that is proud to claim him as her son—[torn] Virginia"—and as the adopted son of Missouri may he prove her redeemer. And may in the selection of your future happiness be the fortunate possessor of such a man, is the only misfortune I can ever wish you.

In behalf of Missouri and her brave sons, allow me to thank you, for the Kindness, and consideration you have ever exhibited in their behalf.

May God remember your actions, and if you are not repaid in this
world, may you receive your reward, where none but pure spirits dwell.

Very respectfully
Your obdt. Servt.
H. W. Tracy

Miss Belle Edmondson

From Major Tracy

Grenada Miss
March 23rd 1863

Miss Belle

Your letter of the 17th instant handed me by Sarah Seath the "American Citizen of African descent." You ask to be excused for the liberty
taken in asking a favour for this person. Did I not request you upon the
short acquaintance of one day to Command me upon all occassions. I
know I shall not if in my power be found wanting when called upon. If
I did I would indeed be an ungrateful being after the many Kind acts
bestowed upon my fellow Soldiers especially the Missourians who poor
banished exiles would have suffered much had it not been for the ladies
(among whom you appear very conspicuous) God bless them. Miss Belle
I now regret my success in obtaining the order I so much desired when
the General [Price] left (of crossing the river) it came two days ago. I
shall not leave for a month at least. And regret the day as it is like
severing a family tie, having made some *few* very agreeable acquaintances since my Sojourn here, you yourself among the number. Excuse
me if I have presumed in claiming you as one of my friends upon so
short an acquaintance. If I am excused I may be permitted to say that—
("It was ever thus from Child hood") the best of friends must part and
in these war times may never again meet. Although I sincerely hope
such may not be our fates. I regreted after you left that I had not accompanied you as far as Panola though I might have been an intruder as you
would then have run the risk of inconvenience from the Villanous Dutch
and interlopers who caused you and Mrs B[redell] so much inconvenience. One of the conditions of granting the pass was that None were
to go but your party. I fear Miss Belle you will consider me a little
presumptive from so short an acquaintance in addressing you so freely
& Candidly, as though the acquaintance were of long standing. If so
blame the pencil which seems as it were to work out its own road (which
causes it to make many mistakes. So overlook them) The old saying
"Out of the heart the mouth Speaketh." I was down to Mrs F[religh's]
this evening and you were many times spoken of (and missed very
much) in very complimentary terms. I would not mention it did I think

you could be spoiled by hearing the truth. I was exceedingly surprised of the deception practiced upon us poor unsophisticated youths—Lads as me were to presume you preferably free. And to awaken to a sad disappointment and find you claimed by another. Well it must be so we are all doomed to disappointment, well I hope in the admiration for the party (who is one of my best friends) you will not forget that there are a few more who feel well if they know they have a passing thought of yours. As you will always hold a place in their hearts for your disinterested kindness. To the poor banished Sons of Missouri most of whom have parents & Sisters at home who would be glad to receive you as an angel who had been sent to them as a Comforter for the Sacrifice they have made in giving their Sons or brothers to their Country. As regards the men their natures are rough, but rest assured let your lot be cast where ere it may, you will find brothers and possibly if not to hard to please one with whom you could ride the waves and rough Sea of this life happily with. "Two Souls with but a single thought two hearts that beat as one." I hope Miss Belle you will not think me as endeavouring to influence you in the selection for your future happiness for I feel it would be a great piece of presumption on my part to undertake such a task being of no experience in matters of the heart. Now that I am thinking of leaving I often ask myself what will be my fate on the west side of the river, subjected to the Caprices of a Military man General Mc [?], who may order me away from my friends instead of allowing me to go where my inclination leads me (toward the home of dear brothers and Sisters) with our noble and gallant Patriot Genrl Price. You will guess that I have a little touch of blues, which is indeed true. Miss Belle may I ask a favour of you and that is to write to my only Sister Eliza R Tracy care Homer, Rex & Tracy St Louis who would be very much reconciled at getting a letter from one whom she knew had seen me. If you knew her I think you would love her. Ask her to write by the address you mentioned and I may get it as I have received but two since leaving home. I would not ask or trouble you did I not know your disposition to serve & make all of your fellow beings happy. You state in your letter that unless you have the selection of your company you will not be likely to come this way again. If the individual himself can clear up this distrust which you appear to have I would endeavour to get him back from Greenwood and sent up to draw you down. Poor fellow he looked very bad the morning you parted at the train you going to see those more dear to you, he to meet enemies that would cavil at nothing that was mean. I did indeed feel sorry for him. This whole and unrighteous war has made many unhappy homes, and God only knows when it will end. Can the just God ever expect us to again live together. I sincerely hope

not. If all were like me they never would as I would as soon be dead as under the same Government again. It is doubtless a sin to express such sentiments, but I cannot help it. Such is my nature and I must depend upon the good angels like yourself to pray for me in order that the wrath of God may not be visited upon me in full vengance—this miserable and uninteresting pencil scrawl I fear will weary your patience as it is rather dull. And no news except the rumour that the Yankees have again appeared at Greenwood after an absence of four days.[9] I hope the last one of the scoundrels may get his six feet of Earth or an over supply of water. I will send this by Henderson's Express. Do send me a paper once and a while a letter would meet with a ready answer if you are not afraid of offending another party. If I go over the other side of the river Miss Belle I will send you my address and the time I leave which will be about the first of May and when you can find no other person to write to I will be more than gratified to read a letter from you.
Very truly your friend H. W. Tracy
PS
Thanks for your consideration for me in endeavoring to get a Newspaper at Panola. If I am living and perfect in limbs I promise *with your permission* to dance at your wedding. It is now one O'clock at night if you were caused to devote as much of the night in reading this as I was scratching it off I think you will say I wish he had not written me so much nonesense

Your friend
Henry W Tracy

25th 1863
PSS We sunk this morning at Vicksburg one Gun Boat & crippled another. Genrl Loring drove the Yankees back on Sunday the 22nd.[10] It now begins to look like work. Capt Henderson read a letter from Dr Moses who is at Greenwood so we drank a glass of your fine Brandy in which your good health was drunk. You were mentioned as the good Samaritan and many regrets expressed that you were so far away from us when good news came

H W Tracy

---

9. The Yazoo Pass Expedition was a flanking operation by General Sherman and Admiral Porter that was stopped by the "cotton bale" fort called Pemberton between the Tallahatchie and Yalobusha Rivers. S. H. Lockett, "The Defense of Vicksburg," *Battles*, 484–85.

10. "General Loring with 3 guns and about 1500 men turned back a large fleet and land force." Ibid.

From Dr. [*John Thompson*] Hodgen

March 26th 1863

Miss Belle,

As my wife is suffering from a boil, which she says is in a very inconvenient place at this time, she turns the pleasant duty of writing to you over to me. We received this evening a box from you brought by Dr Atkins, which I will forward immediately with the suspicious letter to Dr G. A. M. & take great pleasure in doing so.

My little wife *Georgie*, wrote to you last week and will write to you again as soon as she is well. She says she is very glad you will not go to Missouri and thinks you had better return to Dixie. Don't think you are safe among the Yanks. We are all very anxious to see you. Georgie received a very pretty little note from G. A. M. this evening inclosed in which was one for you. His excuse for leaving it unsealed was the want of envelopes. I have not read it yet Miss Belle—Georgie says I shall not positively—but you will allow me; will you not? Say yes and return it by next mail. If I was not the most honest fellow in Dixie (Dr G. A. M. excepted) I would read it any how.

By the way, I hear that you & G. A. M. are engaged. Is it so? My authority is Mrs Kirk & Capt Henderson is hers. He said he has been sending letters from G. A. M. to yourself & he also says an engagement must of course exist. I wish you both much joy & happiness.

"Let the wide world wag as it will" &c you could not do better—as I am not available. Georgie and all send much love to you: I among the rest. Remember—go to the glass and kiss yourself for me twice. You must excuse my dull note, as I have not written one in so long, but however if you are not interested you may skip over it & read on. No news in Dixie—been fighting at Greenwood but no decided result—two Fed Gunboats in it—attempting to pass Vicksburg a few days ago. One was sunk & the other seriously damaged. Au revoir—

Truely your friend
The Doctor.[11]

From Georgie Hodgen

Grenada—April 19th 1863.

My dear friend

Words are inadequate to express the thanks I give you for your kindness to me and I trust it may ere long be in my power to repay you. Had

---

11. Dr. John Thompson Hodgen was Surgeon General of Missouri. The ram *Lancaster* was destroyed 25 Mar. while attempting to pass Vicksburg. The *Monarch* was hit by an eighty-four-pound shell in the same engagement. H. H. Cunningham, *Doctors in Gray* (Gloucester, Mass.: Peter Smith, 1970), 235n; Simon, *Grant Papers*, 471n.

I know the difficulty and danger of bringing things out of Memphis I would not have troubled you. My goods all suit me *exactly*—; the dresses are *very* pretty—shoes are too large but I can exchange them for smaller ones here. Am glad you did not get the sack at the price. The box you sent was forwarded immediately—Mrs Freleigh has gotten home safely with her goods and chattels—Miss Blennerhasset is still with us. She is a dear little creature; we all like her very much. I believe I know of no news of interest. The feds are again threatening Vicksburg, and on Friday last managed to pass our batteries with five gun boats, but I hope it will result in their capture.[12] I enclose a letter to you from our friend, and also one which you will please mail in Memphis for us if you can without trouble; if you cannot *destroy* it. I am sorry we have no Yankee stamps to prevent an infringement on your generosity, but as it is impossible here to obtain one, you will confer a *lasting favor* if you will supply one for us, and mail as directed. If we can ever repay you it will be to us a great pleasure to do so.

Write soon a long letter—You are indebted to me one. I would write more, but am in a great hurry. Any thing we can do for you just say it— All send much love—

As ever your friend
Georgie Hodgen

P.S. As it is difficult to get two envelopes within one you will again be troubled. Please enclose for us the unsealed letter in one envelope and Direct to Miss Mary Hodgen to the care of Mrs M. A. Riggs Norfolk City Virginia. My dear friend to avoid being so often troubled by your friends in Dixie you must leave Yankeedom, and live among us.

From Major Adam Nase [USA] to Major General Hurlbut

Headquarters 16th Army Corps
Memphis, Tenn., May 1st 1863

Maj. Gen. Hurlbut

Dear Sir, I would Most Respectfully ask in behalf of Miss Bell Edmondson that she have returned to her the following property, with permission to take them beyond the lines. to wit: 3 Gallons of Coal Oil 3 Small lamps & a Smiths & Wesson pistol which She has been carrying for her protection beyond the lines. She living in the Country. The Oil

---

12. Rear-Admiral Porter's flotilla of seven gunboats and three transports passed the Vicksburg batteries, 16 April 1863. Grant to Halleck, 17 April 1863, *OR*, 26, pt. 1, 30.

& Lamps She supposing it was not contraband. It was taken from her by the pickets and delivered over to the 4th Division Provost Marshall

> Your Most Obedient Servant
> A. Nase
> Maj 15 Regt Ills Vol

[Endorsed on back]

Headquarters 4th

Div Memphis May 1/63

The Provost Marshall of
the 4th Div will
return the Articles herein
named to Miss Edmondson
and pass her through
the lines

> J. G. Lauman
> Brig Genl

From Major Tracy

> Grenada Miss
> May 5/63

Miss Belle,

Your letter of the Second inst with paper and letters for myself and others reached me safely this day for the papers and my letters and the kind one from you please except my thanks. And the request if ever in my power to repay the obligation you will not hesitate to call upon me. My sister writes that she received a letter from you requesting her if she desired to write that you would be able to send it through, for which she was very grateful. And if you could visit St Louis she would endeavour to make your stay as agreeable there as your appearance has made the Missourians hearts happy whilst in their banishment away from the dear ones at home. Many of whom have left dear Sweethearts who will bless you, when they hear of your many kindnesses. Poor Miss Blennerhasset is now in Mobile did not reach there soon enough to see her brother as he was dead & buried Four days before she left here. I feel very sorry for her indeed as she was very devoted to him and very justly to as he was a devoted Son and kind brother. If you send the Surgical Case for Dr Nidelet to me I will see that he gets it. The news from Virginia is Splendid Genrl Lee whipped Hooker a disasterous defeat we loosing Maj Genrl Paxton killed *Stonewall* Severly wounded Genrls

Heth and one other slightly wounded, the dispatch is Genrl Lee's.[13] We had a terrible fight at Grand Gulf the Missourians poor fellows I fear suffered terribly. Genrl Macy of Alabama was killed.[14] I send you all the late papers up to this date. And will Send them Regular. Miss Belle I fear when your kindness allows you to offer to get our little things down here it may get you into trouble. You ask me when I start over I heard from the officer (who is to relieve me) this evening he will be here to Morrow I will not be able to arrange my business until the first of June. If there was not much doing I would start up with Miss Blennerhasset a part of the way. How far do the Yankees come out; as I would not like to be captured and taken to die in one of their prisons or dens. The Doctor's package and letters shall go direct and if at any time while I am here I can reciprocate by forwarding anything *Even a letter* I shall be most happy. As the night is getting on towards the wee hours and I find I am trespassing upon your time and patience I will close, with this I remain Miss Belle

Truly Your Friend

H. W. Tracy

P.S.

You ask if you can do anything for me. I would say yes if the conditions were agreeable, that is to make the purchases and then bring the things yourself. I think it will require another person persuasions than mine. Enough of this Goodnight. If you can send this letter through by hand to Capt Able. Please do so with the request that he send it by hand to St. Louis.

From Major Tracy

Grenada Miss

May 10th 1863

Miss Belle,

Dear Friend. Enclosed is a letter for Miss Blennerhasset which please have mailed in Memphis as she is very anxious to have it go through safe. It is directed to an old friend of hers and mine who is situated by an association with a Union man in business which will prevent its being

---

13. The Battle of Chancellorsville, 1–4 May 1863. Brigadier General E. F. Paxton was killed; Stonewall Jackson was wounded and died eight days later; and Generals Heth and A. P. Hill were wounded. Frank E. Vandiver, ed., *The Civil War Diary of General Josiah Gorgas* (University: University of Alabama Press, 1947), 36.

14. Grant's forces landed on the east side of the Mississippi River 30 April, near Grand Gulf where the Missouri troops under General Bowen were in a strong position. After a sharp engagement on the road to Port Gibson, Bowen's men retreated. Grant, "Vicksburg Campaign," 3:496–98.

opened. I fear you will think me a little troublesome in calling so much upon you. I can only say that should you ever require the Services of the writer you have but to demand it and they will be readily extended and with hearty pleasure. And any Missourian who would not do the same would indeed be a base ingrate. Your heart being anothers (which I am informed) shows that I have no desire to flatter. If Miss Belle I may be excused for the liberty taken in refering to a matter, which so much concerns your future happiness, (I can but approve of the choice) you must attribute it to a *Brotherly* feeling which I feel for you. And should the future of war permit us to again Meet after the war, I shall be most happy to meet you as the adopted daughter of St Louis. If we are not permited the pleasure of again meeting in this world I hope that my future may be such as to assure me a meeting in that "Spiritual" House, that house where none but Angels and eternal happiness Exist. Enough of this as you will think me tedious. Your Sister, [and] Hal Rodgers were through here this morning on their way to Tennessee and many were sad hearts when they did not find your charming face with them. The former resembles you so much that I almost thought you were present. Her voice, had I heard it in the night would have acted as a magnet to draw me to her, resembling yours so much. I expect you will think I lost my heart. Why shouldn't I if she is as good as her Sister, (Excuse my Candour). I offered my humble services but they remained so short a time that I could be of no assistance in making their Stay agreeable. Besides the name is a passport for them through the Confederacy particularly this portion. I volunteered to forward any letters to you which they would honor me with, was I right? I must thank you for the letters from my Sister & yourself. Also the Newspapers. I return the Southern papers which will post you as to how we are getting along and that we are not starving as the Yankees think and hope. Good night. I hope soon to hear from you, and hope you will maintain the good name which I appear to have credited to me by you at all times and to so many ladies.

H. W. T.

From Major Thomas H. Price

Panola Miss May 11th 1863

Miss Bell

Please write to me at Jackson by *first* opportunity what you know about Mrs Price—how She got along—when She left for home—how She was &c, &c—you dont know how anxious I am to hear from her. I am now waiting here to hear something if possible from her before I return—I will write you soon; but feel to badly to write more now

> Believe me very truly your
> friend & obedt Servt
> Thos H. Price

From Major Tracy

> Grenada Miss
> May 24th 1863

Miss Belle,

This will be handed you by a very trustworthy and reliable man, who visits Memphis for the purpose of getting his family out. We had a terrible fight on the big black river and our army fell back to Vicksburg we have repulsed them from there with a heavy loss. Report says from 9 to 15000 of the Yankees killed God grant it may be So.[15] I saw the Doctor yesterday at Canton looking very well indeed. We have evacuated Yazoo City & Snyders bluff. The bloodiest fight of the war will Soon be fought and the greatest *whipping* the Yankees ever got will be visited upon them. The Missouri troops Suffered terribly in officers & Soldiers killed and wounded—I must again thank you for the papers Sent by Young Atchison the Doctors Step brother. I sent him to Canton this morning in order that he might see the Doctor. I enclose a letter which has been delayed on account of an opportunity not offering for Sending it. I wish I could tell you all that we hope to accomplish Soon you would then be happy. As the party is waiting I must close. Your friend
H W Tracy
P.S. If I can get away I may come up with Miss B. and accept your kind offer. I send $100 Confederate. If you can exchange for Greenbacks without compromising yourself you will oblige ever your debtor

> H. W. T.

From Mrs. Melinda Williams

> Terre Haute Ind June 15th

Dear Miss Edmondson

I heard of you through a Federal Officer in St Louis. He advised me to ask assistance and it would be given. Could you convey this letter to

---

15. Probably the Battle of Champion's Hill, 16 May 1863 that resulted in a great number of casualties. Simon, *Grant Papers*, 8:522.

my Sister, I would feel so grateful. Please read and be the judge whether there is any thing in the contents that could make you hesitate. Please write me a short note if but one word yes or no of the probability of her getting the note. Also tell me if John Overton is in Memphis. Should it ever be in my power I will repay ten fold your kindness.

Address Mrs Melinda Williams[16]

Terre Haute   Indiana

From Major Claudius Mcgivern

Humbolt Ala

June 16" 1863

Miss Edmondson

I take the liberty of writing you in order to request that you will be kind enough to send me, per Mr Brett who carries this, any of the articles you may have been able to purchase for me with the $50 U.S. funds given you at Major Hunt's in Jackson last winter.

If you should not have been able to procure any of the articles as yet, and should obtain them in the future, please send them to me to care of Col Phil Stockton at this place. Major Kimmel and myself spent an evening with your sister in Montgomery a few weeks since.

Mrs Freeman's house was burned when the Yankees captured Jackson, and Major Hunt's and Mrs Martin's pretty well sacked. Miss Gwin lost all her clothing by the burning of Mrs Freeman's house.

I give you the foregoing items to show you that your friends in Jackson were considerable sufferers by the Yankee visit.[17]

Very Respectfully Your obedt Sevt

Claud. McGivern[18]

Miss Belle Edmondson

---

16. Melinda Williams, wife of an east Tennessee U.S. congressman, Joseph L. Williams, owned property in Mississippi. Graf and Haskins, *Johnson Papers*, 6:617n.

17. Grant's forces occupied Jackson, the capital of Mississippi, 14 May 1863. Sherman was given orders to destroy the place as a railroad center and manufacturing location for military supplies. Colonel Fremantle thought the troops wantonly damaged homes of private citizens. Sylvanus Cadwallader, the war correspondent, wrote of damage so excessive as to deserve the charge of "northern vandalism." Ulysses S. Grant, *Personal Memoirs of U. S. Grant*, 2 vols. (New York: Charles L. Webster, 1892), 1:507; Lord, *Fremantle*, 87; Cadwallader, *Three Years*, 75.

18. Major Claudius McGivern, Depot Quartermaster, Canton, MS, Brigadier General Francis M. Cockrell to Colonel T. B. Roy, 19 Sept. 1863, *OR*, 30, pt. 4, 670.

From Captain Thomas H. Henderson

Panola June 16/63

Miss Belle Edmondson,

Many thanks for yours of 13, Inst. I sent the information forwd. immediately, & hope it will reach Canton or Jackson before the *party* gets there.

I am sorry it is out of my power to give you any definate & late good news from Vicksburg. Bro. Sam telegraphed me from Canton 12 Inst. "All well & all right"—his head qtrs are at Vernon 25 miles from there, where he is doing good service with 15 of our Scouts.[19] Rumored that Kirby Smith has captured a wagon train near New Carthage[20] and the enemy were again repulsed Friday last with heavy loss rear of Vicksburg. Genl Johnston still getting reinforcements & I hope will be able to oust old Grant before many days. Genl C[halmers] is moving & I hope you may hear a good account of him soon—where I will not say. Your letters have gone forwd. as well as the dear funny Ladies that bro't them. Many thanks for the papers. I send you some in return which you will please *stamp* & mail. Wishing you continued usefulness & much happiness here & hereafter I am

Yours Most Truly
Tom Henderson

From Shallie Kirk

Canton June 19th/63

My darling Bell

Agreeable to promise, I write to you from the first point at which we remain any length of time: we have been here two days and nights—domesticated at Mrs Speeds, which seems like a second home, we leave, however tomorrow morning for Mobile, thence to Selma: we had a very pleasant trip without incidents, in which but few inconveniences. We staid the first night at Hernando, the second at Uncle Ben's, and the third at Grenada, where we put up at a very nice clean house kept by a Mrs Ebbert. Mrs Freligh sent for me as soon as we reached there as

---

19. Captain Samuel Henderson was a member of the company of scouts his brother organized in 1862. By 1863, the company was divided and part of it sent under Sam's command to the vicinity of Vicksburg. W. L. Alexander to C. P. Newton, 17 Mar. 1917, CC.

20. General E. Kirby Smith was operating in northern Louisiana to create a diversion for the relief of Vicksburg and Port Hudson. Report of E. Kirby Smith, 17 June 1863, *OR*, 24, pt. 2, 457.

Theresa was with her, & I staid all night with her. I found Theresa more cheerful than I expected and very glad to see me: she asked a great deal about you, & so did they all. Major Tracy came to see me that night; & put me on the cars in the morning: I like him so much: he told me Dr Moses was in Canton & he would telegraph to him to meet me at the depot, but as he was not in town when the dispatch came, he did not know I was here until the next morning, when he met John Walker who had been to see us twice already: he came right down & I believe he was *really glad* to see me. I gave him the package, and all your messages, & a great more that was nice besides: he has already been to see me three times & will come again this evening & bring Dr House (who is at camp 14 miles distant) & Capt Lewis Kennerly. I find Dr Moses very little changed, and just as agreeable as ever: we have had two or three long talks about you: he thinks you are the best woman in the world & I am the worst: we however renewed our former pledges of friendship, and I have promised to be a sister to him: so you see he doesnt intend I shall cut you out: he has promised to go with me (after this next battle) to Panola & we will send for you, & all stay at Uncle Ben's, & all have a good time. George [Atchison] is here & has been to see us; he inquired very particularly for you; he devotes himself to Sallie exclusively: he wants to join Henderson's scouts, but I think we will persuade him out of it: by the way! I gave your letter & package to Capt H- and he came down to the cars to see me, said he was under *many* obligations to you: he immediately sent copies of that description through the country: he told me to send my letters to him & he would send them to you: We all went last night to see Gen Joe Johnston who spends part of every day in Canton. I was delighted with him; he is so dignified & gentlemanly. Dr Moses introduced us to him as he is on his staff. I have had a most delightful time since I left home: I think Dixie is the nicest place in the world: I find everything so plentiful and as good as it is in Memphis: I wish I could hear from home: Direct your first letter to Selma Ala. I think that will be the most certain way to reach me. Tell Miss Joanna I left three hats at Dr Esby's as she directed. Give my best to Mrs Dash[iell], Mrs Anderson, & Nannie, remember me kindly to your father. God bless you all! I wish you could be with us. Good bye, I will write you from Mobile. Ever your true friend

Shallie

All send a great deal of love to all of you.

I would write more but Mollie is waiting for the pen & ink to write home: please go in often & see them all then let me know how they are: My love to them all

Shall

From O. F. Prescott

Col Nye A. Q. M. Sir I sold to Miss Edmondson about 10 days since a Brown Horse. The Horse I have owned for nearly a Year and can prove that He has been here longer than that time
June 20/63—O. F. Prescott[21]

PROVOST MARSHAL'S OFFICE, DIST. OF MEMPHIS
16th Army Corps
Memphis, Tenn., June 22 1863

A large dark Brown horse about 7 years old seized from Miss Edmondson is this day return to her, there being no legible brand of "US." upon it

James H. Howe
Col Pro Mar
per Col Howe
Capt [illegible]

From Louise Taylor [Mrs. Clay]

Pendleton June 25th
Dear Belle

I am once more installed in my home in Warren Co. [Missouri], a drear and desolate home to me without my dear husband. As soon as I arrived in St Louis I delivered your letter, and I saw *her* she was the picture of distress but feels so grateful to you. Do write to me let me know where you are? what you are doing and all the news from our friends if you have any. I have not heard one word from Mr T. since I left him I feel so anxious. As soon as I arrived I reported to Schofield[22] the Genl Comg and showed him my pass—he said I could stay at home, but must keep very quiet, which I intend doing. Write and direct outside envelope to F. Bernard & Co St Louis, inside envelope Mrs. Clay Taylor, Pendleton Warren Co Mo. Give my best love to Mrs Kirk, I shall not forget her kindness, also remember me to Mr Seymour and to all your Sisters. Is Miss Johanna still an Exile? Let me know the condition of things down in Memphis. I feel so anxious about Vicksburg. I found

21. O. F. Prescott, a Memphis shopkeeper, may have been a double agent. He was in Mobile the same time as Belle. When he returned to Memphis, he reported to General Hurlbut who called him an "informer." Stephen A. Hurlbut to Colonel J. C. Kelton, 2 Jan. 1864, *OR*, 32, pt. 2, 13.

22. Major General John M. Schofield (1831–1906), West Point graduate, commanded the Department of the Missouri. J. F. Huron to Colonel John A. Rawlings, *OR*, 32, pt. 2, 13.

my children all well, I would give a great deal to see you and have a few moments conversation with you—be sure and write to me. Have you heard from the Dr? Goodby my good friend believe ever yours affectionately

Louise

From Captain Thomas Henderson

Panola June 29, 1863

Miss Belle Edmondson,

I send description of your supposed spy on a Clay bank horse out of Memphis to Capt Williams Grenada, & he wrote me yesterday, saying he thought he had captured the man, to send some one down to identify him. I ordered the Capt to hold on to him till he heard from me again. Will you get some one to make affidavit before a Magistrate describing the man minutely, if possible give his name, age, color of hair & eyes, crooked or broken bridge nose & lame leg. It would not do for *you* to make the affidavit, as the enemy would hear of it certain, & destroy your Fathers House, & maybe seize and put you in prison. Our RR is running from here to Grenada again, & if you could come down here I would send an escort with you to Grenada to identify the Man without letting the object of your trip be known. But your own good judgement Miss Belle, will enable you to decide what is best to do in the premises. I send you a batch of letters, please stamp those requiring them—also enclose a letter that came in one to me. In the way of news, let me tell you that Genl Chalmers was in the bottom trying to sink transports.[23] Genl George & McCulloch had not force enough to meet the 2,200 Feds that crossed at Wyatt & came down here Thursday night & Friday morning.[24] We fell back to Yocona but they the Feds beat our main force to the bridge (RR) cut & burnt 4 pannells & retreated back here, burned all the business Houses & Depot in Batesville, the North side of public square here including Presbyterian Church & steam mill. Our forces pursued & killed & captured about 100 & Genl C[halmers] about the same. Genl Ruggles whipped the other column near New Albany & killing & capturing together over 200. So we done them some 4 to 500 damage but they destroyed & stole a great deal. On Saturday week repulsed another attack on fortifications rear of V[icksburg]—*slaying ten thousand.* Johnston is said to be moving forwd. I have a dispatch saying

23. The attacks on transports took place near Commerce, Mississippi. Summary of Principal Events, 17 June 1863, *OR*, 24, pt. 2, 484.
24. The Federal force was made up of the Second Iowa and the Third Michigan. General Hurlbut to Colonel Rawlings, 23 June 1863, ibid., 486.

we have taken Winchester & 9 thousand prisoners. All other news of Genl Lees movements, you have in Northern papers. Of course you will send me some Papers. I send you all I have. Genl Wilson is captured. Now in Memphis. Cant you do something for him. With most cordial thanks for your many favors, I am

Yours truly,
Thos Henderson

[written on side margin]
NB Many thanks for papers by Mr Webb I sent some forwd & mailed the letters as "requested." TH

From Major Tracy

Grenada Miss
July 5th 1863

Miss Belle

Your kind note enclosing Twenty five (25) Dollars reached me this morning Safely, and places me again under an obligation to you. Please accept my thanks for your kindness and consideration in my behalf. You speak of my visiting you, I can assure that none would enjoy the visit more than I. And it may be that I will see you before leaving for the west side of the river. Miss Theresa has gone to Mobile and will await my visit that point for her. I hardly know what to advise her future course. Sometimes she wishes to return home and I agree that it would be for the best and would so advise her, were it not I fear that her parents and sisters be the Sufferers, which would be to hard for her old Mother to bear—as her trials are great enough, now for one of her age. I send you the late papers, and also two letters enclosed in one for my sister which if you can get my friend Mclye to deliver them to some one who will have them delivered in person as directed and not bring them under the rule of the Burnside order. If I can reciprocate the favour at anytime, I will be most happy to engage my humble self in doing it; with this I remain

Very truly
Your friend
H W Tracy

P.S.
I expect to leave here soon, and if I
do not see you, will cherish the
memory of your name and
friendship as one of a very
agreeable nature.

H W Tracy

From Louise Taylor

5 July

Dear Belle

What is the matter? What has become of you. I wrote you about ten days ago inquiring about your Goings and sayings—but no answer yet— write and let me know what you know of our friends where abouts, and if there is any way of communicating with them. Tell me your plans, in fact all you know or intend doing—any news from the Dr? Has Annie Perdue gone to Dixie? I am well, but always miserable at being separated from my husband and being obliged to live in this land of devils and blue beards. Write soon. Give my love to your father & sisters dear Belle I will never forget your kindness to me. Direct your letter first envelope Bernard Pratte, Pendleton Warren Co Mo inside envelope Louise Taylor. Is there still an exit from Memphis to Dixie—Goodbye

Your friend

Louise

How do you like the Pennsylvania invasion. I find but one fault—there is no retaliation for the murder plunder, arson [illegible] of those hired Yankees—I wish we women could have our wishes and orders enacted [?] ruin & devastation should follow the track of our Soldiers—

From Captain Henderson

Panola July 7, 1863

Dear Miss Belle,

Your favor of 4 inst, came duly to hand accompanied by a batch of papers for which you have my most sincere thanks, & I have no doubt those of Genl Johnston. The package of money I forwd. promptly to Maj Tracy at Grenada, & have also sent the one recd for him since. The package of money for Mr Prescott Mobile I have still on hand and hope to get a safe conveyance all the way thro tomorrow. Your letters were all stamped & mailed. I am largely indebted to you in postage line & hope to get some U.S. currency to send you in this. If I dont get it just pay postage on the letters now sent, some of which require new envelopes also, I hope to settle some day.

Send the best papers you can get about that man, but *dont* you think a moment about coming down here.

Now for news—Genl Holmes comd. in person the forces that attacked Helena July 4 at day light, took some of the Hill batteries but was repulsed with loss of 5 or 600—[25] heard artillery in that direction to

25. The attack on Helena was made by the combined forces of Generals Holmes and Sterling Price in an attempt to do something to relieve Vicksburg. Castel, *Price*, 142.

day, Maybe renewed attack, but the place has been reinforced and can not be taken now. I hope Holmes will fall down and join Kirby Smith & hold some place on the Miss River below this and destroy transports. From Vicksburg we have had reports Yesterday & to[day] of its having fallen. Nothing official 'tis true, but I am very uneasy & fear it has fallen. I would have sent up this morning but waited in hopes of getting a dispatch from my Bro. Sam who is some 40 miles from Clinton, I will still wait till morning in hopes I may get some thing definate to inclose in this. You have full account of Genl Lees glorious exploits in the North, we have dispatch to day that he has whipped Genl Meade at Gettysburg & taken 40,000 prisoners. Most too many to be true, I have no doubt he has whipped him & may get Baltimore & threaten Washington, but avails but little if V.B. has fallen. Genls Magruder & Taylor have taken Kenner Station on Jackson R.R. 12 miles above N.O.[26] & reported to have since taken N.O. I send you all the late papers I have. Command me Miss Belle in any way & I will serve you if possible. Alas *alas* Vicksburg has surrendered, starved out. Staff & field officers retained Horses & Side arms, all paroled & have come out Johnston has about 40,000 & will resist any advance Grant may make. I can't write more

Your friend truly
Thos Henderson

26. Taylor's Scouts pushed down near Kenner, sixteen miles from New Orleans. Taylor, *Destruction*, 175.

4

Romance with Dr. Moses

1863 LETTERS: JULY 13–DECEMBER 20

From Captain Thomas Henderson

Panola July 13, 1863

Miss Belle Edmondson,

Yours of 7 Inst. came duly to hand with the batch of papers for which I am much obliged. The letters were promptly mailed. That *man* has been sent to Columbus & will be kept in custody for a month at least— he gives his name as McGibbon, was driven out of M. because he would not take the oath, has been a Maj. In Fed. army is lame in left leg—the bridge of his nose is broken or deformed, has very serious thoughtful cast of countenance. Says he came out to join our Navy—[1]

Courier got in last Night with Bulletin 8 & 9 & Times of 6 Inst. No letter from you—& I notice you say nothing about getting any letter from me, & that I owe you a great many letters, I have written you 3 times since the last raid & sent you all the papers I could get—have no southern papers later than the 4 Inst, which I sent you by Capt Carroll with flag of truce. In the way of news, we have no official advices of the fall of Vicksburg, but it certainly has been surrendered, & Genl. Grant advanced on Canton 9 Inst. heavy skirmishing that day & 10th when enemy reached our fortifications at Jackson 12 oclock & were repulsed

---

1. Grant had made use of the ruse of having a man, who was in reality a spy, drummed out of Memphis during the Vicksburg campaign. William Freeman Vilas, *A View of the Vicksburg Campaign* (Madison: Wisconsin Historical Commission, 1908), 44. There was a Federal officer, Colonel Joseph McKibbin, "a worthless fellow," whom General Rosecrans sent away for drunkenness. He was in the area and might be Belle's "supposed spy on a Clay bank horse." Simon, *Grant Papers*, 5:328n; Charles A. Dana to Stanton, 1 Nov. 1863, *OR*, 31, pt. 2, 54.

by Lorings Divs. with heavy loss & the capture of 400, prisoners. The enemy then flanged up this way & cut Telegraph between J. & Canton, & we have had no reliable information from Jackson since. Yesterday got dispatch saying heavy skirmishing near Canton enemy advancing up R.R. force small & are felt confident of holding place, no further particulars—We have no southern accounts of Lee's battles since 2d Inst. & feel deeply anxious to know how the Gettysburg fight resulted, was in hopes to have recd. 'Times' of 8 Inst. which is said to contain full accounts, & they are favorable to us. Nothing from Bragg since he fell back to Bridgesport—Communication being cut below Canton we are dependant on Northern papers for our News, do send us as many & as late papers as you can get.

I am almost myself again. Hoping this may find you & yours in good health I am

Your friend

Most truly

Thos. Henderson

N.B. I sent the $2000 by safe hand to Mr Prescott Mobile & hope it will get there safe.

T.H

From Major Tracy

Grenada Miss

July 17, 1863

Miss Bell Edmondson [in another handwriting]

Near Memphis. If you will oblige me by sending a dispatch to the party below mentioned for me, you will render a favor to a poor sick Missourian who I fear will not live long and is anxious if possible to have his father come here before he dies. Telegraph in the name of someone who can see the gentleman and direct him as to the route. It may be that there is no telegraph office at the point if so please ask the operator to forward by mail. I leave tomorrow for the west. Please write my Sister.

The address is   Respectfully

   Mr. Frank Jacoby   Your friend

      Clarksville   H W Tracy [his signature]

P.S. [in Tracy's handwriting]

If you receive or hear of any letters for me from home please send them to Capt Henderson who will forward them by the Courier to Arkansas.

H W Tracy

From Louise Taylor

Home July 20th

My dear Belle

I received your letter this morning, you cannot imagine how it pleased me. I had looked and expected it until I almost gave up all hope of hearing from you. Still I could not think that you had forgotten me so soon now promise me you will write often. You speak of Vicksburg—it made me miserable the day I heard of it I laid aside all else and gave vent to my feelings in a good hearty cry. I cannot but think it was badly managed. It is certain by the horrible loss we have sustained. It was our boasted stronghold—their greatest bug bear—it kept 100,000 men watching it for two years—it was terrible. I shudder when I think of it, but the fall of Vicksburg could not shake my confidence and faith as to the ultimate result. The news from Lee is also bad. I also heard from Mr T. he had arrived safely and was at Jacksonport previous to the attack on Helena—(where by the by they were whipped) if you can write to him, say we are all well. I have not heard one word from Mrs Price. I suppose she was allowed to stay at home. All of Genl Price's property has been confiscated by the thieves. I thought Miss Blennerhasset had returned what keeps her so long. I wish you would try and find out where my brother is. I suppose both Nidelets were in V—[2]as to our friend you say he is with Johnston. I saw Mrs—when I came to St Louis but not since. I think she will go South in the fall—she is sad & low spirited she spoke of you so affectionately in fact all our friends are anxious to see you they have heard so much about you. Your Sister is making quite a stay but I dont wonder. We found Dixie a mighty comfortable place how happy I was with my dear husband may God grant this terrible separation may soon be over. Belle where is Bragg's Army? When you hear from Mrs Hunt let me know where she is, etc. Did the Yankees take Jackson? I am glad you got her things to her—she was so kind to us. As to your going—if I were you I would wait till things were more settled as you say your father is old & feeble and requires all the comfort you can give him. Let me know all your plans—what you intend doing etc. You surprise me when you say Mrs D[uke] & Mrs C[layton] have taken the oath—give them my love tell Mrs D. she promised me her carte de visite and I want it if she is a Yankee—and old Seymour is there yet. I suppose he will marry her yet—I have no confidence in him. Give my best love to your father & sisters. We are all well.

---

2. There were two Dr. Nidelets, Sylvester and James. Dr. James Nidelet served with General Price and was with him when he died. Robert E. Shalhope, *Sterling Price: Portrait of a Southerner* (Columbia: University of Missouri Press, 1971), 289.

Pa is here with me also my Sister Lisa & Mr Taylor's niece Miss Wash—
so I have a very nice time we ride on horseback—in buggy—go visiting
etc and amuse ourselves quietly—Belle do write me often. I hope it will
not be very long before I see you. Kiss the little children for me. Tell
me all Major T & the Dr say about affairs below—

Your true and affectionate friend
Louise

From Captain Thomas Henderson

Panola Augst. 6, 1863

Dear Miss Belle,

I wrote you in reply to yours of 1st Inst. & sent you a batch of letters
in which I hope you find that special one you wanted. Mr W. has gone
up since, but I had nothing to write in the way of News, & am in the
same way still—I saw a Gent who left Richmond 31st ult. The President
was in his usual health then, & he does not believe the report of his
death—There was much talk there, and all along the way of recognition
intervention etc. Some thing of the sort is certainly on the topic, but
nothing definite is yet known—Genl. Johnston is at Mobile where the
next attack is expected to be made, tho his forces are between Meridian
& Jackson some where—Lee has fallen back near his old position on
the Rappahannock—Bragg's forces are at Chattanooga & Atlanta—A
force is said to be concentrating at Helena to advance on Little Rock—
learn what you can about it—Logan's Div is said to have gone up river
above Memphis—How is that, I thought only Cavl force (Griersons) had
gone that far, all the rest were at Helena—A deserter gave me the news
also reported the 1,000 gone to West Tenn. Where is Grierson? Has
Grant gone to Washington?[3] With very best wishes for your health &
happiness

Your friend truly
Thos Henderson

From Lucy A Martin

Jackson Aug 9th 63

Dear Miss Edmondson

It has been several months since I saw you and many eventful scenes
have taken place here since you left us. Our houses have been burned I

3. Grant was in New Orleans conferring with Banks about a movement west of the
Mississippi. Grierson was in Memphis nursing an injured knee. Grant, *Memoirs*, 581;
W. H. and Shirley Leckie, *Unlikely Warriors: General Benjamin H. Grierson and His
Family* (Norman: University of Oklahoma Press, 1984), 106.

mean Mrs Freemans and mine, besides many others and our place does not look like it did when you were here, but still there is much fortitude and cheerfulness shown by our people. Although we have been deprived of nearly every thing. But no doubt you have had an account of the pillaging & burning of many houses in Jackson. I would like if I had time & other circumstances permitting to give you an account of it. However I can only write you a short letter this evening. A lady from this place a Miss Trigg will take this letter & says she will bring down the articles you purchased for Anna Martin, Mrs Frecman, Miss Gwin, Miss Meagle & myself. Please send them all if you can, but if you cannot send all now, send those for my daughter & myself as I need them. I hope you are well and write to me. As I have not heard from you for a long time & suppose you have had no opportunity of writing. Anna joins me in love & kind regards to your family

Yours truly

Lucy A. Martin

From Albert Eyrich

Vicksburg Miss

Aug 10 1863

Miss Belle Edmondson

Esteemed friend

You will perceive this is dated Vicksburg instead of Natches [Natchez]. I was compelled to ship my stock to this point and obtain a permit here for Natchez. I am compelled to remain here for a few days, and concluded to open this correspondence which privilege you kindly granted me.

Vicksburg has suffered but little considering the immense number of shot and shell thrown into it by the "Vandal foeman." Caves in which the citizens found protection from Yankee Shot & Shell are numerous. Opposite the house in which I write this are 8 or 10 of those caves. My present boarding house, formerly Genl Pembertons head quarters, was struck by a shell which went through walls, partitions, ceilings and lastly right through the center of Genl P's bed.

The landlady said Genl Pemberton could have held out longer, had he felt so disposed—provisions were not exhausted, and that Mule meat was not a last resort—but at first merely an experiment, as the troops wanted fresh meat. It is reported here to day that Pemberton with his army is enroute to enforce Genl Bragg at Chattnooga I hope this is true. You have heard of Memphis being the dustiest place etc; Vicksburg is ten times worse—the dust is not less than 4 inches deep—and Soldiers riding through the streets, keep the streets quite foggy.

I think my next letter will be written at Natchez but direct to Vicksburg Care Cole Saunders & Co. till you hear from me again. In anxious expectation of your reply I remain

Your devoted friend
Albert Eyrich[4]

From C. M. Fackler
Per Jno Page

Montgomery Ala
Augt 18th 1863

Miss Belle Edmondson
Shelby Co Tenn
Dear Miss Belle

Please deliver the enclosed letter to my dear wife as soon as convenient. She writes that she has not recd a line from me since we left Memphis. Thanks to your kindness, I have been more favored by receiving *two* letters from her.

Please also take the trouble to write me how my letters can in future reach you for her. I have written about twenty to her, care of Capt Henderson to be delivered to you by him. I refer you to John Page for current news of the day. I was in Selma a few days since. Your brother James H. was there, in good health & spirits. He has secured the command of a privateer on the "blue waters" & will doubtless make name & fame in his new field of interprise & patriotism.

I was in Selma also a few weeks since & saw another brother of yours, who made himself known to me—He was also well. Some one told me they had seen *you* at some town in Georgia a week or two since but I have since learned it was a sister—She was also in good health—

Ed Booker of Memphis, told me a few days since, he was present at La Grange Georgia at the marriage of John Walker & Miss Annie Newell—John had a furlough of only 15 days, and I believe half of that had expired before the ceremony. Ladies of the Confederacy can get married these days & not be troubled with long and embarrassing Honey Moons—

---

4. Albert Eyrich, Julius Eyrich's brother, was a news agent before the war. His brother supplied Belle with northern newspapers, so popular with Henderson. *1860 Directory*, 156.

Ed Kirk is fine, just from Etowah. The girls were all well & had just taken a pleasure jaunt to the Hd Qrs of the Army at Chattanooga—

Miss Belle, please write to me as shown—Direct to Etowah Georgia and your letter will reach me

Very respectfully
Your friend
C. M. Fackler[5]

From Albert Eyrich

Vicksburg Miss
August 19 [1863]

My dear Miss Belle

I received a letter from my brother George, (who has taken my place at Blelock Co and to whom I have issued an "order" to wait on you as I would if present. He is better looking than I am so the girls say but that makes no difference.[)] Vicksburg is a hard place. The Federal Soldiers are very sickly[6]—the city is very unhealthy. I took sick before I had been here a week—a constant fever for 48 hours, but eventually broke it, and am now nearly well. If I get sick again I shall leave Vicksburg. I told you the last time I saw you, I was going to Natchez which was my destination—I had to remain here to wait for Mr Saunders—when he reached here he offered to double my wages, provided I would remain in this place. This was too large an increment to reject and of course I accepted and here I shall have to remain for the present.

I find the citizens of V- & vicinity destitute of every thing. The ladies are without shoes and no prospect to get them until trade is opened, I saw some ladies who told me they had no more than one change of clothes. This is awful—

Vicksburg is not so seriously battered up as some would suppose after the ordeal it has gone through. There are but few houses in the place which were not injured. I wrote you in my first letter that the city was injured but slightly, but I must acknowledge, since looking round that

---

5. Calvin M. Fackler was a Memphis cotton factor who fled when the city fell. His wife, Ann, was the sister of Belle's friend Shallie Kirk. The Fackler home was on Union Street between Second and Third. Ibid.

6. The sickness among the soldiers at Vicksburg was commented on by two Federal soldiers who were there at the same time Albert Eyrich was. An Iowa soldier remembered it as a "siege of fever and ague," and the Chaplain of the 124th Illinois Volunteers recalled a "malarial fever, of a peculiar type." Alexander G. Downing, *Downing's Civil War Diary*, ed. Olynthus B. Clark (Des Moines: The Historical Department of Iowa, 1961), 135; R. L. Howard, *A History of the 124th Illinois Volunteers from Aug. '61-Aug. '65* (Springfield: W. H. Bokker Co., 1880), 132.

there are but few houses which were not struck—either by Shot or Shell—The Catholic Church got a round shot through both walls—A shell exploded, inside the church during service one sunday—but strange to say, injured no one. But few houses escaped some injury. One lady who had been living in a Cave up to 2 or 3 days previous to the surrender ventured out to look after her house and before she had proceeded fifty yards, a shell took her head entirely off. Such as this was of rare occurence. There were but few Citizens killed.

I hope to hear from you soon till then I remain

Truly Yours

Albert Eyrich

P.S. Leave your letters for me with brother at B & Co—We can get more by mail he will put it in our Packages

Albert

From Captain Henderson

Panola Augst 25, 1863

Miss Belle

I am back again at my old post & so anxious to know how you are & all the news that I write this on my knee—The 700 Yanks from above met the 800 from below at Grenada Monday about sunset within an hour of each other. We (Col Simmons comm) skirmished with them a short time, burned the two RR bridges and fell back towards West Point, called a halt at Bellfontaine, the Yanks burned all but 5 engines & 8 or ten cars, the two Depots, Boot mill, one Blacksmith's shop & the Mester block opposite the Collins House.[7] Remained in town all day Tuesday, & crossed Tallahatchie, where some went towards Memphis & the remainder towards different points on the RR devastating the country as they went—Genl Whitfield turned back to Jackson from near Duck Hill. Genl Chalmers came up with him and is now in Grenada. My Co holds the post here again & will likely do so for some time. I have no late news from Genl Lee, Bragg & Beauregard. All quiet on 14 Inst. Please send me all the papers you can get as you have so often done before & write me all the news—Hoping you and yours have escaped without any molestation, I am

Truly your friend

Thos Henderson

[Written in pencil, very faded, smudged and stained]

7. Two Federal expeditions combined forces from Big Black River, Mississippi, and from La Grange, Tennessee, for a raid on the Mississippi Central Railroad, 10–20 Aug. Grant to Halleck, *OR*, 30, pt. 1, 18–24.

From Emily Barr

1 Sept 1863

Dear Belle;

I hear through Jane that you have some goods for me. I am glad to hear you have for I do assure you I need any & every thing in the way of goods. You have probably heard that the Yankees destroyed every thing we had in our House. I left & carried only a few winter clothes. We lost all of our summer clothes & winter ones too except what I carried with me & it is impossible to replace them here. We can not get one yard domestic or calico here. If you can send me any thing of the kind when you send those things you have for me I will cheerfully pay you— tho we can get nothing but Confederate money—though I suppose we can sell that for Tennessee. If you can send them to Pontotoc I can get them. I am not atal particular whether the domestic is bleached or unbleached—which ever is the cheapest. How do you all get on with the Yankees? Where is Shallie? How is Hal Rodgers? give her my love. I am going to Oxford tomorrow. We have almost nothing there—not a sheet pillow case towel—window curtains or any comfort but we can live on almost nothing if we can get clothes. I have been spinning but I think we will suffer before I can clothe my family in that way. I have been with her [?] 4 weeks. I have been from home 9 months—Mr Barr's with Chalmers & think I shall see him oftener at Oxford—& therefore I shall stay there. I wish you would come & stay with me. Emmie sends her love to you & Shallie & Hal. I am busy packing or I would write more. Let me hear from you—& dont let me give you any trouble—if what I ask of you is too much let it pass without complying. I shall always be glad to hear from you.

Yours sincerely

Emily Barr[8]

---

8. Colonel Hugh A. Barr, Oxford lawyer, was paymaster for General Chalmers's division. His wife, Emily, was a friend of the Edmondsons from their Pontotoc days. Colonel Barr may have been the inspiration for the character Thomas Sutphen in *Absalom, Absalom* (New York: Random House, 1936). Colonel Barr owned twelve miles of land from Oxford to Burgess. Faulkner's "Mammy Callie Barr," an ex-slave who worked for his family, once belonged to the Barrs. *Biographical and Historical Memoirs of Mississippi*, 2 vols. (Chicago: Goodspeed Publishing Co., 1891), 346–47; Maude Morrow Brown, "History of Lafayette County" (typescript), MDAHJ; Elizabeth M. Kerr, *Yoknapatawpha* (New York: Fordham University Press, 1969), 87; John Faulkner, *My Brother Bill* (New York: Trident Press, 1963), 48–51.

From Captain Thomas Henderson

Panola Sept 1st 1863

Miss Belle

There is a rumor of fighting at Chattanooga, but nothing certain. 2nd Div of Johnston's Army are there & he may be for what I can learn—Some of our Cavl are coming up this way—The Va Army was quiet last advices. Several of my Boys have chills, please send me $2 worth (inclosed) Shallenburgers Pills—No late paper to send you. Many thanks for your continued Services

Your friend truly
Thos Henderson

From Captain Thomas Henderson

Panola Spt 5, 1863

Dear Miss Belle

The very day your documents arrived I met with a chance of sending them to Meridian & hope the Dr has them by this time. I am truly sorry to hear I shall lose your valuable services, & hope something may yet turn up by which you may act as heretofore. Mr McIntosh tells me you want to use some Cotton—No one, not even the President, under the laws, has a right to grant that authority—I have asked for the priviledge to sell cotton for arms, ammunition & medicine, & it was denied me, but I was told to get those articles & *salt*,[9] & no questions would be asked how they were obtained. I say the same to you & I know Col Blythe will let you use one Bale of cotton in getting Salt & other necessaries.

In the way of news I have nothing of importance—No fighting at Chattanooga last accounts—Bombardment of Charleston still going on—I do hope those English vessels of ours may get there in time to cut off Gilman's supplies & raise the blockade—but I suppose they will go to Boston or New York first. I send you the latest Southern papers—

Your friend truly
Thomas H

9. Salt was a precious commodity in the Confederacy. Grant considered it as contraband as cotton. For a study of the importance of salt, see Ella Lonn, *Salt as a Factor in the Confederacy* (New York: W. Neal Co., 1933); John K. Bettersworth, *Confederate Mississippi* (Baton Rouge: Louisiana State University Press, 1943), 153–55; Simon, *Grant Papers*, 5:240n.

From Belle Edmondson To Captain Henderson [stamped Rebel Archives]

Capt Henderson—

We have been rather bland in the way of news for a week or more—I was near Memphis to day trying to find out what was going on. I saw two trains on Charleston road, 35 Cars crowded with Soldiers going to Corinth so they said, troops moving out in direction of Germantown on State Line Road all morning, they said they all belonged to 18th Army Corps (Shermans) and were all bound for Corinth—Part of 16th Army Corps left—for I saw 3rd Regulars with this train—Grouped in Chetlains[10]—I could fill four pages with rumors about troops &c—but do not think it would be of much importance. Some say they are only moving these troops back and forth to mislead our men—this may be so[11]—but ought to be decided by wise heads—who are perfect in regard to judging of troops and their movements. We never want another Hillson affair—They are evidently making every exertion to relieve Rosencranz [sic]—and from all I can see there are a good many troops still passing through Memphis—Sherman himself had not left Memphis this evening—Hurlbut is still there no one seems to know whether he remains or who commands—They are still buisy with Negro forces strengthening the lower and upper Bateries of Fortifications which have heretofore been very weak—No change in Fort [Pickering] of troops, all just as first news sent—The lines are partially open and I think in a few days will be all right—Then I will try my luck again—and will always remember you in newspaper &c—I sent in to day and got the latest then—no Boat down on account of low water for several days—therefore no very late papers—Resume and send all late southern news—Please forward the Enclosed by courier who will be careful, and oblige your true friend

Belle Edmondson

Sept 8th 1863

From Major Thomas H. Price

Selma Ala Sept 27 1863

Miss Bell

I send you by Miss Wheatley of Memphis a set of Lava jewelry—breastpin & earrings which you will be kind enough to send, or have

---

10. Colonel, later Brigadier General Augustus I. Chetlain (1824–1914), 16th Army Corps, Twelfth Illinois Regiment. Troops in the Department of the Tennessee, 31 Dec. 1863, *OR*, 32, pt. 3, 567.

11. Sherman was moving east to join Rosecrans. Grant, *Memoirs*, 2:24.

sent for me, to Mr J. B. Semoine Commission Merchant St. Louis—by Express I need not tell you they are for my wife, and about which I have written her & also Mr Semoine. Messers Orgill & Bros are friends of Mr Semoine and if you would take or send the package to them they would attend to it for you or if not there I would suggest Mr Abell—get whoever attends to it to take a receipt from the Express Co & if necessary let the agent see what it is & have the value they are willing to pay for it if lost fixed in the receipt and let the receipt be taken *in the name* of the party who sends it so that party can collect if necessary—The case containing the articles should be put into a small paper box & sealed up and directed as indicated to

> "Mr J. B. Semoine
> Commission Merchants
> *St Louis Mo*"

Let the charges be collected in St Louis—I hope you will pardon me for troubling you so much; but I do so relying upon what I know to be the goodness of your heart—

I suppose the late successes will be no news to you—I only hope that they may continue—I saw your brother a few days ago—I believe he is now in Mobile. He was quite well when I saw him and I was glad to hear from you through him—I wish you would write to my wife Mrs Bettie S. Price *under cover* to Mrs Slyvia Cross Brunswick Mo—I have not heard from Genl Price direct for a long time—wish I could write you some good news about him—Please excuse this note & write to your friend & obed servt

> Thos H. Price

You can say to my wife that you heard from me that I am well &c

From Captain Thomas Henderson

Panola Sept 28, 1863

Dear Miss Belle,

Capt Sam [Henderson] reached here two days after you left & was so badly disappointed he did not get to see you—He brot nothing additional about the late glorious victory, but what you find in the accompanying Mss ps [Mississippi papers] of 22nd—A dispatch was recd yesterday that some of our Genl was in Rosecrans rear, trying to cut off supplies coming to him,[12] he having destroyed all supplies with him—

---

12. Confederate troops took up siege positions around the Union forces bottled up in Chattanooga. W. B. Hazen, *A Narrative of Military Service* (Boston: Ticknor & Co., 1885), 148; James Lee McDonough, *Chattanooga—A Death Grip on the Confederacy* (Knoxville: University of Tennessee Press, 1984), 45, 48, passim.

the operator failed to take copy, & cant remember what Genl it is in rear—the Northern accounts satisfy me that we have gained a glorious victory—I hope soon to get full particulars of casualties & will send them to you. I hand you copy of Genl Braggs congratulatory address to the Army, a first rate thing. You dont know how much we have missed you & Miss Tate, hope you reached home safe & found all well—

Your friend truly

Thos Henderson

ENCLOSURE WITH HENDERSON'S LETTER

Genl Bragg's Congratulatory Address. [Henderson's handwriting] After days of severe battle, preceeded by heavy important outpost affairs, you have stormed the barriers & breastworks of the enemy, & driven him before you in confusion. You have destroyed an army, largely superior in numbers, whose constant theme was your demoralization, whose constant boast was your defeat. Your patient endurance under heaviest trials, have been lately rewarded. Your commander acknowledges obligations & promises to you in advance, the countries gratitude. But our labor is not ended. We must drop soldiers tears upon the graves of the noble men who have fallen by our sides and move forward—

Braxton Bragg

Genl

This address was made just after the hard fought battle near Tunnell Hill on the 19, 20, 21st Sept 1863—[13]

From Lt. William Mcconnell

Panola 30 Sept 1863

Miss Belle

After leaving your home I concluded that it would be wise to have a report Thursday if we could get it & so informed your brother—hope it was all right—we sent Mr Harbert up & here after when we send anyone will be very particular to send a prudent & discreet man. Capt Henderson says send your salt down immediately & all will be right—

Reports from the South are that our forces have surrounded Rosecrans & cut off his supplies—Longstreet occupies Lookout Mountain while Buckner is between Rosecrans & Burnside. Of course the federals still occupy Chattanooga.

Below I send you the latest dispatch

---

13. A slightly different version of Bragg's address is in *OR*, 30, pt. 2, 38. In the latter version the date is 22 Sept. 1863, "Headquarters Army of Tennessee, Field of Chickamauga."

Batesville, Miss Sept 29 1863

Capt Henderson

Gen Forrest repulsed the enemy at Cleveland[14]—It is reported there Genl Rosecrans sent flag of truce into our lines asking permission to send some supplies to his wounded soldiers. We captured thirty thousand muskets—Forty five pieces of artillery and some 8 or 10 Thousand prisoners—Some two thousand Feds came out to Canton—our forces engaged them this morning—Captured some horses & Yankees drove them back in direction of Yazoo City. Dont know who commanded on either side—

Marshall Oprt

The Capt would write to you but is too busy. I leave tomorrow for the bottoms—Tell Mrs Dashiell that I am much obliged &c have forwarded her letters—She shall hear from me Soon—Am sorry to have no papers to send—Capt H. sent latest by Mr. Smith.

Yours &c

[torn] McConnell

From Captain Thomas Henderson

Panola Oct 3/63

D. Miss Belle,

Yours by McConnell came duly to hand & I hope & believe the information obtained is all that is wanted & I think will lead to good results very soon, you don't know how thankful I am to you for it. I sent you Southern paper of 26 Ult. by Mr Pope, & have none later to send you. Our telegraph has been down below Jackson 3 days & I have No dispatch Since that McConnell sent you—There is No doubt that we gained a victory—& have Rosecrans in Chattanooga on Short allowance & No chance to get more Supplies unless they whip our Men first.[15] They are reinforcing rapidly or rather send Men forwd whether they get in or not is more than we can tell—Capt Sam got here a day or so after you left, regretes so much not seeing you. May *possibly* get to your house, but this is strictly Contraban, My boys here all getting better & I hope McIntosh is likewise, poor fellow he has had a hard time—If your Salt wagon comes down, I will start a load of *4* [cotton bales] back

---

14. Forrest proceeded via Cleveland and engaged and drove off the enemy at Charleston, Tennessee. Report of N.B. Forrest, *OR*, 30, pt. 2, 523–26; Henry, *Forrest*, 195.

15. The river was closed and the only line of supply for the Union forces was a wagon road forty miles long across Walden Ridge. Hazen, *Narrative*, 148; McDonough, *Chattanooga*, 47.

if I have to stop it the other side of the River & send it after a while.
Kind regards to Mrs D. & Bob—

Your friend truly
Thos Henderson

From Captain Henderson To Lt. Carman

Panola Oct 7. 1863

Dear Carman,

Yours by Bransford is recd—& carefully noted—am Sorry to say all
your labour in getting information from Memphis will avail nothing at
this time—Genl [Stephen] Lee had to defer his attack & go elsewhere,
of which I will tell you in Next communication, Keep the fact of his not
coming to your Self—Genl Chalmers has or will make some demonstra-
tions Some where on the RR—at Moscow I suppose—hope he may Succeed but have my doubts—I send latest Southern papers which look
over, & send to Miss Belle with *this Note*. I have certain information that
2 large Siege Guns are in place on Lookout Mountain & were to open
on Rosecrans about the 1st Ult. & I hope will make him "git up & git"
towards Nashville Soon.[16] Last dispatch says all quiet at Chattanooga—
No fighting in Va. Nothing from Charleston. Lt. McConnell still in the
bottom—Sick here all getting better. With best regards to Mrs D. Miss
Belle & all the Boys—hoping this may find McIntosh still improving, I
am

Your friend
Thos Henderson
Lt. J. S. Carman—

From Tate Dashiell To General [Stephen D.] Lee
[Rebel Archives]

Shelby Cty
Oct 8th/63

There is between twelve or fifteen hundred convalescent *white* Yankees in the Fort [Pickering]:Their Guns are manned entirely by negroes—This lower or south end can be taken with little or no trouble—
The three mounds have been hollowed out and converted to use—one a
powder magazine—one for stores of some kind I know not what—And
there is a Quartermaster store in this Fort:All these places are guarded
by negroes.Arrange a signal of your approach and attack and the men

16. Confederate troops succeeded in planting a battery on the east slope of Lookout
Mountain. Hazen, *Narrative*, 150.

in the prisons will sieze the guns at the south and capture the mounds turn the guns upon the Federals and help your approach. The chief Medical depot is in the Jefferson Block corner of Jefferson and Second Sts—The chief Quartermasters are in the large Block on the west side of Main St between Union and Monroe—The principal government stables are on Monroe St between 2nd and 3rd—also one on Court St and Madison near the Depot and on Union St.

Capture and destroy the houses of Lowenstines & Bros in front of Donohos old stand and W. B. Millers old stand—Hurlbut leaves within the next three days—They are now moving out partly by Memphis & Charleston R.R. Four Regiments leave today for Nashville thence to Chattanooga—

Genl Lee—

The above statement was brought out of the Federal lines today and left with the request they should be immediately sent with the accompanying Map of the city of Memphis to Genl Lee with the compliments of Miss Noble of Memphis—She did not say from whom she got the above *information*—but of course is some one reliable—With the hope that we may soon be blessed with a sight of our *rebel boys*—I am very respectfully yours

T. R. Dashiell

P.S.

My sisters the Misses Edmondsons this evening returned from a visit to a friend above the rail-road and spoke of having seen two trains pass in fifteen minutes of each other one of nineteen and the other of sixteen cars—Both trains filled with soldiers going *they* say to Corinth—they also state troops passing up the State line road Artillery and wagon trains mostly—Those were Hindmans division—I wish I had more information for you but the girls could gain but little from asking the soldiers

Yours &c
T. R. Dashiell

From Captain Henderson

Panola Oct 8. 1863

Dear Miss Belle,

Yours with the three bbls Salt reached here just at sun down & sent one wagon two miles in the country where there are 2 Bls Cotton & will send the other one down tonight, where there are two more bales, & let them get an early start in the morning cross at Randolphs Ferry & get into the main road at Bishops—I got *verbal* permission to send the cotton to you & have drawn up a document which I hope & believe will let the wagons thru. The proceeds of the cotton will surely do *us* more good than the cotton will do them. I am hurried to get Mr Hutchins off tonight, & have a dozen men talking to me & reading the papers you so kindly sent me—I send you the latest Southern papers, & I have nothing later by Telegraph than what was in my letter to Lt Carman which I requested him to send you—Lt McC is still in the bottom—he will send you his Green Backs when he comes up. I will send you the $57 before long—Genl Lee has gone & may not get his things for some time—will keep them till I hear from Capt Sam—by the way only 2 pr Gauntlets instead of 3 pr—all the rest right & have no doubt will give great satisfaction—I sent a sample Cassinett by Capt Abernathy for you to get 4½ yds for the $5 like it, if not to get 2 yds to match it exactly to make a pr of pants—Genl Chalmers had a little fight on Cold Water Northwest Holly Springs Tuesday in which he whipped & drove them back—hope he may yet do something handsome somewhere on the RR—I send Miss Perkins 2 letters & am sorry there is none for you—I must close, wishing you & yours health happiness & prosperity

Your friend truly
Thos Henderson

Had only 4 bls ready no chance to get more yet will report all about the exchange in my next. Take care of certificate & return it to me   TH

From Captain Henderson

Abbeville Oct 23/63

Dear Miss Bell,

Here I am on the front after "Sloshing around" for a week—tolerable hard to leave our good quarters at Panola but Genl C[halmers] prefered my being near him & as I have to report now to both him & Genl Johnston I shall remain with him for the present. Have a hand car every day to Water Valley & can still serve you & your friends in forwd. letters, & hope I wont have to trouble you so much but I send one now to be sent in soon as possible—& one for you, hope it is a good one—No papers to send & don't know when I will have any—Since Wheelers return from his big raid, Nothing important from Chattanooga, we are still shelling there occassionally. The enemy have got but few reinforcements yet. So a friend from there 18 Inst. reports—From Va nothing since the Army of Bull Run Bridge & fight at Cattlets Station. All right at Charleston—Now for our own matters—I was ordered off so suddenly I did not sell our Salt—it is safe & will be exchanged for Cotton if it has not already been done, when it will get to you is more than I can tell. I have two more Bales there that were given me by Mr Sam Tate[17] to get some pistols & ammunition—I send you an order on W. P. Wooten for the 2 Bales if you can send down for them I will give you one for taking in the other, the proceeds of my bale, I want to pay for five Pistols already recd—I haven't got the money yet to pay Genl L[ee's] Bill, will send it up soon as I get it—I am promised for Confederate at 4 for one—Abernathy is just in with late papers. Many thanks for them—No letter, well I know you are sorry you did not write, after reading this long one from me—Lt McConnell speaks for himself to Mrs D—two of his men were captured 14 Inst on Friars Point—I can think of Nothing more of interest—With best regards to you and yours I am

Yours truly
Thos Henderson

From Albert Eyrich

Vicksburg Miss Oct 28, 1863

Esteemed Friend

I was mortified on reaching here, that I could not find your letter. The clerk I left in charge left a few days before my return. I should not be surprised, if he had taken it back to Memphis, as he took a good many papers.

My health is much improved. The weather has been very cold, accompanied by heavy frost, which has had a tendency to make this place much healthier. I think my health will remain good.

The reign of terror such as Memphis and vicinity once experienced has commenced here. Two men have been killed and robbed this week, and to night, in sight of the Washington Hotel, a man was knocked down and robbed, who had not been in Vicksburg 30 minutes. The Commanding Generals are much liked by the Southern people in and near this place. They treat the Ladies with much more respect than those at Memphis. I hope they will remain.[18]

I am afraid my letters will be very uninteresting to you, but you know we have but *little* to write about in this "far off" Country. My duties are very ardous just now. From 6 AM till 8 P.M. I am on my feet, and I have

---

17. Sam Tate, president of the Memphis and Charleston Railroad before the war, was in charge of the Selma to Meridian Railroad project. Young, *Memphis*, 96.

18. When General James Birdseye McPherson commanded at Vicksburg even the "Yankee-hating belles" liked him. Described by one of his officers as young, active and handsome, he was deeply involved with a "handsome Southern grass widow." Lewis, *Sherman*, 299; Andrew Hickenlooper, "Reminiscences," typescript copy of original manuscript, Hickenlooper Collection, CHS.

to keep my own books which I must do after closing the store. My letters I have to write when mind and body are worn out. I hope, therefore, you will excuse dull leters. I hope you are well and in your usual good spirits, of which latter though I am confident, as you have lately read such good news.

Hoping you will find this and Myself worthy an answer, I remain, with high regards

Sincerely yours
Albert Eyrich

From Major Thomas H. Price

Selma Ala Oct 31st 1863

Miss Bell Edmondson
  Memphis Tenn

My dear friend, having an opportunity to write you by your Brother, I do so, without the least particle of news, or anything else of sufficient interest [to] pay you for the trouble of reading, and if I did not know something of the goodness of your heart I might hesitate somewhat about troubling you so much about matters so particularly interesting to myself only—

I had hoped to have received a letter from you before this in answer at least to one of several which I have written you within the last two months—I wrote to you by Miss Wheatley who lives in Memphis, and also sent by her, to your care, some jewelry for my wife—Have you heard anything of it? She may have delivered it with the letter to you to Mr Abel will you please inquire, if you have not already heard & let me know by the return of your Brother—

Write to me at any rate by your Brother when he returns, and if you have heard anything of my little wife for goodness sake let me know, as I have not had a single line from her since she left for home—Please see Miss Annie Perdue before you write, I have understood recently that She has received a letter from my wife, and if so get her to send it to me—

I send a letter by your Brother directed to Mrs Anne Powell in Wisconsin—please mail it for me, and I beg of you to write to my wife at once and insist that she write *to you* a simple *family* letter telling you how all are, that you may convey word to me by first chance—You know our friends in Mo are very much persecuted now, and I know not but that my wife may be under some sort of restraint or watched so that she cannot write to me; but there can be no objection to her writing to you—Now Miss Bell will you write, and write to me and tell me that you have written—I hope you have not forgotten the name (Bettie S) but it would be well to write under cover to her father Mr Thos H. Almand Brunswick Mo—or Messers Marchant & Beasly same place, either will do—I heard about three weeks ago from Genl Price & Staff— all well, none of them killed or wounded in the battles in Ark.

I will likely be here all this week and will expect to hear from you often, and any service I may be able to render you or your friends here I hope you will not hesitate to call on me. I am here under special orders for the secretary of war representing the interests & attending to business for the Dept Trans Miss—the particular nature of which not prudent to write, less the letter by chance should be captured[19]—

Remember me kindly to Miss Hal & all inquiring friends and Believe me most truly your friend & obed Servt

Thos H. Price

From Captain Phil T. Allin

Okalona Miss Nov 23th 1863

Miss Bell Edmondson

Dear Miss

It becomes my painful duty to announce to you the death of our mutual friend George Imes—I met him and Mr Rawlings at Rome Ga after our command had left there as we were crossing the Chattooga River about two miles from Cedar Bluff he was drowned The River was swimming and his horse threw him off he could not swim and before we could give him any assistance he went down and never rose we used every exertion to recover his body but failed—having frequently heard him speak of you as one of his particular friends I write to you hoping that you will have opportunity to break the news to his Sister—Your brother Ed is with the Company and well

Yours with great Respect

Phil T. Allin[20]

Captain-Bluff City Grays

From Madame Levert

[November 23, 1863]

Dear Miss Edmondson

I called this morning to take you to drive, and was very disappointed to find you absent from the Hotel, will not yourself and Miss Kirk come

19. Major Price was to deliver "26,000 stand of arms" sent from Richmond, west of the river. J. Gorgas to James A. Seddon, 15 Nov. 1863, *OR*, 34, pt. 3, 757–59; ser. IV, vol. 2, 955–57.

20. Phil T. Allin, Co. F, Eleventh Tennessee Cavalry, Jordan and Pryor, *Campaigns*, 693; Lenow, *Elmwood*, 97; Mathes, *Old Guard*, 27.

to see me this evening about eight o'clock. Bring any beaux you please
with you. It is my reception evening. If you will do me the favor to ask
Dr Keller to come with you I shall be much obliged to you. Be sure to
come.

Your friend
Mme LeVert

From Major Price

Selma Ala Nov 23rd 1863

Miss Bell Edmondson   Mobile Ala

My dear friend. I start in the morning for Meridian Miss and possibly
will go as far as Brandon and it may be, I will go before returning to
some point on the Miss River under orders from Richmond received
soon after you left here, so you see how *fortunate* as well as unfortunate
I was in not going with you and Miss Shawley [Shallie] to Mobile.

I go on important official business the nature of which I will not
trouble you to relate; but the *time when* I will be back is what I wish to
write you about, and yes this is the big thing that I dont know myself.

My mind is pretty fully made up to go with you to Panola when you
start home if I can find out when this is and I can possibly leave my
official engagements long enough, and I hope to get through with the
matters now upon me by the time you wish to return.I will try to write
you from Meridian or Brandon when I will know better how much time
I will have on this trip long enough to enable me to meet you at Meridian
or Brandon and go with you from there; but this must be determined in
the future; and will depend upon the length of time *you* will remain in
Mobile, as well as my own movements which *shall* be regulated to suit
your convenience as much as possible.

Write upon receiving this and direct to care Capt A. Dauria, Meridian, and let me know when you will go home, if you have fixed a definite
time in your mind, for I doubt not with your present *very pleasant sur-
roundings* you will be at a loss to fix the hour of departure; but for your
consolation let me remind you that *Moses* was once separated from his
people for a long time; but finally "came out of the wilderness" all right,
with a wife wedded while he was away from home.

Don't fail to write to me, for you know I must write that letter home
by you, and that will have to be done before *we*, or *you* as the case may
be, start up to Panola—

I have been to the express office and told the agt that I was looking
for a small package from Mobile (the buttons)Don't forget them—the
tailor is making my coat now—send them by the Pioneer Express Co.,

if you have not already started them. I wish I had time to write you a more decent letter, and a long letter to tell you how I missed you when you left, and then when I think of you and Miss Shallie the morning before you left I almost intuitively give my moustach a twist, and Oh! how pleasant the memory yet—how gracefully—how pleasant you both acquited yourselves, and to me like twin strawberries, or the gathering two ripe peaches from the same limb.

Remember me kindly to Miss Shallie, and ask her how are the lips— at my last examination I thought them better, if not entirely well—

Write me how you found matters when you got to Mobile, and if you do not understand my exact meaning ask Miss Shallie and tell me also how you are spending your time, and whether my friends Mr and Mrs Smith have called on you yet—I wrote to them the evening you left.

> Until we meet believe me your
> friend
> and obdt servt
> Thos H. Price Maj &c

From James H. Edmondson

My Dear Bell

I was very sorry that I did not get to see you before you left this morning, Mrs Clayton arrived shortly after you left and was very anxious to go on at once but concluded twas best to wait for you—You must abandon your trip to Selma Bell and go with Mrs Clayton I know the Kirks will want for you to stay on here still longer but it is by no means advisable to do so—You know what I said to you—With my best love to all at home wishing you a very pleasant trip I am your Affectionate Bro—

> J. H. Edmondson

Nov 26/63

From Shallie Kirk

> Columbiana Dec 2nd/63

Dear Bell

Agreeable to promise I hasten to write you, waiting only long enough to get settled & feel at home. Columbiana is not such a bad place after all and as we are with such pleasant people as Dr McKee & his family, I think I could content myself here even longer than I will have to stay. I have been thinking about you a great deal my dear friend, and my heart has ached with *intense* sympathy for your great trouble. I yearn to administer some healing balm, to offer some soothing remedy for your

wounded heart, but alas for the inability of woman to offer consolation for any such suffering, silence after all is most [healing], and I frequently use that means of showing sympathy, though in your case it often leads to [the un]just charge of *coldness*, even when I was feeling most for you; My dear child, you could not begin to understand or appreciate how deeply & sincerely I felt all you were undergoing. I have been through many a severe trial, & thought there could be none more bitter, but yours surpasses all; I know not what to say: I know I speak idle words when I say: Go; forget him! he is not worthy to be thought of, as you think. Yet I cannot speak harshly of him without violating the trust and confidence placed in me as his friend, which I promised faithfully to be, though all others assailed him: I have never been a *false* friend, & I would not begin now; you see how I am situated. I hope you had a pleasant visit to LaGrange; I wish I could have gone with you, as I could then have seen your sister & Nannie too. I have just finished a long letter to Lou, telling her about our trip to Mobile, but I suppose you gave her a more full and better account. Mollie is writing now to Sue. I will send it with your letter & I will wait until Anna goes, before writing home as one letter can tell all of news from this quarter. We are looking for Anna every day. Mollie says, if Anna goes to Mobile again, we will go too, but I'm afraid I would not enjoy it as much as before as Dick will be away, & I would miss him so much, bless his old heart! Give my best to him & tell him to not forget to bring me something pretty when he returns from Govt lines: and say to Dr Nidelet for me, I [torn] he will not become so much infatuated with the widow Twelve as to forget his friend Shallie; by the way Bell: if you go back to Mobile you will be certain to have the pleasure of her company home with you. Tell Tom Kirtland I sent a kiss to him; I will always love him for his kindness to us. I wish dear child I had something pleasant to say to you, but I know too well nothing that I could say would give more than a transient gleam of pleasure: but be assured of *one* thing you have in me a true friend; and if I can ever serve you, you *know* it would make me happy to do so; don't forget me after you reach home but continue to write & I will always answer. Write to me before leaving Mobile.
Remember me kindly to all of our friends [torn] & say I hope to be with them soon [torn] when you go home say everything [torn] you can think of to Ma, Poppa & Sue [torn] make them as happy as possible [torn] all; I rec'd a letter from Anna last night & she too is charmed with "Dixie." Good bye dear Bell; hoping to hear from you soon I am ever your true friend

Shallie

From Major Price

(Have my letter mailed at St Louis if possible)

Selma Ala Dec 4th 1863

Miss Bell Edmondson

Mobile Ala. My ever Dear friend, I prom.ʒed myself when we last parted, that I would set apart some portion of Today, for the purpose of writing you such a letter, as I even then, while with you, felt, that I wished to write you but things of less welcome, and decidedly more *material* nature have been so crowded upon my attention almost every hour since I saw you that I almost felt unequal to the requirements of the present moment.

I desire to tell you much, *too much*, for the short space of one letter, and yet it may be nothing that has not already passed through your own mind & heart, except it may be some matters exclusively about myself of which it is quite possible I have told you all before.

Friendly letters, to me, are something more than *ink* and *paper*, or *words* and *sentences*, and though there may be nothing new in subject matter, yet there is always a presence of the writer, attended with a sort of spiritual communion hallowed by the sacred memory of the past, that seems to brighten, at least for a time, the *too* often dark pathway of life, and refreshes the soul to pursue its journey with renewed energy, like the fragrance of flowers and the babbling brook to the way worn traveler. Still taking it for granted that the feelings and sentiments which animate my own breast, are common to us both I write with the hope, that the voice of friendship may prove a welcomed visitor though no *special* message is delivered.

Allow me to say to you, my dear friend, that, having lived much longer in the world than you, and having enjoyed as much of its good, and that which is commonly called *happiness*, as usually falls to the lot of most of persons in this life, and, I assure you, upon a retrospect of the past I see nothing to inspire the desire to live it over again, it is true there are many secret memories and sentiments that are welcomed still as precious and refreshing springs of pleasure at which we *should* accustom ourselves to drink *often* rather than in the more turbid pools of bitterness and disappointment.But these green spots of the past, are still in our possession, we need not live life over again to enjoy them, they belong as well to the present, as the past, like precious jewels that have been treasured up, and may be enjoyed now, if we only would, separating from the labor and pain which they cost us.Thus you see all the good of life may be saved to us even in this world, and in the light of revelation how doubly bright and precious these blessings become, if the immortal interest of the soul have been happily not neglected when the sands of life are run out, and this brings me to the great central idea, to which unworthy as I am, I wish with the voice of friendship to turn your attention. You will remember I made some allusion to my own faith and belief in an overruling providence at our last interview, but my heart was then too much affected, and my mind too much disturbed to say what I wished and what, I now believe is all the better by being written. Oh! that I could go with your heart as to be able to bathe it, not in Lethe's oblivious waters, which might rob you of the bright side of past life, but in that precious fountain of blood, and heal it with that safe and effectual remedy, the ever blessed "balm of Gilead"—I know my dear friend, that you will very naturally say that my precept is not in keeping with my example. This, with shame and confusion to myself, I must acknowledge to be true, but nevertheless, whatever *appearances* may be, and so unworthy and ungrateful as I feel myself to be, you may rest assured I am not recommending the waters of an untried fountain; but rather one from which many a refreshing draught has been drawn, and that too when the dark clouds of gloom & bitterness hung heaviest over my future. There is much of [illegible] a philosophy in disappointment and adversity, and I believe, in almost every instance they are heavens choicest blessings in disguise, though we may from the blindness & weakness of poor human nature fail to see & enjoy the good this providence holds in store for us. Of course, I predicate what I have said, as well as what I have to say, in this connection, upon your acquiesence in my belief in the truth of Revelation. You know that there is but *one* object according to the teachings of Revelation, that is [worthy] to be loved with *all* of our hearts soul and strength without the sin of idolatry on our part: That is, according to my understanding we are not permitted to so concentrate our hearts & affection on any earthly object as to neglect the higher interest of the soul, and when we do it, we are in danger, and having the nobler part of our nature so jeopardized by the poisonous draught which we so eagerly seek; we must admit that providence to be a blessing, which takes from us the cup before it is drunk to the bitter and everlasting dregs though we may be almost overcome, for the time, by the dark billows of disappointment. I feel assured there is a higher destiny, a brighter day in store for you, yet in the future, and I must believe that one who has exhibited *so much* fortitude, and encountered so many dangers for the good of others & a beloved country in distress, will at least exercise some of that large store of virtues for self protection. In the goodness of your noble, womanly and patriotic heart you have doubtless been too confiding; but while the quiet of the crystal fountain may be disturbed, yet thank god, its limpid waters are still pure, and in spotless inocence & truth will continue to reflect, and perpetuate the deformity and blackness of the heart that would dare disturb its rest.

Despise not, nor think not one particle the less of yourself my dear friend, for you have almost innumerable friends with true hearts & loving whose good opinion and appreciation is richly worth living for, and that too with the *highest* opinion of yourself.

And now allow me to say to you in writing, what I have already promised verbally, that *all* that you have intrusted to me in confidence shall be kept most sacred; and allow me to say that I thank you most heartily for the compliment you have paid me in making me your confidant, and in return I can but remain *at all times* your obedient servt. And now, the balance of my paper about my dear wife & children and myself; and first if you go to Mo, see them for me if you can, for I am in dispair of hearing from them otherwise & if you go they will send me by you such things as I need, a memorandum of which I herewith send you, if you do not go you will please call on Mr George T. Hubbard whom you can find through Mr Seymour and get such of the articles as you can & I will come to Panola at any time you will agree to meet me there, or you can send the things to Maj Mellon at Panola or Grenada—he is the purchasing commissary for this part of the country—if you send them to him instruct him to keep them & communicate to me by letter. The things you have for my wife you can send or carry to her as the case may be—the letter herewith is for "her"; but if you do not go I want you to write to her as soon as you get home and tell her all you know about me. Believe me very truly your friend & obdt servt

Thos. H. Price Maj CSA

[marginal note] I shall expect a letter from you soon after your arrival at home—don't let me die of suspense—You must answer this also from Mobile—T H Price

From Captain Henderson

Panola Dec 20, 1863

Dear Miss Belle,

Yours & Mrs D.'s trunks have been here 3 days, & I have done my best to send them up, but the bad weather, bad roads, & high weather [water] have prevented so far. I have a promise to get them taken to Hernando tomorrow & if I can get them no further will leave them at Sim Tates—So if you send down for them, stop at his house—In the way of news I have not a word of interest, & I don't think you will find much in the papers herewith Sent, except their Presidents Message. I am suffering from a bad Stye, & can hardly see, can't you send me "an eye opener" for Christmas. With kind regards to your Father & all the family I am

Truly yr friend
Thos. Henderson

P.S.
I send you a letter from Maj Hunt of Genl Polk's Staff to his Wife Mrs Sallie Ward Butler, that was. Get Some of your Memphis friends to put in note saying how she can answer so he will get it if possible

T.H

5

The Meridian Campaign

1864 DIARY: JANUARY AND FEBRUARY

January

FRIDAY 1 'Tis New Year, a happy one to our household. Lieut Spotswood and Eddie came last Night. Poor Eddie is greatly in need of
Clothes.[1] I do not think we will have much trouble in out Gen'ling
the Yanks. I have $50 G[reen] B[acks] left I intend to devote to that
purpose. It is very cold, all nature is robed in Ice. Notwithstanding
the Yanks are such near Neighbors,[2] we have a house full of Rebels
all day, four of Hendersons Scouts, Lieut S., Eddie, Jim & Ebb
Titus. Nannie and I went in the buggy over to the Smuggler's Joe
White, to see if we could not get some things there for Eddie, failed,
bro't Tate some soap. Almost froze to death. Got home at dark, all
just finishing dinner, had a splendid time to Night. Our Armys all
seem to be Status Quo. God grant successful may be the termination
of 1864. Oh! my savior I have buried the past. Guide and leade me
from temptation. After you my God, then I live for my Country.
God bless our leaders in Dixie.
SATURDAY 2 Bettie and Uncle Elam went in town this morning on

1. Two problems that faced General Forrest as the new year began were an "extreme want of clothing" and the return of stragglers to their commands. Jordan and
Pryor, *Campaigns*, 382–84.
2. Probably a reference to the picket posts at Nonconnah Creek and the Holly Ford
Road. The Holly Ford Road was an early Indian trail that crossed the creek at a
shallow or hollow ford. Map of Memphis (1863); Thomas Frank Gailor, *Some Memories* (Kingsport: Southern Publishing Inc., 1937), 11; Elizabeth Avery Meriwether,
Recollections of Ninety-Two Years (Nashville: Tennessee Historical Commission, 1958),
65: Anna Leigh McCorkle, *Tales of Old Whitehaven* (Jackson: McCowat-Mercer
Press, 1967), 16–17.

horse-back. I sent $50 to Mr Armstrong to get Eddie's suit of clothes and other articles which he needs. Poor Soldiers this bitter cold weather I wish I had money to buy every thing they need. Lieut Spotswood went with two of Hendersons Scouts over Nonconnah to Mr Deadrick's[3] to get them to bring him every thing he needs out. They promised to do so. It has been sleeting all day. Three of the Bluff City's called this evening got their dinner, warmed, and went on over Nonconnah. Cousin Frazor[4] came this evening, and we have a house full. They are all Rebels, and we always have room for them if a hundred would come. All we can do is sit round the fire, laugh, talk and try to keep warm. Bettie and Uncle Elam have not returned yet. I feel very very uneasy as she is to smuggle Eddie's clothes.[5] Tate is out of humor, Eddie is troubled, but I think it will all be right. Yet suspense is terrible.

SUNDAY 3 Another day has passed and not one word from Bettie or Uncle Elam. No communication with Memphis to day. Too cold to go out side of the doors. Still sleeting. House still full, if not a little fuller. Tate is growing very impatient to leave for Dixie. She is really cross about Bettie, but I still have hope that it will all be right. Eddie feels badly about it, as the risk was run for him. God bless the Rebels. I would risk my life a dozen times a day to serve them. Think what they suffer for us. Henry Ferguson[6] and Lieut Spotswood left

---

3. The Deaderick plantation was located off the Pigeon Roost Road, adjacent to the Memphis and Charleston Railroad. The owner, Michael Joseph Deaderick, was the son of John George Deaderick, an early Shelby County settler. The Deaderick family once owned downtown Nashville and the hill where the state capitol stands. A Memphis street is named for the family with the same misspelling of the name [Deadrick] that Belle used in her diary. Map of Memphis (1863); Paul R. Coppock, *Memphis Sketches* (Friends of Memphis and Shelby County Libraries, 1976), 43–46; 1860 Census of Shelby County, 29 Aug. 1860.

4. Frazor Titus was a "violent secessionist" and president of the Vigilance Committee before Memphis fell to the Federals. He fled to northeast Mississippi and took refuge in various places between Pontotoc, Aberdeen and Columbus. His diary for 1864 rounds out the picture of life at Elm Ridge during this year. After the war, he was one of the people who made bond for Nathan Bedford Forrest after his indictment for treason. Keating, *Memphis*, 1:484; Frazor Titus Diary for 1864, privately held, copy of original in editors' possession; Henry, *Forrest*, 442.

5. The use of Negroes for smuggling was widespread. If caught, they were punished less severely than white southerners. It was said that few ever betrayed their owners. Parks, "Trade Center," 289; John Hallum, *Diary of an Old Lawyer* (Nashville: Southwestern Publishing House, 1895), 306–7.

6. Henry Ferguson, Second Lieutenant, Eleventh Tennessee Cavalry, was associated with the firm of Edmondson and Armstrong before the war. Jordan and Pryor, *Campaigns*, 694; *1860 Memphis Directory*, 153.

for Dixie. Henry F. bought Helen's Pony, gave $200 for it, he rode
it off. It does not seem like the Sabbath, though this is the first one
of 64. We spent the day as usual, laughing, talking and trying to
keep warm. Julian Simmons and Dashiell Perkins[7] came over from
Col Perkins. Dashiell staid, we sat up very late, and Poor old [. . .
][8] looks like the noise will drive him crazy.

MONDAY 4 I always try to see the bright side of every picture. I have
never given up hope but Bettie would come right side up, and I
think she is a star darkie. She and Uncle Elam arrived safely at
home. Bettie was loaded with contraband. Eddie a suit of clothes,
pr Boots, Gauntlets, socks, blacking and in fact every thing he sent
for. He is so grateful and real proud of all his things. Laura gave
him the Gauntlets. He went with me to my room, and I packed his
valise. He now has every thing in the world he needs, and Company
to go South with him. Sam Alexander one of the Bluff City's came
and stoped over Night to go on in the morning, old Mr Jaison[9] with
him. Dear Eddie this is his last Night with us. We all sat up very
late. Weather gloomy, bitter cold, ground still covered with snow.

TUESDAY 5 Still cold, cloudy and gloomy, has not moderated at all,
it is real dangerous traveling, the ground covered with Ice. Eddie,
has on his new suit ready to leave for camp. Mr Alexander and old
Mr Jayson are going with him, and we are better satisfied. I would
not have him stay any longer for any thing. I am perfectly disgusted
at the way in which our Soldiers are lying about, shirking their
duty.[10] Eddie has every thing to make him comfortable for this winter. Two more of the Bluff City's arrived, got their dinner, warmed
and went on over Nonconnah. Our house still full, we have a gay
time picketing for the Yankees, but I expect the boys think they
have a gayer one running in the cold at their appearance. As usual
we all sat up very late.

---

7. Julian Simmons, Chief Paymaster for Brigadier General W. H. Jackson, was
from Sardis, Mississippi. By 1864 Dashiell Perkins was color-bearer for the Seventh
Tennessee Cavalry. Mathes, *Old Guard*, 174, 191.

8. Belle left this space blank. A possible reference to Frazor Titus.

9. Possibly John A. Jeancon, a Memphis druggist. T. M. Halpin, comp., *Memphis
City Directory* (Memphis: Bingham, Williams & Co., 1866), 132.

10. The regiments and companies of the state troops which were consolidated with
Forr... Command were in the habit of staying in the field "at their own will and
pleasure . . . and returned even by large squads to their own homes." Jordan and
Pryor, *Campaigns*, 383.

MONDAY 11

Like a weary actor in a play,
Like a phantom in a dream,
Like a lost boat left to stray
Rudderless adown the stream—
This is what my life has grown,—
Since thy false heart left me lone,—
And I wonder sometimes when the laugh is loud,
And I wonder at the faces of the crowd,
And the strange fantastic measures that they tread,—
Till I think at last, till I half believe I am dead.

February

THURSDAY 4 [This date is an error. Frazor Titus reports the incident in his entry for January 28. See Helen Edmondson to Belle from Como on 4 February 1864.]

We had a terible accident to Night. Jack had Mr Wilson's[11] pistol fooling with it and shot Jane right through the body. Poor fellow he was frightened to death—it was an accident. Mr Wilson went for the Dr, he came in a great hurry. As it was Night he could not tell how serious it is, but very much fears it has struck some vital point.

FRIDAY 5 [This date is in error by one week. Frazor Titus reports this incident on Friday, 29 January. He also writes, "Belle returned from her work."]

Jane doing very well, the ball although passing so near, the kidneys, & spine, missed both. Dr Shaw has examined it by daylight and thinks she will be up again in five or six weeks. Peter and I went over to Mrs Duke's. I went to Memphis in Mr Armstrong's wagon—got the Morphine & Choroform.[12] Mr Armstrong drove me out to Mrs Duke's. I mounted old McGruder, Peter old Sam, we got home early. Jack ran off this morning we dont know where to, but I expect he has gone to Memphis.

SUNDAY 14 [Belle is still off a week. Frazor Titus reports this incident on Sunday, 7 February.]

Tate and Helen came from Dixie today.

11. One of Henderson's Scouts. There were four Scouts named Wilson. List of scouts Paroled, CC.

12. Belle's smuggling of morphine and chloroform for Dr. Moses [see Helen's letter of February 4, 1864] took place on 29 Jan. Women's clothes, especially hoopskirts were an asset in smuggling. A Confederate doctor wrote that the most fearless and successful smugglers were "shes." F. E. Daniel, *Recollections of a Rebel Surgeon* (Austin: Von Boeckman, Schutze & Co., 1899), 117.

MONDAY 15 [Frazor Titus reports the same incident for this date.]
I did not get up very early, was eating breakfast in my room, when
I was startled by the report of six or seven guns. Dressed hurridly,
on arriving at the gate found all the family, both white and black, in
the greatest state of excitement. One of the 2nd Mo[13]—Mr Brent—
relating to them the particulars of the skirmish which had taken
place only a few hundred yards from our home. A family of Negroes
had got this far on their journey from Hernando to Memphis, when
Mr Brent met them, and they ordered him to surrender at the same
time firing. Of course no Southern Soldier would ever surrender to
a Negro, he fired five times, being all the loads he had. Killed one
Negro, wounded another he ran in the woods and we saw nothing
more of him. One of the women and a little boy succeeded in getting
off also. The other woman with three girls were carried back to Hernando. The soldier got a splendid Cavalry horse & equipments, two
Mules and another horse. He left expecting the Yankees. Father had
the Negro buried where he was killed. No Yankees. Mr Wilson
came, no late news.

MONDAY 22 I mounted Mr Brent's condemned steed which proved
to be a very nice riding horse, but rather wild. I had a lovely ride,
found Mrs Morgan's after some difficulty. Mrs. Plunkett[14] was with
Missie, her Mother has been very sick, but they think she is now
recovering. I do not think so, she looks dreadfully, and poor Missie,
my heart aches to look at her and think what trials she must in my
opinion pass through. I staid until 1 o'clock arrived at home just as
they were all eating dinner. Found Mr Wilson had arrived. No news,
no courier up lately.

THURSDAY 25 Sallie Hildebrand[15] sent down for me this morning to
go with her to Mrs Morgan's, poor Ladie, she has at last gone to
rest, she died yesterday evening at 4 o'c. I went with her and staid
until sundown. Returned home to try to get Joanna to go and sit up
but she would not do it. I went back with Miss Mary Robinson, met
Helen and Nannie got them to go back with us. They had been
down to Col Perkins to spend the day. Ben Henderson went with us.

13. The Second Missouri belonged to the Second Brigade, Chalmers Division. It
was commanded by Colonel Robert McCulloch. Composition of the Army commanded by Lieutenant General Polk, C. S. Army, 20 Jan. 1864, *OR*, 32, pt. 2, 585.

14. The Morgans and the Plunketts were early settlers in Shelby County. John Hall
Morgan purchased land in 1836. Dr. John Plunkett was the oldest son of Lord Plunkett of Ireland. He became a citizen in 1840. McCorkle, *Whitehaven*, 28–29.

15. The Hildebrands and the Robinsons were also early settlers in the region. Ibid.,
26, 42.

We did not get there until dark. Poor Missie, I feel so sorry for
her.

FRIDAY 26 Nannie, Helen and Miss Mary Robinson and myself sat
up last Night with Mrs Morgan's corps. It was a sad and lonely
Night. Poor Missie, how my heart sympathizes with her in this great
affliction. Helen and Nannie came home very early. Miss Robinson
and I staid until after breakfast, when Miss Huchens [Hudgens]
came we left. Tate & Joanna went to the funeral. After that Joanna
and Cousin S[allie] returned Memphis. A squad of 7 Confederates
stoped at the gate—belonging to 2nd Ark.[16] I went to sleep directly
after breakfast and did not awaken until after dinner. I was never in
such a cross humor as I have been to Night. I feel ashamed for the
way in which I have spoken to Bettie and Laura. Nobody knows
what I have to try me sometimes. Bettie left early. Laura fast asleep.
Beulah & Tippie Dora both nodding. Here I sit at 3 o'clock morning, with four packages of 300 letters for our Rebel Soldiers, which
it has taken me until this time of night to finish. I will lie down and
take a nap. I had to waken Laura to get me fresh water. I was so
sick. She is always kind to me.

SATURDAY 27 Anna Nelson and myself went to Memphis this morning. Very warm, dusty and disagreeable. Accomplished all I went
for. Did not go near any of the Officials and was fortunate to meet a
kind friend Lucie Harris, who gave me her pass.[17] Tis a risk, yet we
can accomplish nothing without great risk at times. I returned the
favor by bringing a letter to forward to her husband, Army of Mobile. I sat up until 3 o'clock last Night, arranging poor Grimes[18]
mails to forward to the different commands. It was a difficult job,
yet a great pleasure to know I had it in my power to rejoice the hearts
of our brave Southern Soldiers. Most were Kentucky letters for
Breckinridge's command. The rest were Mo. letters for Johnston's,
Polk's and Maury's commands. God grant them a safe and speedy
trip. We have glorious news from Dixie. Forrest has completely

16. The Second Arkansas belonged to the First Brigade, Chalmers Division. Composition of Army, *OR*, 32, pt. 2, 585.

17. A person could enter the city freely, but a pass was required to leave, and an
oath of allegiance was required to obtain the pass. Lucie Harris was the wife of Captain Edward R. Harris. Anna Nelson was a member of another family of early settlers
in the area. Hooper, "Memphis," 56; Hallum, *Diary*, 281–83; Harris Papers, CC;
McCorkle, *Whitehaven*, 30.

18. Perhaps a reference to Absalom Grimes, a Confederate mail runner, who was
captured in Hernando late in 1863. The mail he was carrying eventually came into
Confederate hands. For an account of how Grimes worked with women carriers of the
mail, see Quaife, *Grimes*, 121.

routed [Brigadier General William Sooy] Smith and [Brigadier General Benjamin H.] Grierson at Okolona. God grant my Bro Eddie may be safe. We hear his Col, Jeff Forrest was killed. The Yanks are perfectly demoralized. All that escaped have arrived in Memphis. I never witnessed such a sight as the Stolen Negroes poor deluded wretches.[19] Praise God for this Victory.

SUNDAY 28 Cloudy and raining all day. Much colder than yesterday. Anna Nelson and myself went to Mrs Morgan's. I went to take those letters to Cousin Campbell Edmondson.[20] He left for Dixie and will see that they are safely forwarded. Met a great many persons there, all in fine Spirits, topic of conversation our glorious Victory, which was added to this morn by news that Sherman was in full retreat for Vicksburgh—had not reached Canton, and we were confident of ruining the whole army as [Major General Stephen D.] Lee with his Cavalry force was between him and Vicksburgh, while Polk was close on his rear.[21] Merciful Father crown our Armys with Victory. Spare so much bloodshed of the bravest and best of our Sunny South. Enlighten the minds of the miserable Yankees, of their sinfulness. Drive them from our soils! Oh, just and merciful Saviour, give us peace, and our independence. I received a letter from Dr Moses and Maj Price by Mrs Fackler, through them heard from my friend Maj Maclean, with Gen. Price. Laura and I sat up late to Night, I slept all evening. Still raining. 12 o'clock sleeting cold.

MONDAY 29 The last day of Winter. Gloomy, oh! mercy how dreary, sleeting all day, the shrubery is all bowed to earth with the weight

19. The engagement at Ivey's Hill, on the road from Okolona to Pontotoc, 22 Feb. 1864. Dashiell Perkins witnessed the death of the general's youngest brother who was shot through the neck. He saw the general holding his brother's head in his lap and crying. Sherman blamed Smith's defeat on his encouraging slaves to desert from plantations along his route, slowing his movements. One Federal officer at Memphis who witnessed the return debacle wrote that Smith returned with 1500 slaves. Henry, *Forrest*, 229–33; Perkins, "Record," 12; George E. Waring, Jr., "The Sooy Smith Expedition," *Battles and Leaders*, 4:417; John Merrilees Diary, 27 Feb. 1864, Merrilees Collection, CHHS.

20. Cousin Campbell was married to the sister of the deceased Mrs. Morgan. EFP.

21. The Meridian Campaign was ruined by the failure of General Smith to reach Meridian. Instead of the combined forces of Smith and Sherman striking out for Selma and Mobile, Sherman had to return to Vicksburg on 21 Feb. Both Polk and Lee followed his infantry columns for a time, but neither attacked. One Confederate officer believed Sherman's forces would have been annihilated if General Hardee had not arrived too late to join in the pursuit. A Union officer wrote that Smith and Grierson were responsible for the failure of the expedition. Henry, *Forrest*, 233; Report of the Meridian Expedition, *OR*, 32, pt. 2, 798, 811, passim; Cash and Howorth, *Nellie*, 158; Merrilees, "Diary," 36.

of Ice. All nature is crowned with it, yet it is so gloomy out. There is some happiness in our house hold, the two children Mamie and Robert are all life—though, like all children troublesome and noisy from their imprisonment. Father & Cousin Frazor have spent the day reading in the Parlor while we have [been], as women usually are, buisy sewing. I fixed Laura's new dress waiste. The Servants have done little except to try to keep fires in the house. We have seen no one to day, therefore have heard nothing later from our glorious Victory. God bless our noble soldiers, and protect them from this miserable bad weather. Tate and Cousin Sallie both very much disapointed not being able to go to Memphis. Laura and I as usual sat up late. I drew the pattern on my swiss to braide, she ruffling her Apron. I finished the book of Luke.

6

Smuggling through the Lines

1864 DIARY: MARCH

TUESDAY 1 First day of Spring. Laura awakened me for my breakfast. I looked out of the window, and to my surprise, one of the hardest Snow Storms I ever saw was prevailing, lasted until 11 o'clock when the Sun shone out brightly, a more magnificent scene I never witnessed. The forests glistened like thousands of diamonds, sun set was glorious. It moderated a great deal, until Night when the freeze came again. Laura and I spent evening alone, except Beulah and Tippie Dora, buisy sewing, Laura just finished her ruffled apron. I am really proud of her, she sews so nicely. I spent the day in Tate's room, braided one width of my white swiss. If my chest was only stronger, I would enjoy sewing but oh! I am so weary—both in body and spirit. My Angel Mother, you would not have thought your two youngest born could grow so indifferent. I pine for a companion, tis not my fault, she loves me not. My poor old Father you are all that binds me here. Helen is to be married, they are all buisy, but do not wish me to share it. Have seen no one, or heard more from Dixie.

WEDNESDAY 2 Bright and beautiful. Ice glittering magnificently, moderating a great deal, by 12 o'c. all snow gone, real pleasant to Night. Father went to Mr Holmes,[1] our victory confirmed by news from below. Mr Wilson dined with us, gave the same news Father heard at Mr H's. Nonconnah out of its banks, still rising. Tate and

---

1. John Holmes was an early settler. His home was on a road that ran between the Holly Ford Road and the Tchulahoma Road. It was about a mile south of Nonconnah Creek. McCorkle, *Whitehaven*, 29; 1863 Map of Memphis.

Cousin S. very much disapointed, as they seem in great haste, to go to the City. I sat in Parlor after Mr Wilson came, braided another width on my swiss, tis real fascinating work, but oh! my chest aches so badly, no one but my sainted Mother ever knew or sympathized with me, in this affliction. Laura washed to day, although my only companion, she has fallen into the arms of Morpheus and left me real lonely. She and Bettie are improving very much in their lessons. Poor Father he too is alone. I have forgiven the past heavenly Father, give me strength to forget it. Nothing late from Jimmie or Eddie. Lord be with them in all hours of danger, and bring them safe to us.

THURSDAY 3 The monotony of our life was some what changed to day, by a visit from Lt Bayard of the 4th U.S.R. to Nannie, he is her cousin, and came this distance with only six escort to make a call. They behaved themselves very well, ate dinner with us, and they all admit our dear Rebel Gen Forrest defeated them badly in their raid to Okolona.[2] Decatur Doyle came this evening from Dixie. Jimmie sailed for Europe the 6th of Feb. Eddie and all the boys safe through the fight. Pontotoc suffered very much. Sister Mary [Anderson] with the two youngest [Kilpatrick] children will start home some time next month. Col Jeff Forrest is really killed.[3] Sherman has returned to Vicksburgh. Our Army of Johnston advancing. Grant reported falling back.[4] I have been buisy braiding all day, one more width finished. Laura has provoked me, and I feel real cross. She or I should certainly have less temper at times. All of them received letters to Night except me. Tis now 10 o'c. and I think I

---

2. William Bayard, Fourth Regulars, U. S. Cavalry, was stationed at LaGrange, Tennessee. His unit was in the fighting at West Point and Okalona. He was a double cousin [brothers married sisters] of Brigadier General George Dashiell Bayard [Federal] who died at Fredricksburg in December 1862. Their mothers may have been Miss Em's cousins. Samuel Bayard, *The Life of George Dashiell Bayard* (New York: Putnam's Sons, 1874), 304; Waring, "Sooy Smith," 417.

3. Mrs. C. M. Stacy, a refugee at West Point, Mississippi, wrote an account of Jeffery Forrest's death to her son. She mentioned the general's weeping and said it would take many "Yanks" to pay for his brother's death. C. M. Stacy to James Hamner, 14 Apr. 1864, Hamner Letters, Special Collections, MSUM.

4. Sherman arrived in Vicksburg on 27 Feb. In Georgia where General Johnston had his headquarters at Dalton, there was activity: "We have been skirmishing in the Gap and driving the enemy into the valley." Perhaps the reference to Grant had to do with the Kilpatrick raid around Richmond when Ulrich Dahlgren was killed. In Memphis, a Federal officer wrote in his diary of the same rumors. Sherman to J. A. Rawlings, 27 Feb. 1864, *OR*, 32, pt. 1, 173; Report of General J. E. Johnston, 25 Feb. 1864, *OR*, 32, pt. 1, 476; Report of Kilpatrick's Raid, 8 Apr. 1864, *OR*, 33, pt. 3, 3, 170, passim; Merrilees, "Diary," 34.

will try to get to sleep early to Night. I suppose they are all happy in the house. I can never content myself with the lonely life I lead.

FRIDAY 4 I do wish Nonconnah would fall, and let a visitor from Memphis return home, for I am always in an ill humor when she is about.[5] Tate and Helen went over to see Missie Morgan this evening. I have been in Tate's room all day buisy sewing—almost finished my dress. Mr Hildebrand was here to day, bro't nothing later from Dixie, nor have we heard any thing to day. I wish one of the Scouts would come, and bring us some news. It has been very cloudy and disagreeable all day. This evening we had quite a Storm. I received to day another batch of letters from Dixie, to be mailed in Memphis for Yankee land. Decatur told us Gen Armstrong had been ordered to Miss.[6] He has taken Mariah to Mobile to be confined. Poor girl I pity her, no Mother or relation to be with her. Laura as usual nodding, and I all alone. Beulah and Tippie Dora also enjoying their nap. I feel real sick to Night. Oh! I am so lonely. What is to be my fate. Oh! God shield me, have I not suffered enough. Make my future bright.

SATURDAY 5 Nonconnah has fallen at last, and crowds of wagons are passing loaded with provisions in exchange for their cotton.[7] Joanna and Cousin S went to town this morning. Mr Wilson came early and staid until after dinner with us. Tate, Helen, Nannie & Decatur all spent the day sewing in my room. Decatur excepted of course from the sewing. We had a pleasant time. Only this morning I did wish I was a man. I never read a more insulting note in my life, than Father received from Dr Malone.[8] I will not stain the pages of my book, writing of such a dog, and hope God will give me strength to forgive it. Coldwater and all streams below so high that we have no com-

5. A reference to Frazor Titus's wife, Cousin Sallie.

6. Brigadier General Francis C. Armstrong was transferred from the Army of Tennessee for assignment in Mississippi. General Longstreet to General Cooper, 8 Feb. 1864, *OR*, 32, pt. 2, 681.

7. By the winter of 1864 trade with the enemy was allowed. "I can see no sound reason why we should not use our cotton to purchase supplies we can not get otherwise." [General Polk] By March 15, however, a Confederate officer was writing to the provost marshall general at Mobile to complain that "not less than 2,000 bales were carried in [to Memphis] and that in many cases the traffic resulted in speculation, extortion and providing information that the Yankees could use in future raids." Bettersworth, *Mississippi*, 177–79; W. A. Goodman to General Polk, endorsed by Polk, 21 Jan. 1864, *OR*, Ser. 4, 3, 9–10, H. Winslow to Major J. C. Dennis, Provost Marshall General, Mobile, 15 Mar. 1864, *OR*, 32 pt. 2, 633–37.

8. Probably Dr. R. C. Malone of Memphis who treated Belle for an unnamed illness in 1859.

munication with Dixie, therefore have heard no news to day. I would give any thing if I could send the things I have for the poor Soldiers. Poor fellows I know they need them, would to heaven I had Money to get all I could bring through the lines. I finished my dress to day, and made Laura a beautiful apron. 12 o'c, no Beulah yet. Laura, Tippie Dora & I alone, they asleep.

SUNDAY 6 A bright and beautiful day. Tate and Nannie went to Church. Col Perkins came home with them, to take Nannie home with him. Prior [Pryor] leaves for the Army in the morning was anxious to see Nannie before he left. Tate saw Cousin Campbell, just arrived from Dixie. No news, waters up, telegraph all destroyed, floating rumors that Sherman had arrived safely in Vicksburgh. Forrest moveing this way—that is glorious news for us. Cousin Mat, Frazor [Titus Edmondson], and Joanna came from Memphis about 1 o'c. Mary [Dashiell] was delighted with the arrival of Frazor. Joanna went to the Provost Marshall yesterday to get her a pass and he started to arrest her, thought it was me. I heard some good news, she heard one of the 4th U.S.R. swear he would shoot old Gibbert, the Dutch detective. I have not received a letter for over two weeks and expect old Williams[9] has intercepted them in the Post Office. Oh! God how long must we suffer. Beulah has run off again to Night. Laura, Tip and I alone. Laura and Bettie had a good lesson. We all sat in the Parlor after Tea. One month to day since Jimmie left for Europe.

MONDAY 7 The quiet of our life was disturbed to day, by the arrival of 150 Yankees—only two came to the house. We gave them their dinner. Mr Wilson and Decatur were down in the Orchard. Helen sent for them to come and capture the Yanks, we saw the rest coming & Tate and I ran to tell them it was too great a risk. Mr W. and D. were nearly to the gate; I was never so excited. We turned them in time, the two Yanks passed while we were standing there. Mr W. and D. came to the house and spent some time with us, when Mr W. followed the Yankees. They returned about 9 o'c, on their way to Memphis. D. and Cousin F. had a run again, with the horses, but fortunately none of them came in. I have not done any work today, have suffered death with my spine. Tate and Helen at work in my room all day. I sat in Tate's room until bed time. Beulah, Laura and Tip all in time. I amused myself reading Artemus Ward's book.[10]

9. Captain George A. Williams, First U. S. Infantry, provost marshall of Memphis. Pay voucher for Secret Service signed by Williams, 7 Apr. 1864, Special Agencies of the Treasury Department, Memphis District, RG 366, NA.

10. Artemus Ward, pseudonym of Charles Farrar Browne (1836–1867), American humorist. *Artemus Ward: His Book* (New York: Carleton, 1862).

We did not hear what the Yanks went for. We heard from Eddie &
the boys, all safe. One of Henderson's scouts arrived.

TUESDAY 8 Cousin Mat, Frazor and Joanna went in town this morning. Joanna was to have returned this evening, did not come. We
heard what the Yankees were after. Old Frank[11] the detective carried
them to Felix Davis's and took him and his Wife both to Memphis.
They are now in the Irving Block.[12] We did not hear the offense,
only t'was some old grudge he had against Mrs Davis. They stole a
great deal from Widow Hildebrand's[13] but she has taken the oath,
and I dont care much. I pity poor Mr & Mrs Davis, they have been
so kind to our Soldiers. Nannie Perkins came home this morning.
Joe Clayton, Memphis Light Dragoons,[14] came on short furlough,
Tate & I are going after Mrs Clayton & Hal tomorrow. We all spent
the evening in the Parlor, singing and playing. I am almost crazy
with my Spine took a dose of Morphine. I am in so much pain it
does not affect me. All spent day in my room sewing. Laura, and
Beulah in, Tip not arrived. Oh! I am so lonely, and suffering so
much.

WEDNESDAY 9 Tate and I went over to Mrs Claytons early this
morning,[15] had to pass through a Yankee Camp, no trouble, spent
the day, and came back this evening. Hal and Dink came with us.
Tate's horse threw her, not hurt, I was never so full of laugh.
Reached home about dark. After Tea we were all sitting in the Parlor, when in walked Joe Clayton and Mr McCorkle, our little St

11. Captain Whitney Frank, Chief of U. S. Detectives, Sixteenth Army Corps. Pay
voucher, 8 Apr. 1864, RG 366, NA.

12. The Irving Block Prison was in a row of office buildings on Second Street,
opposite the northeast corner of Court Square. Before the fall of Memphis, it had
been a Confederate hospital. As a prison, conditions were so deplorable that Captain
George A. Williams, the provost marshall and prison commandant, was temporarily
cashiered in the spring of 1864. A report of the inspection found it "the filthiest place
ever occupied by human beings." General Grant intervened and Williams was later
reinstated as provost marshall and commandant of the prison. For description of the
terrors of the Irving Block, see Elizabeth L. Saxon, *A Southern Woman's Wartime
Reminiscences* (Memphis: Pilcher Printing Co., 1905). The Irving Block was condemned and demolished in 1937. Hallum, *Diary*, 334; Meriwether, *Recollections*, 82;
J. Holt to President Lincoln, 24 June 1864; George A. Williams to Judge-Advocate
General, 24 June 1864, *OR*, Ser. 2, 7, 404-9; "Unsafe City Now Says of Doomed War
Prison," clipping, *Memphis Press Scimitar*, 29 June 1937, vertical file, MSUS.

13. There were three property owners named Hildebrand who were neighbors of
the Edmondsons. 1863 Map of Memphis.

14. Private J. J. Clayton, Company A, Seventh Tennessee Cavalry, John P. Young,
Seventh Tennessee Cavalry (Nashville: Barbee and Smith, 1890), 154.

15. Mrs. Sophie Rodgers Clayton, sister of Hal Rodgers, lived four miles east of
Memphis on the Germantown Road. Lenow, *Elmwood*, 107.

Louis friend. He has a furlough, and is going to St Louis and New
York to see his Father and Sister. We were all delighted to see him,
all sat in the Parlor until 11 o'clock singing, playing and had a real
nice time. Laura and I were not so lonely, Hal shared my little room.
I heard of my letters in town, but could not get any one to bring
them to me. Mr Wilson took one of those Yankees prisoner the other
evening and got him a fine Saddle and Bridle, so he has made up for
his loss at the Party. Oh! I am suffering so much with my Spine,
what is to become of me. Mrs Dupree arrived from Dixie,[16] sent
Helen two letters by me. I was so disapointed that I did not get one.
I expect my friends will all for get me now that I cannot run to
Memphis and bring what they want.

THURSDAY 10 Mr McCorkle and Tate went to Memphis this morning. I hope he may have a safe and pleasant trip. Cousin Frazor left
for Dixie this morning. We were delighted to see Mr Wilson & Harbert this evening, they staid with us until after Tea, bro't a letter
from Eddie and Bro George [Dashiell]. Tate was kind enough to
bring my letters from Memphis—one from Miss Em, two were for
Surg[eon] Leonard from Mo to my care. Our house is crowded to
Night. Mrs Clayton and Hal share my room. I sat up very late wrote
to Maj Price & Dr Moses. No Yanks near to day. I have suffered, no
one can tell how much with my spine. Mr Bob Wallace and friend
came to spend the night with us. I am so lonely, and my Spine hurts
me so much I cant sew. And it's impossible to fix my mind on any
reading for ten minutes, in the excitement we live in. I am unhappy,
and I tremble for fear there is something more fatal to befall me, as
the Spine so much influences the brain. Beulah & Tip & Laura all
here. Sat up until 12 o'clock.

FRIDAY 11 Mrs Clayton, Hal and Dink all went home this morning.
Mr Wallace & friend left. Decatur Doyle and Joe Clayton both left
for Dixie—they both got all they came for. It has seemed quite
lonely all day. I have been compelled to lie down most of the day
with my Spine, it is getting worse all the time. Tate & Helen sat in
my room all day sewing. I am happy that poor Father can have some
quiet now. I sat in the Parlor a little while after Tea, have spent the
evening in my own lonely little room. Laura and Bettie said a good
lesson. I tried to keep Laura awake, but she nodded so, it worried
me, and I sent her to bed. Tip is also asleep and Beulah has not yet

16. Probably Mrs. Lewis Dupree whose husband was an associate editor of the
Memphis Daily Appeal. Mr. Dupree and the newspaper moved from the city as the
Federals took over. Hallum, *Diary*, 156.

made her appearance. I wrote to Miss Em to Night. Tis half past 12, and I feel afraid. Joanna would not let me have the key to lock my door. Two robbers were killed near here yesterday. The country is full of them.[17] Oh! God protect me. One year ago Mrs Bredell & I arrived in Grenada—Wednesday.

SATURDAY 12 Tate and Bettie went to Memphis this morning—did not succeed in getting any thing through the lines. The Picket was very insulting to her. She brought me a letter, but not for myself— only my care, to Mr Lawson in Hendersons Scouts.[18] I forwarded it to Capt H. also a package of late papers, by Mr Harbert, who spent the evening with us. We all sat in the Parlor and have had a pleasant evening. Mr Harbert vacxinated Father, Helen, Nannie, and I, also Jane and Laura. I have made the skirt to my swiss Mull, and fixed me a beautiful braid pattern, and drew on the skirt ready for my work Monday morning. I have not suffered much with my spine to day, though only on account of taking morphine last Night, which has made me insensible to the pain. 11 o'clock, so I will to bed. No Beulah. Father gave me a key to day. Tippie Dora & Laura both here.

SUNDAY 13

> Hopes, what are they? Beads of morning
> Strung on Slender blades of Grass,
> Sweet is hope's wild warbled air
> But oh!—its echo is despair!

Today is the first anniversary of the happiest day in my life. Just one short year ago, twas then on Friday morning, he came for me to walk on the hill to listen to the echoes of our triumph at Fort Pemberton (Greenwood). I rushed to meet my fate, oh! God that it had never over taken me. Yet tis the brightest spot in my sad life—his love. In reviewing my diary for 63, I find in this day a quotation from Raphael which has indeed found its moral. Oh! who in the course of his life has not felt some joy without a security, and without the certainty of a morrow. Time hath power over hours, none over the soul. Time had power over his heart, yet none over my true and holy love. To day he wooes the daughter of a more sunny

17. Perhaps the Dick Davis band which consisted of fifteen to twenty men, mostly deserters from both sides. This band was active in the area during 1864 and committed depredations on civilians and military personnel from both armies. Thomas S. Cogley, *History of the Seventh Indiana Cavalry* (Laporte: Harold Co., 1876), 188; Hallum, *Diary*, 188, 293.

18. J. Lawson, Fourth Sergeant, Henderson's Scouts. List of Scouts, CC.

clime—Miss Sallie Anderson of Mobile, may she never know the pangs of a deceived heart. I have spent the day alone in my little room, finished the book of John. Bright and beautiful though rather cool. Laura & Bettie went to Mrs Nelsons. All the whole family walking and enjoying themselfs. Tis just four o'clock—I will wait until after Tea to finish. I sat in the Parlor with Father after Tea. Laura & Bettie speled at Baker to Night. No Beulah or Tip. Laura & I alone. Oh! my heavenly Father humble my heart, and give me Christian patience.

MONDAY 14 I have had a miserable cold, and not fit for society—yet we have been delighted by the visit of a Rebel Major, Maj Allin who spent the day with us. I tried to braid on my dress, only a little while, my Spine pained me teribly. Maj A. went down to Col Perkins, to stay until Thursday when I will have returned from Memphis—having attended to his wants. Mr Wilson and Harbert came this evening. Mr Harbert has bought him a new horse, very pretty one. Poor Anna, I think Mr Wilson ought to give her a rest. They staid right late, we had a pleasant evening—music, conversation &c. Anna Nelson & I have made our arrangements to go in to Memphis to morrow and not return till next day. Oh! Lord deliver me from getting in any trouble with the Yanks, this will be a hard trip, I have a great risk to run. No Beulah to Night. I think she has forsaken her post. Laura & Tip both here nodding. I feel like I had been stewed. Oh! God protect, guide, and make me a good girl.

TUESDAY 15 Anna Nelson and I started to Memphis about 9 o'clock. Suffered very much with the cold, stoped at Mr Roberts to warm. From there we passed through the Pickets to the Pigeon Roost Road. Found Mr Harbert's after much searching. Did not reach Memphis until 1 o'clock. Left our horse & buggy at Mr Barbiers[19] [Barbierre], went up town, and not one thing would the merchants sell us—because we did not live in their lines. I consoled myself with a wheel that would not turn—could not spin. Went to my friend Mrs Fackler, she went up town and brought the things for me. Poor deluded fools I would like to see them thwart a Southerner in such an undertaking as I had. Spent a very pleasant evening with Mrs Facklers family—all Rebels, and we talked just as we pleased! Mrs F and I did not go to sleep until 2 o'c this being the first time I had seen her since she returned from Dixie. I have finished all my provisions and will have nothing to do tomorrow except fixing my things for smuggling.

---

19. Joseph Barbierre, agent for Barbierre Brothers, Marseilles, France, sold liquors, sundries, etc. *1860 Memphis Directory*, 63.

1864 Diary: March 97

MARCH 16 Went up Street directly after Breakfast to finish a little job I
forgot on yesterday. At one o'clock Mrs Fackler, Mrs Kirk & I began
to fix my articles for smugling. We made a balmoral[20] of the Gray
cloth for uniforms, pin'd the Hats to the inside of my hoops, tied
the boots with a strong list, letting them fall directly in front, the
cloth having monopolized the back & the Hats the side. All my buttons, brass buttons, Money &c in my bosom. Left at 2 o'clock to
meet Anna at Mr Barbiere's—started to walk, impossible that,
hailed a hack—rather suspicious of it, afraid of small-pox. Weight
of contrabands ruled—jumped in with orders for a hurried drive to
Cor Main & Vance. Arrived, found Anna not ready had to wait for
her until 5 o'clock, very impatient started at last. Arrived at Pickets,
no trouble[21] at all—although I suffered horibly in anticipation of
trouble. Arrived at home at dusk, found Mr Wilson & Harbert, gave
them late papers, and all news. Mrs Harbert here to meet her Bro,
bro't Mr Wilson a letter from Home in Ky. Worn out. 8 yds Gray
cloth, 2 Hats, 1 pr Boots, 1 doz Buttons, letters &c, 2 cords, 8 tas-
sels. Laura, Beulah & Tippie Dora all in.

THURSDAY 17 My cold is no better—miserably hoarse, got up rather
late, Laura brought my breakfast to my room. Fixed my work to go
in the Parlor, found Mr Wilson, Mr Harbert arrived. All buisy sewing, laughing & talking—when the Yankees were reported coming.
Mr. W. & H. in the greatest haste retreated through the Garden, left
their horses. The report was a mistake, it being Maj Phil Allin. All
quiet again, enjoying ourselves very much. Maj Allin liked his Hats
very much. Mr Harbert, Sr. & Mr Bedford came. After a little Mr
Falls and Miss McKinny, they brought the rest of Maj Allin's
clothes. Mr Wilson left early to start a curior below. The rest remained until after dinner then returned to Memphis. Mr Harbert &
Maj Allin staid late, left together, oh! how I hate to see the last Gray
Coat disappear. Father & I sat alone in the Parlor after tea. Laura,
Beulah, & Tip all in to Night, all asleep except L. I shall read myself
into the arms of Morpheus. When, oh! when will it be bright, My
Savior. I trust in thee, hope & faith oh! God give me strength.

20. A kind of petticoat showing below a hooped-up skirt. *Webster's*, 210. Mrs. Kirk
was probably Mrs. Fackler's mother.
21. Some pickets were reluctant to search women. One Federal soldier wrote to his
wife: "It is no joke standing picket here, for you don't know what moment something
may happen. Besides we have to search all persons and vehicles going from town for
contraband articles. . . . Some of the old and ugly ladies make a great fuss about
being searched but the young and good looking ones are a great deal more civil."
Parks, "Trade," 289; Quaife, *Grimes*, 111; George Cadman to Wife, 24 May 1863,
George Cadman Papers, SHC.

FRIDAY 18 One of the loveliest days I ever spent—bright and beautiful—I have been buisy braiding my dress, finished 1½ yd. It is very fascinating work, and with my natural abhorance of sewing I think this particular kind would give me much pleasure, if it were not for my miserable old spine. I am suffering intensely to Night from my hard days work. I fixed Mr Noe's grave this evening, it is a lovely spot but oh! so sad, my heart aches when I think of his long suffering, and so young taken from his widowed Mother.[22] Oh! God drive those miserable wretches from our Sunny land, and give us freedom and peace. I have been alone to day except Laura sewing. Tate came twice to sew on the Machine. Joanna & Anna Nelson went to town this morning, got back safe, no late news. Mr Wallace, Henry Wilson[23] were here to tea. I came to my room very early— heard Bettie's & Laura's lessons. Beulah & Tippie Dora both here. Read myself to sleep.

SATURDAY 19 To day has been just as gloomy as yesterday was bright—cold, windy & cloudy. Helen & Nannie had a general cleaning up in the house. Laura was unusually particular about my room, kept me waiting until dinner time to get to my sewing. I made up for lost time, finished one width of braiding, and drew the rest of the pattern off. I dont know what I shall do, if I am to spend so much of my time alone, no companion except my sewing, which is almost too much food, for a mind, in the present state of my own. However tis all for the best, God's will not mine be done. Tate & Anna Nelson went to town this morning, got back safe. Mr Eyrich sent me a nice lot of papers. Tate brought me a letter, as usual not my own, from Capt Hohenstine to his wife in Mobile. No late news. Laura & Bettie recited a very good lesson to Night. Every thing in my room status quo. Anna Nelson did not come, went with Helen & Nannie up stairs.

SUNDAY 20 Another Sabath passed, and I read only eight chapters in my Bible—first of the Acts. I did not get up until rather late. Laura brought me a nice warm breakfast to my room. I dont know what I would do if it were not for her. A disagreeable day cloudy, gloomy and real cold. I spent the morning alone in the Parlor reading. Mr Wilson and Mr Harbert arrived about 12 o'clock. No news, except that which we regretted very much. Gen Chalmers relieved of his command, ordered to report to Gen Polk. Missouri McCulock

---

22. There is a tradition in the Edmondson family that Confederate soldiers were buried on their land. What became of the graves in the twentieth century is not known.

23. He was not one of the Wilsons in Henderson's Scouts, CC.

[McCulloch] takes his place.[24] Forrest is on the wing again, no one knows where to. God bless Eddie and keep him safe, wherever they may go.[25] Tate, Nannie, Helen & Mollie Strange all went to church, got back late of course were delighted to see our Scouts. Mr Wilson is going to Camp to morrow. I am so sorry. I had a nice bundle of papers to send to Capt Henderson, one also to Dr Moses. Oh! if I was only sleepy, and nothing to read. What shall I do. Laura, Beulah & Tip all asleep.

MONDAY 21 Wake'd up almost suffocating with the Smoke, wind from the East, Laura had to throw all the fire out of the stove. Began my work early, nothing to disturb me all day. Finished two widths on my dress in braiding. Sat in the Parlor, no companion. Father came in once or twice, sat in his easy chair and read. Laura and I sat an old Goose this evening—and I think she acted her name to perfection about the nest we fixed her. How cold to day, it is real winterish. I am afraid we will not have much fruit this Year. I sat in the Parlor a little while after Tea. Father was reading, so I thought my own little room much more agreeable as the rest all went in Tate's room. Beulah has run off again to Night, and I expect will certainly get herself in trouble. Bettie and Laura in the same old style with their spelling lesson. All over and here I sit alone, rocking, rocking, rocking,—with the few embers in the grate for my only reflection to the thousand thoughts which crowd my poor clouded mind. Oh! for sleep, deep sleep to relieve me.

TUESDAY 22 Sunshine has greeted us once more—it has been a lovely day. Nannie & Anna Nelson went to town this morning got back safe, no news. My Eyrich sent me the late papers. I sent them on to Capt Henderson by Mr Harbert, he spent the day with us. His Bro & Mr Bedford came down to meet him, brought him a fine horse. We all spent the day in the Parlor. I finished braiding my dress. Just as we had finished Tea, and were quietly chatting in the Parlor, Peter ran hurridly in and announced Jim Titus and Mr Jack Doyle. Of course we were all astonished, imagined Forrest near, and many other such ideas, ran out to meet them, instead of Mr Doyle,

24. Forrest relieved Chalmers 9 Mar. 1864 after a petty dispute. Chalmers appealed to General Polk who decided Forrest had exceeded his authority. Chalmers was reinstated 17 Mar. and returned to his command 25 Mar. 1864. The details of this episode can be found in the *OR*, 32, pt. 3, 602, 606, passim; Henry, *Forrest*, 236–37.

25. Forrest left Mississippi 16 Mar. 1864 for a campaign into west Tennessee and Kentucky. A Federal officer wrote in his diary that the Federal command in Memphis had "Forrest on the brain," and that Forrest had returned to his old hunting grounds at Jackson, Tennessee. Henry, *Forrest*, 237; Merrilees, "Diary," 39.

met old Bose Pugh.[26] We were delighted to see them but sorry to hear Forrest had passed us and gone to Jackson, Tenn. Jim & Mr Pugh have only a short leave to see us, and then return to Columbus [Mississippi], where part of the command are. Eddie went with Forrest—I expect we will hear glorious news from him in a few days. God grant successful may be his career. Sat up rather late. As usual my little family all right.

WEDNESDAY 23 Tate & I went to Memphis this morning bright & early. Stoped at Mrs. Aperson's first, from there to Cousin Frazor['s home]. Tate met me at Mrs Worsham's room, we then went up street,[27] walked until three o'clock, attended to all affairs entrusted to our care, ready to leave at half past three. All of the Yankee Cavalry moving, destination not known—could hear no particulars. Think they are going after Forrest, who we think is on his way to Kentucky. The Yankees are evidently on a great fright about something.[28] God grant they may be defeated in all their undertakings. We came through white Pickets. I think we will not try them again—the Negroes are ten times more lenient.[29] We came by Wash Taylor's, got two hats for Soldiers. Came through Yankee camp, if the Lord forgive me, I will never do it again.[30] Yankee Soldier drove our horse in Nonconnah for us—seemed to be a gentleman for which we were very grateful. Found Mr Harbert awaiting our report. Mr John & Henry Nelson & Mr Harbert took tea with us. Jim & Mr Pugh completed the list for a nice Rebel meeting. Brought a great deal through the lines this eve—Yankee Pickets took our papers.

THURSDAY 24 I slept very late this morning—had breakfast in my

26. Probably Frank M. Pugh, Seventh Tennessee Cavalry, Jordan and Pryor, *Campaigns*, 695.

27. The Appersons were grocers, cotton factors, and commission merchants. Mrs. D. P. Worsham's family ran a hotel, the Worsham House. *1860 Memphis City Directory*, 53, 350.

28. Belle and Tate may have been in Memphis on an information gathering mission for Henderson's Scouts. They knew all the right people and just where to go for military information. Grierson was sending a force to "hang upon, harass and watch the movements of the enemy." Grierson to T. H. Harris, 23 Mar. 1864, *OR*, 32, pt. 3, 131–32.

29. Hurlbut authorized the use of white soldiers for picket duty, 18 Mar. 1863, but by the spring of 1864, Negro soldiers from Brigadier General Chetlain's Black Brigade were on picket duty on the Horn Lake Road. *OR*, 32, pt. 2, 244; *OR*, 32, pt. 3, 286.

30. Perhaps a reference to false swearing or flirting with the Federal soldiers on duty. A tradition in the Edmondson family had Belle flirting with the soldiers to distract them from searching for contraband. Thomas Ridgely Edmondson tape; EFP.

room. I would rather have slept than have the choicest dishes from old Schwab's.[31] Ready at last, arrived in the Parlor found Jim & Mr Pugh with the girls having a nice time. Spent the morning fixing my old Bombazine dress. Enjoyed my dinner finely. Did not stay in the Parlor very long after dinner, came to my room and prepared for a nice evening siesta with London Papers for companions. Soon fell into the arms of Morpheus, slept soundly but have had no spirit since awakening. Joanna got back from Memphis bringing Mammy to see Prince.[32] Anna Nelson will ride her Bro's horse, through the lines to morrow. Mr Harbert came early this eve. I left them all in the Parlor—Father allows them to sit up late as he is reading the Papers. I got tired and came to my room but found it very cheerless, no fire, smoking. Laura, Beulah & Tip all asleep. Oh I am so lonely. I feel a presentiment something good is going to turn up for the Confederacy. God bless my dear Bros and bring them safe home again.

FRIDAY 25 As usual late and breakfast in my room. Found Nannie, Jim & Mr Pugh having a nice time in the Parlor. Have not done any work scarcely, only hemmed Eddie two handkerchiefs. Mr Pugh & I had a game of drafts—I beat him the best three in five. Helen and Joanna went over to Mr Armstrongs—did not hear any late news. Mr Harbert came this evening, he had no news. No couroir up for several days. Heard from Mr McMahon, in 2d Mo Cav, he is very sick, and cant tell when he will come for his clothes and boots. Mr Matthews a Soldier from Jackson Cavalry is staying with us tonight, Mr Harbert staid too, and we have spent a very pleasant evening— Jim & Bose Pugh the life of the Party. Father was very lenient with us to Night, let us sit up until 11 o'clock. We Rebels are having a gay time although the Yankee Camp is only three miles off. God bless our servants for they are certainly very faithful. Laura is sitting in a chair now fast asleep. Bettie did not wait to say her lesson. Beulah & Tippie Dora both asleep—here I sit, solitary and alone— my mind giving birth to a thousand thoughts yet none mature. God bless my brothers and oh! make me a better and more useful woman.

---

31. According to Hallum, Schwab's was "the Delmonico of that day." The spelling may have been Schwoob and pronounced as Schwab. Hallum, *Diary*, 183; *1860 Memphis City Directory*, 252.

32. Prince Moultrie, a Titus slave, was with Jim Titus when he was killed near Franklin, Tennessee in the winter of 1864. He remained with the Titus family after the war. He and his wife are both buried in the Titus plot at Elmwood Cemetery. Frazor Titus Diary for 1864; Elmwood Cemetery Records, EFP.

SATURDAY 26 To day every thing in commotion, as it is a general cleaning up day. Laura did not give me possession of my room until 12 o'clock—have not set a stitch in sewing to day. Mr Pugh and I spent the morning playing Drafts. I beat him badly. After dinner he very kindly offered to fix my lock, so he and I with Gimlet and other instruments proceeded to my little domicile to accomplish the task. I think I shall recommend him as a no 1 Carpenter, although he filled my eyes with sawdust. He fixed it very securely and nice, and I shall always think of and bless him, at the still hour of Night, when thoughts & fear of a raide from the Yankees or Robbers are soothed only with its security as my faithful slave Laura, my dog Beulah, & kitty Tippie Dora are always securely in the arms of Morpheus. I feel so much better about our affairs. I think the bright day is fast approaching. Tate & Anna Nelson got safe from Memphis—Anna got her Bro's horse through the lines. We have glorious news from Forrest, to morrow I will give full particulars. God bless my Bro who is with him.

SUNDAY 27 Rather lazy as it was Sunday. Laura fixed me a very nice breakfast which I enjoyed in my room. Helen and Nannie went home with Anna Nelson, all rode horseback. The girls did not stay very long. I spent the morning reading my Bible, finished the Acts to day. Took a long walk after dinner with Beulah as a companion— she enjoyed it very much, especially the creek. Tate & Helen went to ride over on the Plank Road this evening, they did not hear any news. Mr Harbert came this evening, brought me a package of letters from Capt Henderson to be mailed in Memphis, also a note for myself from the Capt, with it a Dixie newspaper, which I shall carry to Mr Eyrich. I sent Capt H a package of Yankee papers in return. Forrest captured Union City Thursday taking 800 prisoners.[33] God grant he may be successful in all his attempts to gain our lost territory. The Yanks as yet have not started after him. Oh! heaven keep my Bro safe. All my little household asleep and I am lonely, oh! so lonely. Staid in Parlor until 10 o'c. Father made us all retire. Mr Harbert, Mr Pugh & Jim he took with him.

MONDAY 28 Tate and Anna Nelson went to Memphis this morning— got back safe. Mr Tommeny [Tomeny][34] gave Tate up all of her

33. Forrest was at Paducah while Colonel Duckworth and a detachment captured Union City, Tennessee, taking 475 prisoners. Young, *Seventh*, 83; Henry, *Forrest*, 238– 39.

34. James M. Tomeny was Assistant Special Agent, Treasury Department, District of Memphis. Goods and furniture left behind by Confederates and Confederate sympathizers when they fled the city were often seized by the Abandoned Property Divi-

things the U.S.G. confiscated. She brought them all safe through the lines, they belong to Mr Wallace—who will be delighted to hear they are recovered. Mr Harbert & Jim went off scouting did not return until late this evening. We have heard glorious news to day. Mo. McCulloch captured Germantown,[35] Forrest is having glorious victory in Kentucky, Hickman & Paducah both held by our forces. The Yanks are shelling Paducah.[36] We are not afraid of GunBoats. Father of justice & mercy crown our armies with victory, drive the wicked tyrants from our Sunny land—we humbly crave thy pardon & blessing—oh! give us peace—guide my Bros, protect them from harm. I made my swiss skirt, played drafts with Mr Pugh, he beat me badly, trimmed the Rose trees, have spent a very pleasant day, and am so happy to Night after the good news. God bless our dear Soldiers and Officers. I worship Jeff Davis and every Rebel in Dixie.

TUESDAY 29 A merry heart maketh a cheerful countentance, but by sorrow of heart the spirit is broken—Proverbs [15:13] I am sitting in my little room, alone with the exception of my little family, who are more inclined to the silent embrace of Morpheus, than any pleasure the quiet of my own society could give. Father was tired, went to his room early, gave us permission to sit up until 11 o'clock. I availed myself of it for a short time, finally withdrew to a more quiet scene, leaving Mr Harbert, Mr Pugh & Jim together with the girls having a gay time. I have spent the day, how? I think it is how, Mr Pugh & I played drafts most of the time he beat me badly. I wonder in after years if I can recall this day, and imagine the same feeling of je ne sais quai [I know not what]—which I have experienced. There is a bright day fast approaching, I can't say why, but I feel it. Oh! my beautiful savior, only teach my heart to be pure and good, let no unholy thought or action lead me astray. Oh! keep me near thee, let thy influence & protection guide me from wickedness, in the paths of rightiousness. Hasten the day I am to be free from this melancholy, then I will prove my punishment has been great enough, and through my afflictions, I am a child of God. Oh! give me thy love,

sion. Signed permit, 23 Feb. 1864, NA; Hooper, "Memphis," 102; Hallum, *Diary*, 278–79.

35. McCulloch was ordered by Forrest to "sweep the country." No mention of a skirmish at Germantown can be found for this date. Jordan and Pryor, *Campaigns*, 406–7.

36. Forrest held Paducah until midnight, 25 Mar. 1864, then marched southwest to Mayfield, Kentucky. Two Federal gunboats shelled the city after the Confederate forces left. Henry, *Forrest*, 240–41.

make me a christian. God bless my Brothers, and my dear old Father.

WEDNESDAY 30 It seems I can never go to Memphis without some disagreeable arrangements and sayings. I was greatly disapointed in my trip. Tate and I went together. I stoped at Mrs Fackler's on Union St—she went on up to Cousin Frazor's in the buggy. Mrs. Fackler and Mrs Kirk in great distress, old Hurlbut[37] gave her ten days to abandon her house. She took an old Yankee, his wife & two children to board with her, hoping he would recall his heartless order to make her and her little children homeless. I did not smuggle a thing through the lines, except some letters. Mr Tomeny gave me a permit to bring 2 Gals of Whiskey and 5 bbs Tobacco, which I got home safely. Frazor came out in the buggy with me, cousin Mat and Tate came together, we did not have any trouble at all. They all sat up very late in the Parlor, I came to my room early. Jim and Mr Pugh came with me to try my whiskey, which they pronounced very good. I received a letter from Mrs Moses to day, and am really distressed she did not receive the last I forwarded to her. Forrest is having his own way in Ky. God grant Eddie may be safe.

THURSDAY 31 Laura awakened me standing by the bed with my breakfast. I was too sleepy to eat and only drank my Coffee. I have felt very badly all day, did not do any sewing, lying down most of the day. Mr Pugh, Jim and Mr Harbert with Jim's body guard the Prince of darkness left for Dixie. Mr Harbert is to meet the other Scouts a few miles below here, where they will all cross the R.R. together, joining Capt Henderson somewhere in Tenn. All of troops have crossed Charleston R.R. and I expect we will hear glorious news in the next few days. Jim & Mr Pugh are trying to find a way to join Forrest. They had not been gone more than five minutes, when four Yankees belonging to 6th Ill. Cav came riding in, asked if we had seen any Confederate Soldiers,[38] of course we said no. I

37. Major General Stephen Augustus Hurlbut was in command of all forces in the district of Memphis. He was an unscrupulous political general, who along with his provost marshall, Captain George A. Williams, ran an extortion ring in the city. Two of his other appointees, Captain Asher Eddy of the Abandoned Property Department and Whitney Frank, Chief of Detectives, broke into and burglarized certain Memphis homes. Jeffery N. Lash, "Stephen Augustus Hurlbut: A Military and Diplomatic Politician" (Ph.D. dissertation, Kent State University, 1980), 196; Hallum, *Diary*, 278–79, 317.

38. The Sixth Illinois Cavalry, Second Brigade, Grierson's command had been out on the Holly Ford Road before. Part of the command were under orders to follow and intercept Forrest, while the remainder were kept near Memphis to fend off small

think they came to steal but we were polite to them, and they left—only wanted some milk, which they got. Tate & Nannie went to town to day, Mr Perryman got them a pass. They got home safe, but saw Anna Nelson and Sallie Hildebrand arrested and carried back with a Negro guard—for smugling a pr of boots.[39] Forrest is still moveing onward through Ky., having every thing his own way. I came to my room early. A terible rain storm raging. My pets all in. May my heart still be humble, and trust that God will in his own time, brighten my life and happiness.

bands of Confederate raiders left behind. Lucius B. Skinner to Captain F. W. Fox, 3 Jan. 1864, *OR*, 32, pt. 1, 65; Leckie, *Warriors*, 113.

39. "One of the pleasant or unpleasant features of provost duty was the arresting of secession women who had become expert at smuggling and carrying rebel mails . . ." an Illinois soldier on picket duty in Memphis wrote. Howard, *124th Regiment*, 260.

7

An Arrest Order

1864 DIARY: APRIL

FRIDAY 1 A gloomy day, raining, cold and dreary. I have managed to exist, have not done much sewing. I came to my room after dinner, and spent the evening reading the Caxtons—although quite an old book, I have never read it, I began with high expectations, and recommendations as Bulwer's best—must confess I was greatly disapointed. I think 'What will he do with it?' is one of the best novels I ever read. With that as my last rememberance of Bulwer, it would scarce be expected I could admire old Mr Caxton's eccentric disposition, or Ladie Caxton's great lack of spirit, through fear of her liege lord.[1] Beulah was my companion. I could not listen to her distressed whine, unfastened her chain, she went out as I came to my room after Tea, and has not yet returned. I fear they will all get into trouble. Poor Beulah, she is my best friend, but I do not think she has many friends outside of my little room. Laura and Bettie said a very good lesson. Laura and Tippie Dora both asleep. No late news from Forrest. I am so lonely, how long oh! Lord, how long must I wait.

SATURDAY 2 Ever memorable, and (to me) sad day. I was awakened this morning by the piteous howl of poor Fosco. As I feared when Beulah left the room, they all killed seven sheep last night. Uncle Elam knocked Fosco in the head. Beulah ran to my room thereby saving her life. Father sent for her, and then came for her—but oh! he knew not what he asked. To give my dog, my best friend, my Beulah, who had so often defended me in danger, my only protection in the dead hour of Night—to drive her from my side, to be murdered. I would as soon, thought of kneeling myself on the block,

---

1. The books Belle mentioned were: Sir Edward George Bulwer-Lytton, First Baron (1803–1873), *The Caxtons—A Family Picture* (New York: Harpers and Brothers, 1863); *What Will He Do With It* (Philadelphia: J. B. Lippincott, 1860).

106

as to see my best friend. Father positively forbids my taking her off.
I hope God will forgive me for the disobedience, but I was obliged
to do it. Mary Robinson and Joe Smith took her to Memphis in the
buggy to Ed & Rhoda [Seymour]. I know they will love her. None
of them sympathize or appreciate the sorrow it gives me to part with
poor Beulah. Old Wright's drunken son has been prowling all over
the place to Night, shot Ben's dog. Edmondson's battery both white
and black started after him, met him in the lane, he cocked his gun
and flourished it, cowardly dog, sneaked off after that. Laura, Tip
and I all alone. Oh! my poor, poor Beulah, how can I do without
you?

SUNDAY 3 This has been a sad and lonely day for me—I miss my poor
Beulah so much. Tippie Dora has not come to Night, so Laura and
I are all alone. Tate, Joanna, Nannie, Robert and Uncle Elam all
went to Church. Father went up to Mr Hildebrands, Helen was at
home, spent the morning in her own room. My sainted Mother how
different from what you wished. To see your two youngest born, so
widely separated, both in thought & feeling. It is not my fault,—I
pine for a companion—yet she is happier with those of her choice. I
spent the morning in Father's big chair, reading. I read the book of
Romans. Father returned but had no news—we have not heard from
Forrest since he crossed the Cumberland at Eddyville.[2] God grant
us success throughout the State, and return my Bro safe to us again.
I spent the evening alone, grieving for my lost friend. Just one week
ago this eve, I had a long walk, with her as companion, but now I,
oh! it makes no difference to any one but myself, why do I thus
complain. A hard storm of rain and wind is raging. Laura learning
her lessons, Bettie did not come to Night. Father of mercy give me
hope—brighten my life—oh! give me a companion, or my mind is
lost. Thy will not mine oh! lord be done. Tip just arrived.

MONDAY 4 The days now passing are of so much pain and unhappiness to me, it is with the greatest difficulty I can have patience at
Night to make a record of my sad life. The weather to day as gloomy
as my feelings—cold and drizzling. Anna Nelson spent the morning.
I went in to sit with her, did not stay long. Oh! for happiness, and
peace. There is no love or sympathy for me there. I did not sit in the
Parlor long after Tea. Father retired early. Laura and Bettie had a

2. Forrest did not cross the Tennessee and Cumberland Rivers as expected but
went to the southwest. At Mayfield, Kentucky, some of his troops who were raised in
that vicinity were furloughed so they could return to their homes and replenish clothing and horses and gather up recruits. Henry, *Forrest*, 241.

very good lesson. Laura now deep in slumber. Tippie Dora in bed asleep, but my poor Beulah, alas the best of friends must part. I am alone, all alone there is a mournful spell in the heart echo of that simple word, even when it bounds through the warm blood of youth! I have thought until my brain feels like a burning fire. It is 1 o'clock, yet where is sleep or rest for my weary spirit. Oh! heavenly Father have I not suffered enough—remove this trouble, and if I am not humble, then return it to me—oh! try me once again, bless me and brighten my hopes—and guide and lead me in the paths of Rightiousness.

TUESDAY 5 I was awakened at daylight, by a servant with a note from Miss Hudson who has succeeded in getting all she wants out of Memphis, and promised to take the things I had for Mrs Hudson to her. I regretted not having all the things through the lines, but sent what I had. Although awakened I did not think it too late to take a nice little nap, which thanks to Laura lasted until 10 o'clock. Breakfast I have not taste for, yet as Laura brought it to my room, I tried to treat it with politeness. Nannie, Helen and Father were all gone to the funeral of Mrs. Bartons little girl. I spent the remainder of the morning alone, met all at dinner, no definite news, some say Forrest has returned, I think though tis only prisoners sent through. Sewed some to day, all together a dull, lonely time. Tip and Laura as usual asleep—I thinking, and wondering when I can be so relieved. God be with me, Guide, protect and make me a christian.

WEDNESDAY 6 Laura awakened me this morning with the news that Beulah was at my door. Oh! it seems there is always something to trouble me. Father allowed her to be chained and so far has not killed her. We were very much surprised this morning by the arrival of five of Forrest's men—Eddie & Ebb, leading the advance, while Capt Jim Barber [Barbour][3] Capt Farrell & Mr John Kirk brought up the rear. Oh! I was so happy, we have spent a delightful day, have taken it turn about standing Picket—with the horses hid in the woods. Geo Anderson came running up, had just had a nice race with the Yankees. In a little while Joanna & Nannie came from town with the news the Yanks were camping on Horn Lake creek to Night, having heard Forrest had a good many of his men in here on leave.[4] They will have to be right smart if they get our five, with the

3. Captain J. G. Barbour, Company B, McDonald's Battalion, Forrest's Old Regiment. Jordan and Pryor, *Campaigns*, 695.

4. The officer in charge at Fort Pickering worried about an enemy attack from the direction of Horn Lake. Grierson reported a strong picket around Memphis com-

assistance of Edmondson's battery for Pickets. We all sat up very late, I left them in the Parlor. Tis so much happiness to see so many of our Rebel friends. Oh! I am happy, yet miserable, my heart is never free from pain, have mercy upon me, oh! my savior guide and give me happiness.

THURSDAY 7 I feel dull and stupid this morning. We have had a happy day—although the Yanks are still down the road. Tate and Nannie went to the Pickets this morning, were turned back, the lines closed. Capt Barbour & Mr Kirk cannot get their things. I had not the heart to see them disapointed, so rob'd old Mr McMahon of 2d Mo. Mr Kirk took his Boots, Capt Barbour his Uniform. I will get him more through the lines before he comes for them. I beat Capt Farrell two games of Chess to Night. Father let us sit up as late as we wanted to, and we had a delightful evening, Music &c. Very buisy sewing all day. Nannie & I made two shirts for a Kentucky'n, who is far from home, and has no one to take an interest in his need. I sent him a pair of Pants too. Joanna, Helen & Tate made Eddie two. Oh! I would give any thing if I had it in my power to give them every thing they need. My poor Beulah is fast asleep at my feet, to morrow I must give her up again. Thank heavens, Father is not going to kill her. All my little household all quiet in slumber.

FRIDAY 8 A bright and beautiful day, yet a lonely one, our Rebel friends left us, and my poor Beulah was taken away again. Helen & Nannie went over to Mr Harbert's and took her to Willie Duke. Capt Barbour, Capt Farrell, Mr Kirk, Eddie & Ebb went over on the Plank Road nearly to Nonconnah,[5] did not see any Yanks, heard of a squad going in to Memphis just before them. They came back just before dinner did not have time to wait, as Laura was just done churning, they drank heartily of Butter milk. I made them each a nice julip, they went off in fine spirits, yet I can answer for one sad heart they left behind. I went to sleep after dinner, and slept until very late. Poor Mr Noe just two years to day since he was wounded. I decked his grave with flowers, and his suffering during the eleven weeks I nursed him, after his wound, until the time of his death,

---

posed of Forrest's old regiment. Forrest had sent McDonald's battalion to the Memphis vicinity to report on any hostile movements. Colonel I. G. Kappner to Captain G. W. Dustan, 7 Apr. 1864, *OR*, 32, pt. 3, 286; Grierson to T. H. Harris, 4 Apr. 1864, ibid., 253–54.

5. Perhaps the Horn Lake Road, though several other roads in the area were planked. McCorkle, *Whitehaven*, 40–41; Young, *Memphis*, 92.

were ever present in my mind.[6] Father and I sat in the Parlor a short
time after supper. Laura and Bettie worried me a great deal with
their lesson. Poor Beulah I miss her so much—will my troubles
never cease. Hope is my Talisman—every dark cloud hath its silvery
lining.

SATURDAY 9 What strange weather, cold, bitter cold & raining.
Laura awakened me with the news that Lieut Buchanan of the 2
Mo. Cav. with two of his men were here, I hastened to dress, as I
expected they would have some news. They came here last Night
about 1 o'clock to see if we could tell them anything about the Pickets. I dressed and went in the Parlor, he did not stay very long, had
twenty men with him on an expedition to capture Cav Pickets. I
regreted to learn from him this morning, they had failed. They took
french leave, we thought we heard the Yanks coming. They did not
get this far, rob'd poor old Mr Isbell of all his meat, and a great deal
of corn—fourteen in the squad, how I wish those Mo's could have
known it in time to have captured them. Oh! mercy I am so lonely—
have not sewed much to day. Sat in the Parlor with Father a little
while after tea. Poor Father his heart is as sad as my own. L. & B.
did not say a lesson to night. Laura, Tip and I all alone, poor, poor
Beulah! I sat up very late, alone, ah! the heart's echo of that simple
word.

SUNDAY 10 Oh! what a relief to the weary, aching brain when there
seems naught for which to live; when this beautiful earth holds no
joy; when the glorious sunsets, with their rose tinted clouds have no
beauty; when our lifes barks seem drifting ceaselessly on, and we
are powerless for good or ill—oh! what a relief to lie down, and
closing our eyes forget it all. To feel that at least while we slumber
the scorpion-sting of memory is robbed of its poison—the goading,
burning lash of human thought stayed,—and then comes day glar-
ing again and so it goes on to the bitter end. We are all alike in this
wicked, human world. Let us strive as we will to soar above it, at
last it all comes back to us—human hearts full of passion, love, and
beauty—full of sin, sorrow, and suffering; the world overflowing
with good and ill. Sometimes in life our value is appreciated, and we
can claim true, affectionate friends—meet with lofty generous souls,
whose very beings thrill with instinctive love for the whole human

6. If Mr. Noe was wounded 8 Apr. 1862, he may have been one of the seven soldiers
wounded in a reconnaissance from the battlefield the day after Shiloh. They were
members of Colonel Wirt Adams's cavalry under the then Colonel N. B. Forrest.
Report of Thomas Harrison, 11 Apr. 1862, *OR*, 10, pt. 1, 923–24.

race, but mostly we are not understood until the flowers and shadowy, green grass bloom and fade above us and we lie mute below. Such is my life, how long it must be, no matter. God in his own good time will brighten my life. A beautiful day. Col Perkins & Jimmie Greer spent the day with us, Helen &Nannie came home. I finished Corinthians. Father and all of us sat in the Parlor after tea. Laura & Bettie said a very good lesson. I am as usual alone, my two companions fast in slumber. God grant peace we humbly crave, give us our liberty and make us a Christian land. God bless my Brothers.

MONDAY 11 Helen, Father, the children and myself spent the day alone, the rest all in Memphis. Joanna came home, succeeded in getting Father's permit for supplies, brought no late news. Miss Perdue & Noble[7] banished, leave to morrow. I expect I will be next. I was so happy to hear Miss Em, is expected to day, my future plans depend on her advice. Tate and Nannie staid in M. all night. Col Overton[8] came to see us to day, just up from Dixie—every body hopeful and confident of a bright day soon. Mr McMahon, 2d Mo Cav came this eve, I was so disapointed about letting his things go— though he seemed perfectly satisfied, as he had replenished his wardrobe from Yankee Prison in Grierson's raide.[9] He has been quite sick, is now on his way to Camp at Jackson, Tenn. He has his fine horse again. God grant him a safe journey for he is a splendid Soldier. Gen Armstrong with his brigade at Water Valley moveing up. Ah! God is just, and I feel that we have not suffered in vain. We humbly pray for a cessation of this horrible war, oh! give us our independence & peace. We all sat in the Parlor right late. Mr Mc went further below. Tip & Laura both sleep, poor Beulah I wonder where she is.

TUESDAY 12 Mr Jim Rodgers arrived from Texas to day, he and Mr

7. Miss Annie Perdue had a ladies' dress shop in Memphis in 1861. After the war she married Lieutenant Colonel W. H. Sebring. A Florida chapter of the United Daughters of the Confederacy is named for her. She was involved with Absalom Grimes in moving the mail for Confederate soldiers. Miss Molly [Mary] Noble worked along with Annie Perdue and Absalom Grimes. Quaife, *Grimes*, 153; Mathes, *Old Guard*, 291.

8. Colonel John Overton (1821–1899), son of Judge Overton, Andrew Jackson's associate, declined a commission from Governor Isham G. Harris of Tennessee because of physical disabilities but served the soldiers in other capacities. "Travelers Rest and Its Owners During the War Between the States" (clipping), unnamed, undated newspaper, CC.

9. Probably not the famous raid of 17 April–2 May 1863. Grierson's command was still active in the area after that raid.

Farrer [Farrow][10] came over, Col Perkins, Jimmie Greer and Col Overton spent the day. Capt Bissel was here, left two Pistols for me to take care of until he came back the last of the week. I went with Col Overton over to Mr Brays,[11] he took me to protect him from the Yankees, we had a terible trip. He went on down to Col Perkins. We heard there was a Yankee Negro Soldier dead on Day's Creek, so Bettie, Kate, Robert and Mary & myself started in search, we found him, and it was an awful sight, he was in the Water in full uniform, his napsack on the bank of the creek. Oh! I would give anything if I had not seen it. I have not done any sewing, house full of Company all day. I received a letter from Maj Price & Mrs Hudson, one to forward from Dixie, two from Memphis, one for Mr Sam Wilson,[12] one from Mo. to be forwarded to a Soldier of Mo. Brigade. No late news from Forrest. The Yanks in Memphis are frightened to death—think he is coming there. Miss Em has not come, I was so disapointed. Tate & Nannie got home. Bettie and Laura had a very good lesson.

WEDNESDAY 13   This has indeed been an exciting day. Heavy fireing all last Night & this morn. Forrest has captured Fort Pillow. Still in his possession up to this evening dispatches. Captured on yesterday. The fireing we heard was between the Fort & Gun Boats.[13] The Yanks in Memphis are frightened to death. A squad of 15 came and made us feed them & their horses. Staid here nearly three hours,

10. The Farrows were early settlers in Whitehaven. Brother Eddie married one of the Farrow daughters, Floy May Farrow (1869-1931), in 1892. McCorkle, *White-haven*, 37.

11. Edmund Dozier Bray (1811-1880), a neighbor. Sister Mary Anderson married Bray in 1871. Their daughter, Susan Tate Bray (1874-1955), kept the Edmondson Family Papers intact.

12. S. B. Wilson, one of Henderson's Scouts. List of Scouts, CC.

13. Fort Pillow was built on the east bank of the Mississippi River, forty miles above Memphis, by the state of Tennessee in 1861. After the loss of Corinth, Memphis, and the Memphis and Charleston Railroad, the Confederates abandoned it. The Federals occupied it immediately but never with a large force. In April 1864, the garrison was made up of Negro troops and "Tennessee Tories," mostly local men of the Thirteenth Tennessee Cavalry. The assault was begun on 12 April and by nightfall ships in the river began firing on the fort. The fort was captured next day with great loss of life. Forrest was accused of killing some after they surrendered. "The affair was from all accounts disgraceful to the enemy," wrote Lieutenant Merrilees in his diary. For an account of the action at Fort Pillow, see Albert Castel, "Fort Pillow: Victory or Massacre?," *American History Illustrated* 9 (April 1974): 4-10; Jordan and Pryor, *Campaigns*, 440; Young, *Memphis*, 342; Merrilees, "Diary," 41-42; Captain George B. Halstead, A. A. General to Tom J. Jackson, 19 April 1864, RG 94, Regimental Papers, NA.

hateful old thieves. I wish a squad of Confederates had come and captured the last one of them. They stole Mr Withers horses. Late this evening 9 of our Soldiers passed the gate, too late to get those rogues. Yet I think we will hear from them on Nonconnah very soon. Tate, Annie Nelson and Joanna, with Uncle Elam and the wagon went to town, succeeded in getting through Fathers supplies and a good many things. The Yanks stole three hats out of the wagon in Nonconnah bottoms,[14] oh! how I hate them. Col Overton came, Nannie went down to Col Perkins with him. Mr Henry Nelson & Mr J Hildebrand came to see us after tea. I have not sewed much today, L & B said no lesson. Thank God for this glorious news today. Oh! that my Bro maybe safe.

THURSDAY 14 A comparatively quiet day to yesterday cold, cloudy and disagreeable. I have spent it with little use to myself, or any one else. Done no sewing at all. Mr Rogers [Rodgers] spent the day with us. Brought no late news. Col Overton and Anna Perkins came after dinner, staid a very short while. Anna Nelson & Rebecka Robinson came by and borrowed a horse to go to Memphis. We did not hear whether they returned or not. Indeed we have heard nothing reliable to day. Father heard a rumor this evening that our Virginia Gen (Robert Lee) had ruined the left wing of Grant's Army.[15] God grant it may be so. Grant is a fool to think he can whip Gen Lee. Gen Stephen Lee is at La Grange, Gen Forrest still at Fort Pillow last account we had.[16] God grant we may humbly receive the blessings which have brightened our little Confederacy. Drive this wicked band from our Sunny Land. Give us Liberty and peace. Oh! make us a christian Nation. We have suffered yet we deserve thy punishment, we humbly crave thy pardon, and beseech thy blessings. The Night spent as usual with me, sit in the Parlor with Father a short while after Tea.

FRIDAY 15 To day I have spent sewing, all for nothing, tried the waiste on to Night and it will not fit at all. I am so diapointed. Mr Mancont [?] came this evening from Memphis. Forrest still holds Fort Pillow, the Yanks are frightened to death in Memphis, how I wish we could get possession of our city once more. Navigation of

14. Nonconnah Bottoms was a dangerous place during the Civil War. Three Federal soldiers were court-martialed and shot for committing rape in the bottoms. James H. Malone, *The Chickasaw Nation* (Louisville: John P. Morton and Co., 1922), 65–66.

15. A rumor. Only skirmishing took place in the Virginia theatre during the month of April while Grant planned his spring campaign.

16. Forrest was already at Jackson, Tennessee. Henry, *Forrest*, 269.

the Mississippi above blockaded for the present.[17] And I hope forever to the Yankees. They have begun to forage on the Country, supplies rather short in Memphis. Just as I was wondering what there was in this day, worth recording, Kate came in and announced to my great surprise, Margaret had a baby. I left her Cabin about an hour ago, she said she had not felt well, and asked me to bring the little Goslins in my room. I have not heard how they are getting along. No one with her except Bettie, Harriet, and Myra. I did not stay in the parlor long after Tea. Laura and I have spent the evening nursing the Goslins. We heard the sad news that Mr Gates and Mr Cy Smith were both dead, belonged to Hendersons Scouts, captured at a party, died in Alton Prison.[18] Oh! so many of our bravest, and best young men are passing away. God spare my Brothers and bring them safe to the heart of my poor old Father.

SATURDAY 16 Another day of excitement. About 30 Yanks passed, early this morning, only six came in, for their breakfast, they did not feed their horses.[19] They behaved very well, and seemed to be gentlemen, in fact we so seldom see gentlemen among the Yankees that we can appreciate them, when they are met with. While the squad with us were sitting on the porch, the squad which went to Mr Hildebrands passed with two of his horses, which they were taking to Memphis. Anna Nelson came down this morning. The Chicago Times of the 12th has a good letter in it from X. Forrest has left Fort Pillow haveing accomplished all he went for. We have not heard where he is or what his movements are, yet are perfectly satisfied that we will have good news from him in a day or two. Margaret and baby, both doing well, she says I may name it, so I have named her "Dixie." Mr Rodgers came over this evening. Hal was down to day, but did not come to see us. We have no news of importance to day, I have had a great deal of trouble with my Goslins. Sewed some little, yet feel that I have spent the day with little profit to myself or any one else. Beat Tate playing chess to Night. My little room as usual, my Lamp all right again.

SUNDAY 17 For what am I living? Why is it that I am spared, from

17. Hurlbut believed the Confederates at Fort Pillow had closed the river and that Memphis was practically in a state of siege. Hurlbut to A. J. Smith, 13 Apr. 1864, *OR*, 32, pt. 3, 348.

18. John W. Gates and two scouts named Smith were paroled at Gainesville, Alabama, in May 1865. List of Scouts, CC.

19. Cavalry patrols were increased south of Nonconnah Creek after the capture of Fort Pillow. S. L. Woodward to G. E. Waring and W. P. Hepburn, 13 Apr. 1864, *OR*, 32, pt. 3, 346–47.

day to day with no happiness myself, and I am sure my poor weary life adds not moiety of pleasure or happiness to any one in this household. Oh! give me strength, give me patience my blessed redeemer to receive thy punishment with meekness and humbleness—and faith that in thy own good time, all will be well. Tate and Helen with the Children went down to Col Perkins to spend the day. Came home this evening in the rain. Col Overton came this evening, did not stay many minutes, went to Col Perkins to meet his friends. Father, Joanna and I have spent the day alone, indeed I have been all alone, only saw them at dinner. Read two books in the Bible—Galatians & Ephesians. We heard Forrest had Columbus Ky, cant vouch for the correctness of the report.[20] God grant it may be so and that Eddie is safe. Laura & Bettie said a very good lesson to Night. My Goslins have given me a great deal of trouble. Did not stay in the Parlor long after Tea. Spent the evening alone as usual, Laura and Tip both asleep. My poor Beulah I wonder where she is to Night. How much I miss & grieve for her, no one cares or knows.

MONDAY 18 Well I expect our days of peace and quiet are over, another squad of Yanks passed. Four stoped here, staid until after dinner and went on back to Memphis. All of them except one, seemed to be a gentleman, this one was a black abolitionist, oh! how I heartily despise him. I promised to make a Confederate Flag for one of them, Mr Greer, and he promised he would not reenlist. So I have spent the evening making one, and will give it next time he comes. We were fortunate in their visit, they only ate their Dinner. Forrest was fighting at Columbus Ky on yesterday, no particulars. God grant he was successful, and my Bro is safe. I have sewed all day. Yet not accomplished much. Did not stay in the Parlor long after Tea. No use in my recording why. Laura & Bettie are improving very fast recited a very good lesson to Night. The Goslins are a great deal of trouble. Laura and they are fast asleep on her pallet. My Mother, oh! my Mother how long must I leave thee. My heart yearns for thy sympathy, thy advice. Oh! God have mercy on me. No news from my dear Miss Em. Oh! hasten her arrival I shudder for my mind. Oh! my dear my beautiful savior, have mercy on me.

TUESDAY 19 No Yanks to day, a heavy raide passed down on Pigeon Roost Road, do not know their destination. No news from Forrest, and the Yanks do not seem to know where he is. We have not seen any one to day, or heard a word of news. Joanna and Bettie went to

---

20. Forrest was not in that vicinity. A detachment from Buford's brigade made a demonstration in front of Columbus on 13 Apr. 1864. Henry, *Forrest*, 245–46.

Memphis to day, Sallie went with them—got a permit. I am going to try my luck in the City to morrow. I scarcely know what to think about it, or expect, but I do not believe all I have heard. Father is not willing I should go. I must change though, I cannot live always thus. Sewed all day, finished my white wrapper. My poor little burnt Goslin died, I have a great deal of trouble with them. Bettie and Laura did not say a lesson to Night. Bettie said she was too tired,and it was not five minutes until Laura was asleep. I am right sick to Night—and so lonely. No news from Miss Em yet, I am very much afraid she will give up her visit. Forrest keeps so buisy on the Miss River. The days of my present life are not worth recording—and I am sure the trouble and sorrow are indelibly ground on my memory and heart.

WEDNESDAY 20 Tate and I arrived in Memphis quite early, put the horse up then walked up Street together, met Nannie and Anna Perkins. Nannie gave me two letters one from St Louis to Mrs Welch, an exile in La Grange, Ga, one from New York, from a stranger, asking assistance to through me to communicate with Mrs Van Hook at Selma Ala. I received a letter from Maj Price at Selma, by Mrs Flaherty. I dined with Mrs Jones and Mrs Kirk. Went round for Hal after dinner, she went with me to see Capt Woodward,[21] to know what I must do in regard to an order which I heard was issued for my arrest. He advised me to keep very quiet until he could see the Provost Marshall and learn something in regard to it. I came to Mrs Fackler's although she has a house full of Yankees boarding with her—they seem to be very gentlemanly. Dr Irwin and Dr Sommers [Summers] the latter has his family, Wife and two children.[22] We spent a pleasant evening at chess &c. Mrs Fackler has been very fortunate in her selection of boarders.

THURSDAY 21 I went round according to appointment met Capt Woodward at 11 o'clock. Col Patterson went with me, Capt W. had not seen the Provost Marshall, he went as soon as I left. Came round to Mrs Fackler's after dinner and brought me bad news. Though having approached Capt [George A.] Williams as aid for a Heroine of Jericho he could not treat me as the order read—it was issued

21. Captain Samuel L. Woodward, A. A. G., General Grierson's staff, known as "Sandy," was a handsome young man and a personal friend of Grierson. Leckie, *Warriors*, 73, 84, passim.

22. John W. Summers, medical inspector, made a critical report on conditions in the Irving Block Prison in January 1864. Major B. J. D. Irwin was in charge of a military hospital at Memphis. *OR*, Ser. II, 6, 864; G. W. Adams, *Doctors in Blue* (New York: Henry Schuman, 1970), 82.

from old Hurlbut. I was to be arrested and carried to Alton on first Boat that passed—for carrying letters through the lines and smugling, and aiding the Rebellion in every way in my power. He [Williams] sent me word I must not think of attending Jennie Eanes wedding, or go out of doors at all, he would be compelled to arrest me if it came to him Officialy—but as my Father was a Royal arch Mason, and I a Mason,[23] he would take no steps, if I would be quiet. Mrs Fackler, Mr & Mrs Goodwyn, Mr Leach and Dr Irwin all went to the wedding. I staid at home and spent the evening with Mrs Summers and the Dr, they are very pleasant, and not the least bitter in their feelings towards the South. Ah, but they are Yankees, I cant forget it when with them.

FRIDAY 22 All ready for breakfast this morning notwithstanding the late hour of retiring last Night. They all spent a delightful evening— the Bride looked beautiful, the groom charming and all passed as merry as the marriage bell.[24] It was a great disapointment to me, but rather too much of a risk, a trip to Alton would not be very pleasant. I ventured with a thick veil on, to go up town this morning and purchase me a few articles which I would be compelled to have, if I am banished, only went to one Store, went to see Mrs Worsham and Vine sent some letters to St Louis to Mrs Moore's from her husband. Anna Nelson came after me but the detectives have been looking for me to day and I was afraid to pass the Pickets. I have certainly escaped wonderfully. Mrs Summers seemed very much distressed that I could not get through. We spent a very pleasant evening. Dr Summers and Mr Goodwyn discussing the war, I enjoyed it very much. No anger or hard words they both agree to disagree. Beat Mr Clark three games of chess, did not sit up very late. I am miserable for fear old Gibbert[25] [Gilbert?] gets me at the Picket tomorrow. God grant I may get through safe.

SATURDAY 23 All ready for breakfast, and very much refreshed after

23. According to Edmondson family tradition, Andrew Jackson Edmondson saved Elm Ridge from the torch of the Yankees several times by giving the sign known only to Masons. Other examples of Masons helping each other among the enemy can be found in the Confederate Collection at Nashville. Cheairs, "Memoir"; F. F. Foard, "Memoir"; J. Rufus Hollis, "Memoir."

24. Virginia Eanes married Noland Fontaine at the First Presbyterian Church on Poplar Street, 21 Apr. 1864, at 8:30 P.M. One of the homes in Memphis's restored Victorian Village is named for the Nolan Fontaines who built it in 1883. Invitation, EFP; Perre Magness, *Good Abode* (Memphis: Towery Press, 1983), 63.

25. Possibly Gilbert. Men of Gilbert's brigade [no other designation given] were on picket duty on the Pigeon Roost Road, week ending 22 Dec. 1863. Perhaps this is the same person Belle is referring to. Report of Pickets, RG 366, NA.

a good nights sleep. Dr Summers leaves for Vicksburgh to day, inspecting hospitals. I would not care if they had no hospitals, however he is very agreeable. I prepared for my trip directly after breakfast. Mrs Summers came in the room and seemed very much distressed that I was in trouble, and said she would get the Dr to get me a pass if I would wait until he came. I knew it was of no use to ask, the Provost Marshall said I must not, but consoled me by saying where there is a will there is generally a way. This was hint enough so I went to Mrs Worshams and Kate went round to the Provost's Office and got a pass for herself and Miss Edmunds. I shall ever be grateful to her for it. I then started for Mr Barbierre's came by & told Mr Eyrich good bye. Came by Miss Perdue's found Miss Mary & Annie just having their baggage searched to leave for Vicksburgh—banished never to return. I got through Pickets safe, Jack was on. Anna Nelson came out with me, we were caught in a terible storm no trouble otherwise, found all well at home.

SUNDAY 24 This has been a terible day of excitement, two wagons from Memphis came out and camped in front of our gate all day, the Yanks did not bother them this morning only to take some Whiskey. Two Confederate Soldiers were sitting in the Parlor all the time they were here, they did not see them coming in time to run, but fortunately they did not come in the Parlor. Mr Fallis and Miss McKinny, Sister of one of the Soldiers came out to see them, the other Soldier was Mr Hutchinson. I sent a package of Papers and letters to Mobile by Mr. McKinny. They had not more than rode out of sight when five Yanks came up all drunk, they robbed those people with the wagons of all their money, drank all the whiskey and treated them shamefully. They had not been gone long before three Confederates, John & William Hildebrand and Ben Henderson came riding up, we told them about it, they rode off full speed, in a little while we heard firing, continued about five minutes, then all quiet. Father and Uncle Elam went down to Dave Hildebrands after tea, our boys just left all right. They met the Yanks returning, only four, and they frightened to death almost, no particulars. I am very much afraid. Laura, the Goslins, Tip and I all alone.

MONDAY 25 Father went first thing this morning to see if he could not hear something more about those thieving Yankees—could not hear whether the Confederate squad gained any thing or not. They went down to poor old Mr Isbell's and beat him nearly to death because he would not show them the way to the plank road. Father and Mr Madden went down there this evening to see him. A squad of Yankees passed, only two came in to get some buttermilk. Luce was one, we told him how those had acted yesterday, he reported it to the Officer, and Father said they stoped at Mr Isbell's and enquired very particularly about it, and said he would have the man arrested. Miss Annie Perdue, Sister and Bro all sent through the lines to day banished, Washburn countermanded Hurlbuts order[26] and sent them by land instead of River. Miss Annie came over to see us, and get me to go over the creek for her. Father is rather afraid, but I will try it in the morning—though I expect not. Father has just left my room, and says he is afraid for me to go. I am so unhappy about the trouble I have got in. Oh! what is to become of me, what is my fate to be—a poor miserable exile. Poor Tip is very sick, and I am very much afraid she is going to die. The Goslins are well, Laura and I complete my lonely little household.

TUESDAY 26 I arose very early this morning, Father was not willing I should go over the creek, went over to Mr Farrer's [Farrow] to tell Miss Annie Perdue so she would make other arrangements about sending for them. I was so distressed to think she must be so disapointed, and I did not get to see her again. No Yankees out on our road to day, all very quiet until this eve, we were all very much excited, surprised & happy to see Maj Crump. He is just from Jackson, Tenn, where Gens Forrest and Chalmers still have their Hd. Qts. Lee's Cavalry have gone to Ala to check the raid advancing by way of Decatur. John Hildebrand and Henry Nelson came down and spent the evening with us. John Hildebrand beat me badly at chess again. We have had a very pleasant evening with our Rebel friends, in spite of Yankee visits. Father retired very early, all left the Parlor except Maj Crump and Helen. Poor child may God shield her from all dark clouds. Oh! may she never know the anguish which has been mine. God grant them a happy and peaceful union. Tip is still quite sick, Laura and the Goslins have retired, my poor lost Beulah I wonder where she is to Night. And me, poor miserable being. Oh! heavenly Father have mercy and brighten my lonely life.

WEDNESDAY 27 Tate and Nannie started to Memphis very early this morning, got back home without any trouble, and Tate was fortunate enough to get a permit, and kind enough to me, to bring out what few things I had to me. No news except they are just realizing

26. Major General Cadwallader C. Washburn succeeded Hurlbut as commander of the District on 17 Apr. 1864. Sherman relieved Hurlbut because of dissatisfaction with his performance in curtailing attacks from Forrest, not because of Hurlbut's personal corruption. W. T. Sherman to General Brayman, 16 Apr. 1864, *OR*, 32, pt. 3, 382; Gaillard Hunt, comp., *Israel, Elihu and Cadwallader Washburn* (New York: Macmillan Company, 1925).

the terible thrashing they received in La.[27] Maj Crump went to the
woods this morning did not come in again until late this evening.
Laura and I have been very buisy all day cleaning and arranging my
room for summer. I had a splendid bath, enjoyed it very much. The
day has been so warm and disagreeable, tried one of my new white
wrappers, first change of the season. Two of Henderson's Scouts
came here after dark, Mr Benson and Alexander,[28] got their supper
and fed their horses—did not stay long, sent a bundle of papers and
letters to Capt Henderson by them. Four Soldiers came in after
Tea—the same who broke up the abandoned farm, (Ball's) Saturday
Night, and I think they are on such an errand to Night, did not stay
long, only until the storm passed over. Yanks—three passed this
evening, did not stop. All my household quiet in slumber.

THURSDAY 28 Maj Crump left for the bushes early this morning, did
not return until the rain began. He sat in my room until supper was
ready. Helen, Tate, and Nannie have all been out here all evening
buisy sewing on Maj C. shirts. I finished mine before the storm
came up. Mr Wesson came after Mr Wallace's things. He has not
left yet, will start in the morning. Seven Yankees and a cotton buyer
came today, just after dinner, did not harm anything, only wanted
some milk, and to know the way, to the plank road. We were very
fortunate once again—they did not even come in the house. We have
not heard a word of news to day. All spent the evening together in
the Parlor, Music &c. I beat Maj Crump at chess. Father & Mr
Wesson retired early. I sat up right late, trying to get Mary to sleep,
succeeded at least. Left Nannie, Helen and Maj Crump in Parlor,
found Laura sleep in the chair with her work in her lap. Tip had not
arrived—the Goslins taking their lunch—and I, poor miserable
being, praying for strength, and patience, for thy will oh! Lord.
Tate had a letter from Eddie & Capt Barbour.

FRIDAY 29 Joanna and Nannie went to Memphis early this morning,
and have not returned yet. Father is very uneasy about them for fear
they are in trouble with the Yankees—none have been out to day.
Maj Crump spent the day in the woods again. Another storm this
evening, which bro't him home rather early, he came in my room
where we were all buisy sewing. Tate is making Capt Barbour's
shirts—Helen buisy getting ready to go South, which she thinks will
be about the first of June. I have made "Dixie" five dresses, and

---

27. Perhaps the engagement near Cloutierville, Louisiana, 22 Apr. 1864. Long,
Civil War, 488.

28. William L. Alexander, First Sergeant, and N. J. Benson. List of Scouts. CC.

have one to make yet, then I will have fulfilled my agreement for the privilege of naming her. Mr Crawford spent the day with us, waiting for Nannie. Mr Wesson left early this morning with his goods. We have no late, reliable news to day. All spent the evening together in the Parlor. Father and I retired early, left Tate, Helen & Maj Crump in there. All my little household together—poor Beulah I will always miss her.

SATURDAY 30 Laura brought my breakfast to my room—very late—every body slept late this morning. Raining, raining, raining—oh! such a gloomy day as it has been. Joanna & Nannie have not come yet. Nonconnah is swiming, but Father is miserable for fear that is not what keeps them. Maj Crump left about 10 o'clock, we have not heard how he got through, but heard of no scouts, and reckon he is all right, some where in Panola to Night. Mr Bray brought Nannie a letter from Dashiell. All of the fords on Nonconnah are heavily picketed. The Guerillas ambushed a scouting party of fourteen, at Pigeon Roost crossing on yesterday—killing the Yankees three horses, wounding two Yanks and capturing three and one horse, only six out of the crowd got back to Memphis. They are very much exasperated. The lines have been closed since, and that may have detained the girls. Hurrah! for the Dick Davis, and his band. I hope they may break into this thieving band of Yanks roving over the Country.[29] Both of Helen's little pups died to day. God bless our armies and give us success.

29. For conflicting accounts of the Dick Davis band and their depredations and skirmishes, see Cogley, *Seventh Indiana*, 188, 238; and Hallum, *Diary*, 188, 293.

8

A Fateful Visit

1864 DIARY: MAY

SUNDAY 1 I slept very late this morning. Tate and Helen ready to
start to Church when I went in the Parlor. Uncle Elam went with
them. Father, Mary, Robert & I were left at home. Mr Hildebrand
and Mr Madden spent the morning with us—they had no late
news—neither did we hear any from the girls. Five Yankees found
where John, William, Ben & David Hildebrand and Ben Henderson
were hid on Day's creek about a mile from here and surprised them,
although they were fast asleep, they made their escape. The Yanks
fired twice only, our little band were not armed for a fight, therefor
beat a hasty retreat. The Yanks then came to old Mr Hildebrands,
did not stay long, we saw them pass on the ridge returning to Memphis. Nannie and Joanna have not returned yet, cannot imagine
what keeps them. The Yanks sent out a heavy force after Forrest on
yesterday.[1] God bless our little band and crown them with victory—
guide my Bro, and keep him safe through all danger. Came to my
room early. Father retired so early. We think the Yankees are at Mr
Hildebrands now, so much noise, and two guns fired. God bless my
dear Father—and protect him from the Yankees.

MONDAY 2 Very cold and disagreeable—had to keep large fires to
keep warm. No Yankees have been out to day. The lines are still
closed. Nannie and Joanna have not got home yet. Cousin Frazor
[Titus], John [Titus] and Mr Wormsly got here from Dixie to day—
every thing is cheering from below, Gen Price has demolished
Steele's entire army, capturing all of his Artillery, Wagon trains, and
demoralizing his entire command.[2] We have not heard from Forrest

1. Scouts informed Forrest that a large cavalry force under General Sturgis was two
miles west of Bolivar, Tennessee. Jordan and Pryor, *Campaigns*, 457.
2. Perhaps a reference to the defeat of General Steele in the Saline Bottoms in
Arkansas 30 Apr. 1864. Shalhope, *Price*, 255–56.

yet, but our faith in him is implicit, he will be successful. Oh! I
think the bright day for Dixie is dawning. God is just, our prayers
are answered. Oh! let us be humble, and pray constantly in our success, thy will not ours be done. I made Laura a dress to day. Sallie
Hildebrand & Mary Robinson came down and spent the evening.
Mr Wormsly went on over to Mr Holmes. The Hildebrands all got
off safe last Night. Every thing has been unusually quiet in the
Neighborhood to day. I did not stay in the Parlor very late. Bettie &
Laura both buisy sewing.

TUESDAY 3 The lines still closed, no news from Memphis, cant tell
when Nannie and Joanna will be home. I did not get up until nearly
dinner, spent the remainder of the day sewing for Laura, trying to
get her clothes in order, it seems I can never get her again for any
length of time. No one has been here to day, John spent the day hid
in the woods with Cousin Frazor's horse. Father as usual running
round trying to hear the news. I think the Country is rather dull,
since the blockade. This is a lonely day in my weary life, and I can
record nothing which would give, either pleasure or profit in after
years to look back upon. The children have been happy at play, and
I expect Helen and Tate have passed the day pleasantly together.
Mine has been alone. Father and Cousin Frazor left the Parlor early
after tea. John & I sat up right late—talking, and I played for him.
Laura is still sewing and nodding. No bread for Goslins, they are
very noisy.

WEDNESDAY 4 I have sewed buisy all day, finished my white braided
swiss —I think it is so beautiful. Laura finished her new Calico, we
both had to sew very late to Night to finish them. Bettie got sleepy
and went home some time since. We all had a considerable fright to
Night—by Anna Nelson sending to warn us of danger if any Confederate Soldiers were here. So poor Johny, although he has spent
the day in the woods, shouldered his blanket, took his Pa's horse
and went to the woods. Cousin Frazor will stay in and take the
chances. Capt Floyd with 20 men passed about dusk, going cross
the Creek, dont know their destination. The lines open this evening—Joanna and Nannie got home. No news of interest. We are
still victorious on all sides. The negroes have raised the black flag—
gone out on a raide after Forrest, and I will bet, but few will ever
return.[3] God grant not one life of our dear Soldiers, will be sacrificed

---

3. The black flag was once flown in warfare to signal that no mercy would be shown
to the vanquished. According to Bennett H. Young, the events at Fort Pillow were
used to inflame and incite Negro troops. Young also wrote that Forrest considered the

to those cowardly dogs. Oh! give us victory, that peace may once
again smile on our Sunny land. God bless my poor old Father and
dear Bros.

THURSDAY 5 I have spent a most unhappy day—half sick, and the
"black spirits" haunted me teribly. Oh! I don't know what is the
matter with me, or what on earth is to become of me. I spent the
evening sewing on Harriet's dress. Laura and Bettie both sewed late,
yet I am left alone, and no prospects of sleep relieving my poor
weary, aching heart. I pray for hope, and patience, yet virtue is lost
in every thing to me in my present state of feeling. Old Mrs.
Holmes, Mr Wormsly & Bedford came over this evening, no news
except a rumor that Forrest had beaten the Nigger troops who left
Memphis.[4] God grant it may be so. Poor Danie Donelson's body has
been found, at Pounder's ford, he was murdered, on his way back
to the Army. His only Bro, was killed at battle of Chickamauga.[5]
Oh! heavenly Father give us peace, give us peace, crown our sunny
land with victory & peace, guide my dear Brothers, and return them
safe to our Father's now lonely fireside. We humbly crave thy pardon, thy forgiveness and peace.

FRIDAY 6 I got up very early this morning, finished Harriet's dress a
little after dinner, just one day making it. I have picked my finger
almost to the bone, and will have to rest for a few days, and let it
recruit. I slept all evening, have spent the day alone, and it has
seemed terribly long. No Yankees out on our road to day, a heavy
scout passed down the Hernando road, a very heavy picket on Nonconnah, since Floyd's raide yesterday. Poor old Mr Farrow got in
trouble yesterday, the Yanks carried him in Memphis and put him
in the Irving Block, we have not heard any of the particulars. Cousin
Mat, Frazor & Cousin Sallie [Titus] came out this evening. News
we have another victory on Red River, captured three more Gun
Boats.[6] Oh! how thankful we are for the bright days which are dawning. We humbly crave thy blessings for victory and Peace. Received

---

raising of the black flag "the most economical and merciful way of ending the war."
Bennett H. Young, *Confederate Wizards of the Saddle* (Boston: Chapple Publishing
Co., 1914), 5, 11.

4. The skirmish at Bolivar, Tennessee. Federal troops broke and left the field in
disorder. Henry, *Forrest*, 275.

5. Daniel Donelson, son of Major A. J. Donelson of Memphis, was murdered in
January in DeSoto County, Mississippi. His brother, Captain John Donelson, Preston
Smith's adjutant, was killed at Chickamauga. *Memphis Bulletin*, 1 May 1864; Mathes,
Forrest, 143.

6. At Dunn's Bayou. Long, *Civil War*, 493.

a letter from Jimmie in London, the crew seem all well and in fine spirits. God bless both my dear Bros and guard them from all danger and temptation. Bless my poor old Father, and keep trouble from his last days. Oh! make me a better woman. Frazor is 9 years old to day. We have not heard from Eddie for several days.

SATURDAY 7 I went over to Mrs Claytons early this morning to make arrangements with Hal about going South, did not find her at home, waited until after 3 o'c but did not get to see her. Spent a very pleasant day—heard no news. Came by Mrs Duke's to see Beulah, poor dog she was almost crazy when she met me. I could not stay many minu. 's, and it almost broke my heart to. see Beulah begging to come. Peter and I started on home, met two Yankees, they were drunk and frightened me very much. We had a very rough trip home, came through to Hernando road, the pickets on Nonconnah did not ask me for a pass. Saw old Mr Farrow just getting home, he has only one week to be out of this country. A Yankee detective, with a woman came to stay all Night, Father was afraid not to take him. Just after they stoped, in came two of the 2nd Mo Cav. Mr Crile and Mr Davis. They did not come in when we told them who was here, for fear it would get Father in trouble. The detective (Lewis) was very uneasy for fear they would take—I hope they will get him after he leaves here in the morning.

SUNDAY 8 I had a nice time sleeping late this morning, and Laura had a nice Breakfast to tempt my apetite when awakened. The detective and his lady friend had left before I got in the Parlor. John and Cousin Frazor kept in the dark all morning, though every [thing] was quiet. We have not heard what the raide was for which passed down Hernando road yesterday, they staid in Hernando last night. Old Mr Hildebrand came down after dinner, though we have not heard a word of news to day—in fact it will be almost a nonentity in the pages of my sad and weary life. I have read in my Bible mostly—went to sleep after dinner and did ot wake up until late in the evening. All went to walk except myself. Anna Nelson & Mrs Lewis came here for some Soldier clothes, but they had not been left here. I did not stay in the house late, Bettie and Laura gave me a great deal of trouble about their lessons to Night. All quiet now, Bettie gone home. Laura & the Goslins both fast asleep. I trust sleep will soon relieve my weary brain.

MONDAY 9 I slept very late, Laura came in to clean my room, did every thing but make the bed. I told her if she would let me alone I would make the bed. I have been sewing on my white mull, did not get much done, have it all arranged, and hope to finish it tomorrow.

We had a delightful rain this evening. Cousin Frazor bought John a horse to day, from Mr Maddon. The two Miss Robinsons came over this evening, trying to find out where their Bros were, whom Floyd conscripted, we could tell them nothing, Poor things. I feel sorry for them, although they are such wicked people. Three Confederate Soldiers came riding up while they were here, I am very much afraid they will report it to the Yankees. I did not go in the Parlor after Tea the rest were all in, singing and playing, which I enjoyed all alone on the Porch. Father sat a while. Laura and Bettie had a very good lesson. All asleep now except myself, and I am prepared for a nice feast in one of the Waverleys—the Abbot,[7] it will draw my mind for a while at least, from its own sad and weary thoughts.

TUESDAY 10 Cloudy and rainy, I got up to breakfast as Mr Harbert came, he is cut off from his command, and has no news. We heard Forrest had got safely out of Tenn. Tate and Joanna went to Memphis this morn, did not get back and we have not heard a word, suppose the rains must have kept them, we had a very hard storm this evening. Mrs Franklin & Miss Kate Daugherty arrived from Dixie this morning.[8] They say we have had a glorious victory in Virginia, but a dearly bought one—loss heavy on both sides—the Conferates Victorious as always under our brave Gen. Lee. A sad loss will be our gallant Longstreet. We hear he is mortally wounded.[9] Heaven forbid the correctness of the report. Oh! my heavenly Father enlighten the hearts of our wicked foe, and let them leave our lovely land, think of the thousands of Souls hastened into eternity—we humbly crave thy pardon, grant us thy blessings, and give us peace, Oh! give us peace—all we ask —drive them from our land. We have sinned, but now are humble. God bless my dear Father, and Brothers and unite them once again.

WEDNESDAY 11 Tate and Joanna went to Memphis this morning—what a mistake —on yesterday they went in, did not return until this evening. Joanna and Miss Em, and little Emie all came. Oh! I

7. Sir Walter Scott (1771–1832), *The Waverley Novels*, 30 vols. (Edinburgh: Cadell & Co., 1830–33): *The Abbott*, vol. 21.

8. The adventures of Mrs. Ann Franklin of Columbus on a trip from Mississippi through the lines of Memphis to buy a trousseau for her daughter may have been inspiration for some of the episodes in William Faulkner's *The Unvanquished*. She was the grandmother of Estelle Faulkner's first husband. A. E. Franklin, "My Experience as a Blockade-Runner," included in *War Experiences of Columbus, Mississippi and Elsewhere*, comp. by Stephen D. Lee Chapter, United Daughters of the Confederacy (West Point: Sullivans, 1961), 11.

9. The wilderness, 5–7 May. General Longstreet was not mortally wounded. Long, *Civil War*, 494.

was so delighted to see Mrs Perkins. Nannie came out very early. Started to go to Germantown, for John a horse, too late. Poor cousin Mat and little Frazor had to return with Mrs T[itus] to M. No news from Mr Harbert yet—he is always very prompt—we think it very strange he did not return. We all spent the evening in the parlor. Mr Tom Nelson came this evening. Brot intelligence of Poor Mr Fackler's death —he killed himself drinking, died with Mania potin.[10] I do pity his Wife, and poor little children, and such a horrible death. No late news from either side. Miss Em and I talked nearly all night.[11]

THURSDAY 12 Miss Em and I took breakfast in our room. It was bitter cold this morning, and I have taken my stove down. Mr Nelson very impatient, Mr Brett arrived about 11 o'clock, had succeeded in getting a pass for Mr N. from Genl Washburn good for one week. They left about 12. We all sat in the Parlor in the morning. After dinner Miss Em and I came out to my room and spent the evening—Nannie and Emie came also. Oh! I wish they would quit speaking of the war, or Politics. Cousin Frazor was tight at dinner and as he and Mrs Perkins differed, he was very rough and disagreeable.[12] We did not sit up so late. Bettie & Anna Nelson reached home safe, but very late. No important news. No news from Mr Harbert yet.

FRIDAY 13 Miss Em, Joanna, Anna Nelson, Tate's children and Kate all went to Memphis this morning—all returned except Mary who they left with Tate. We have had a quiet day comparatively speaking—no Yankees. Mr Wilson and Mr Pope came this evening—been up several days, no late news. Poor Mr Harbert was captured on yesterday, at Mr Rutland's on the plank road—both of his fine

10. Mr. Fackler's death was possibly the reason his wife's letter remained with Belle's papers. (See p. 197–201.)

11. Frazor Titus recorded his reaction to Miss Em's visit in his diary. "Mrs. Perkins and others are here. The old lady is full of Union. I am tired of the war." Frazor Titus Diary entry, 7 May 1864.

12. The incident between Miss Em and Cousin Frazor was noted in a letter to Miss Em from her sister: "You said at their house [the Edmondsons] to Mr Titus rather than this Union should be dissolved, you would see every man, woman and child destroyed, yes utter annihilation of everything and everybody. They were all shocked, his reply was, reflect what you say, Madam, not only humanity but ties of family and friendship & you turned and looked at him. *I am aware sir what I say* and I alone am responsible for it. . . . The only view they could take of the whole thing that you *were deranged on that subject*. The whole affair is known and commented upon throughout the South. It had scarcely happened before it was the talk of Jackson [Tennessee]." Anna to My dear Em, 29 Sept. 1864, PFP.

horses captured. No news from him since he went into Memphis.
Mr Keene who came out with Cousin Sallie said Banks had certainly
surrendered with 35,000 men.[13] God grant it may be true. Nothing
deffinite from Virginia, though the slaughter has been terrible on
both sides. Oh! my Father in heaven crown our army with Victory.
God give us peace, I am so weary of so much bloodshed. Bless my
dear Father and Brothers.

SATURDAY 14 Miss Em and I slept until almost 12, o-clock. I finished Emie's dress after getting up. Miss Em cut out her new Calico
and run on the skirt. No Yankees to day, neither have we seen a
Confederate. Joanna and Anna Nelson went in this morning with
the wagon to get supplies, as this is the last day the lines will be
open.[14] All of them got back safe with a permit for all they wanted.
Tate came out with all of Helen's Bridal trousseau. Still no decisive
news from Va. Papers all suppressed, which appears rather ominous.
Oh! heaven hear the humble, and heart rending prayers, of our poor
suffering South—drive the wicked Northman from our soile, protect and guide my Bros safely through, may they do their duty
nobly—bless my poor old Father. I am miserable, what is to become
of me.

SUNDAY 15 This had been an unpleasant, unhappy Sabbath. Oh! we
differ so in politics from Miss Em—I am afraid her visit will be
miserable. Helen & Nannie went to Church. Col Perkins came home
with them, spent the evening. Capt Wormsley came over to spend
the Night, preparatory to leaving at day light in company with
Cousin Frazor and Johnie, poor John. He has not got him a horse,
or his clothes—Mrs Titus his step Mother has treated him shamefully. Miss Em had a talk with Nannie this evening, and she has been
miserable ever since. I do not know what it is, but they are so widely
different in Politics. I pray that Miss Em may not insist on Nannie
leaving. I shudder for the result, she says she will not go. We heard
our Army in Va. was victorious—I pray that it may be so, and this
horrible war closed. No communication with the City to day. Miss

13. Banks did not surrender, but in an inglorious end to the Red River Campaign,
Banks's army and Porter's fleet escaped from Alexandria, Louisiana where they had
been bottled up and surrounded. Taylor, *Destruction*, chap. 10 passim.

14. The lines at Memphis were ordered closed 15 May 1864. No one was allowed
to enter or leave without a special pass. Those who wanted to leave the city had to do
so before the deadline, and those who entered the city would not be allowed to leave.
Parks, "Trade," 308–9; Hooper, "Memphis," 102–3; General Orders No. 3, General
C. C. Washburn, 10 May 1864, *OR*, 39, pt. 2, 22–23.

Em speaks of going tomorrow—she has a free pass. She is sick in bed to Night. All retired very early.

MONDAY 16 Laura awakened me at daylight, to see Cousin Frazor, John, and Capt Wormsley leave for Dixie. They left early for fear they would meet a squad of Yanks later in the day. Miss Em and Nannie went to Memphis this morning,[15] got back safe, no late news except Yankee lies—which say that we are beaten in Va, and I do not believe one word of it—never will hear the truth until we get the Southern account. Mr Wilson came this evening, bro't me a package of Southern papers (Mobile & Richmond) though not very late date—therefore nothing deffinite from Lee's army. He had no late news, currier up yesterday. Nannie saw Mr Harbert at the Provost Marshall to day—he will be sent to Alton in a few days. Mr Crawford came for Nannie to day, was very much disapointed. I read all the morning, made me a dress waiste after dinner. Oh! how my heart has yearned for this visit from Miss Em, and how sadly disapointed. Yet I have learned to bury my sorrow within my own breast. There is a terible gap in our social circle, we are so widely different in Politics.

TUESDAY 17 Oh! most miserable day. Mrs Perkins almost made me mad at her deep distress. Poor, poor Nannie my heart aches for her would to God, I might be the medium through which all could be made happy. Miss Em is so widely different in her political feeling, there will never be any happiness I fear with poor Nannie. May God guide the dear child, keep her firm to the cause she has espoused. May she never have her pure noble Southern feelings polluted with Yankee treachery or tyranny, keep her firm and true to her noble Brother Dashiell and his Country['s] rights. She dreams not but oh! my heart trembles and bleeds for her in this great trial and affliction. I received a letter from Dr Moses. Tate did also. Oh! why am I tempted, Guide oh! comfort me my Savior. Poor Father is quite sick. Joanna went to Hernando this morning.

WEDNESDAY 18 When, oh! when will this wickedness and strife end. My heart how sadly, and how sorely it has been tried. God have mercy and keep it pure, through all temptations. Bless poor Miss Em be with her in this affliction, guide dear Nannie in the right path. I pray that it may all be right—thy will, and I am content. Col

15. Although the lines were closed Miss Em was able to make trips through the lines. She may have had one of those "special" passes from Washburn's headquarters. She knew General Grant, according to her son, Dashiell Perkins, "Record," 1.

Perkins came this morning, Nannie had not decided to stay when he was here. Mr Nelson took dinner with us, on his way to Dixie. Mr and Mrs Lake came down here to meet him, missed only a few moments. Mr Crawford came this evening. Miss Em sent a note to Col Perkins by him. Mr Huchins [Hutchenson][16] was here also—with all the arrivals, of persons and newspapers no reliable news. My dear redeemer I pray, oh! I humbly beseech thee to bless our brave little bands in Va and Ga—crown them victory, oh! give thy blessing to our sunny land. Give us peace then will we praise thy great and glorious reign through all eternity.

THURSDAY 19 It seems that trouble and misery will never cease. Miss Em almost killed herself with Chloroform last Night, did not get up, until late this evening, and is still very feeble and miserable, from the effects. Nannie has been in bed all day—seems to be quite sick to Night. Poor old Father he is almost prostrated with trouble. I wish I had some influence, oh! that I could be the medium of reconciliation & peace between Miss Em, and the family. There is a breach which can never be healed. She is raving mad whenever she speaks, or thinks of Tate and Helen. Poor little Emie, the child is miserable. Heard from Dashiell last Night, but do not dare to show the letter to his Mother. I think the scriptures are truly fulfilled in this war, Child shall be against Parent and Parent against Child. Col Perkins did not come. We have heard nothing deffinite from our Armys. Joanna got back last Night with Helen's cotton. I have been unhappy all day, no one could be in this house at this time and not be.

FRIDAY 20 Mrs Perkins went to Memphis this morning in an awful state of mind. Col Perkins came up to see her before she started, but I do not think she was much releived by his visit. Nannie would not go. She did not come back to Night although she said she would be certain to come. I am entirely weaned from any affection I ever had for her. Any Southern woman to talk and express herself as she does I have no use for her. I wish to heaven she would never come to our house again. I went over to Mr Clayton's on old Gray, took Peter with me—did not get to see Hal. Arrived at home safe, but very much fatigued. Laura and I had a very quiet, pleasant night all alone. Joanna tried our fortunes with the cards, if they are true I do not think we will have a very exciting life for the next few days.

16. Probably S. A. Hutchenson of Henderson's Scouts. The scouts were in the area hanging around the various Federal units. List of Scouts, CC; Colonel G. E. Waring to General C. C. Washburn, 18 May 1864, *OR*, 39, pt. 2, 37.

SATURDAY 21 Nannie still sick in bed, got up this evening when Mr Wilson came, I think that is the only thing which could have aroused her. Nothing unusual happened to day, the news from Va still glorious. Oh God! we praise, we humbly bow to thy glorious favor, of our struggle for Liberty—crown our Armys every where with decisive victories, and oh! we pray thee for peace. Mrs. Perkins came home this evening, I am afraid she has made her arrangements for some vengeful feelings—her plans are entirely different from when she left. I did not imagine one I loved so much, I could so soon hate. Poor old Father is almost crazy with his troubles, yet the happy news from the army keeps him up. Mrs. Perkins staid in my room and I had anything but a pleasant Night.

SUNDAY 22 Every thing has been in commotion and any thing but a quiet day. Mrs Perkins is still disagreeable in her Politics. She and Nannie and Emie started down to Col Perkins broke down, came back did not go until this evening. Hal and Mr Clayton came to day we made our final arrangements for our trip and will get off one day this week. Mr Bray came over and made arrangements for Miss Tollison [Tarleton] to go with us, she is going to marry Gen Pat Claiborne [Cleburne].[17] We have had anything but a pleasant day. Mrs Perkins has been spouting forth her Unionism. Every thing has gone, and we are quiet once more. I wish the day could have been more pleasant for Hal & Mr Clayton. I wish I did not feel so bitter towards her. Thank God the news is still glorious for us from all quarters. Laura and I will have a pleasant Night alone.

MONDAY 23 I was up bright and early this morning, went over to Mr Hudgins [Hudgens] to get his Wife, who 's going to Memphis to morrow, to bring me out a few articles, which I am compelled to have before leaving. The day I have spent trying to get my clothes arranged to have them done up to morrow—it has been an unpleasant task, and altogether any thing but a pleasant day to me. Until this evening we were all made glad by the arrival of Sister Mary [Anderson], Aunt Patsy [Buchanan Edmondson], and our dear Sister's [Jane Scott Edmondson Kilpatrick] two youngest little Orphans—Sallie & Frank,[18] also their nurse Nellie. Both of the Chil-

17. Major General Patrick Cleburne met Miss Sue Tarleton, the daughter of a wealthy cotton factor, at the wedding of Major General Hardee in Marengo County, Alabama 13 Jan. 1864. She was bridesmaid, and he was the best man. Irving A. Buck, *Cleburne and His Command*, ed. Thomas Robson Hay (Jackson, Tennessee: McCowat-Mercer Press, 1959), 51.

18. Jane Kilpatrick died 4 Sept. 1863. Aunt Patsy was Martha Buchanan Edmondson (1789–1865), the widow of William Edmondson (1780–1838), Andrew Jackson Edmondson's older brother, genealogy charts, EFP.

dren are beautiful, poor little things how my heart aches for them. How sad is life to me without my Mother's love. Sallie is a sad little creature, very like her Mother in appearance. Frank the baby, is all life & happiness. They came all the way from Pontotoc in an Ox wagon just one week coming. Mr. Wilson was here to day—no late news, from our Armys.

TUESDAY 24 Little Frank waked me up this morning bright and early, I managed to get up, and send Nellie, who was with him to the kitchen for his breakfast, he is prettier every time I look at him. Laura did not get to washing my clothes until 11 o'clock, but finished all except three dresses and has done them beautifully. Annie Nelson & Missie Morgan came out this evening—though the lines are closed. I dont know whether Mrs Hudgens went in or not, if she did not I dont know what I am to do about the things I sent for. I finished my Peasants waiste and think it beautiful. Oh! I am so unfortunate, and unhappy. I pray for patience and submission. No late news from Va or Ga. I did not go in the parlor after Tea, the rest all spent a pleasant evening I suppose. My heart is too full to venture in company. I put little Sallie & Frank to bed.

WEDNESDAY 25 I have been quite sick all day, was taken some time in the Night, Laura was very kind to me—and has been the only one in my room to see me today. Miss Em & Nannie & little Emie got home from Col Perkins just before dinner. Poor Miss Em, she seems almost heart-broken that Nannie wont go with her. I pity her, and have forgiven all hard thoughts which ever existed in my heart towards her. I wish this horrid war, would not uproot so many social ties. I dressed late this evening—went on the Porch, very cloudy and cool after tea, so we all moved in the parlor. Sister Mary, Miss Em, Father and I spent the evening alone. The rest did not seem socially inclined, even Nannie did not come in although it was her Ma's last Night with us. Poor old Father he tries to smooth over the ruffles all the rest make. God bless him and my dear Brothers.

THURSDAY 26 Miss Em was almost dressed, when I awoke this morning. I was very much distressed, to see her leave, in remembrance of the wickedness which filled my heart a day or two ago. I have entirely forgiven, and all unpleasant feelings have passed away. Poor Miss Em, she was the picture of dispair, did not get to see Dashiell, and little Emie, oh! tis hard for horrid politics to interfere with social feelings. They all left quite early for Memphis. Joanna and Robert got back safe, did not bring me anything I sent for. I am very much disapointed—but must think of some other way. Capt Farrell arrived this evening—left Tupelo on yesterday morning. All the boys well, most of the Batalion had gone to Alabama Eddie was among the number.[19] News is all we could wish for. By the grace of God Lee is still victorious. God bless our Armys, my dear Father and Brothers. Yankees gone to Hernando on a raide. Have mercy and make me a better and more useful woman.

FRIDAY 27 Sister Mary and I started early over to Mrs Armstrongs—found both Mr & Mrs A. at home, and as usual my best friends in trouble. Mrs. A. is going to Memphis to morrow and will get all the things I need and bring them out to her home. Sister Mary has made arrangements to go to town with her to morrow to get her watch. We spent the day with Hal & Mrs Clayton. After dinner we all came over to Mrs Seymours to welcome she and her husband, who had just returned from their bridal trip. Poor Beulah, I met her again, she was so delighted to see me, and it almost broke my heart to part with her. How much I love my poor dog. Laura, Tip and I have sat up very late. I have been talking to Laura. Father will not let her go with me. I trust and pray that she may be guided through all temptations and come to me just as I leave her. I am very unhappy to think of leaving home.

SATURDAY 28 Sister Mary and I arrived at Mrs Armstrongs quite late. They went on in town, I drove over to Mrs Claytons and spent the day. Hal is not ready to start yet, so it is doubtful whether or not we leave Monday morning. Maggie Cockrell was there, we spent a very pleasant day. I got back to Mrs Armstrongs quite late, found Sister Mary impatiently waiting. Mrs A.'s kindness I shall never forget. She bought all my things, and brought them through the lines. They are all just as nice and pretty as can be. I left my bundle, with the dress in it, when we started, so that will make another trip to-morrow, which I hope Nannie & Helen will take for me. Father gave me a deed to Laura this evening.[20] I am grieved to leave her, exposed to so many temptations, but hope the principal, I have always endeavored to instill, may save her. My room is all confusion. Trunk not packed—every thing scattered.

SUNDAY 29 Today has been an eventful one in the dull pages of my life. Bettie awakened me, standing by the bed with a hot cup of Coffee, which I enjoyed very much, after refreshing myself with a cold bath. Mr Wilson came by, with late dispatches, letters and pa-

19. A portion of Chalmers's command was sent to Alabama 26 May 1864 to meet a Federal raid anticipated against the iron works in that area. Jordan and Pryor, *Campaigns*, 460.

20. The Deed to Laura contains an interesting provision: "unless the said Belle marries with my consent during my lifetime."

pers—the latter containing news which paralyzed me for a while.
Oh! such a shock, yet I had expected it. At Arcola, Ala, April 27th
1864, by Rev Mr Beckwith, G. A. Moses P.A.C.S. to Miss Sallie S.
Anderson, of Mobile, Ala. There is a future, oh! thank God, thy
will not mine be done—in thee I trust, in thee I shall be saved——
Father went over to Mr Brays, but failed to get a conveyance for me
to go to Dixie in. Helen and Nannie went over Nonconnah to get
the bundles I forgot, and also to see Hal. She has not all arrangements made, and will not be ready before Wednesday. Our news
today is very encouraging—thanks to the Almighty the day for our
glorious Confederacy & independence is brightening. Packed today.
Laura & I spent the evening alone. God bless my servant & take care
of her. God bless and protect my dear Father and Brothers.

MONDAY 30 Began the day quite early, drew off the pattern on Nannie's dress first thing. Tate asked me to fix the Machine, she sewed
for me while I did it. Father went over to Mr Farrows to see Mr
Hodge, and try to trade for his spring wagon—he asked so much for
it, I hope Father will not get it. I and Peter went over Nonconnah to
try and get one from some place, failed three times, when Joe, Mrs
Claytons gardener told me of a Mr Smith who had one. Dink and I
went over to Mr S. We made a trade, only $75.00 for the wagon,
tied the wagon behind, started for home again. Stoped at Mrs Duke
(Seymour) saw her and Hal—no news—had a rough and troublesome trip home. Arrived safe. Father likes the wagon very much. So
I am all ready for Dixie, dont know what day Hal will be here. Laura
finished my dress and hemed three handkerchiefs. I dont know what
I would do without Laura. Glorious news from the South, we have
been successful in all battles. Lee whipped Grant, Johnston vs Sherman, and Forrest old Dutch.[21] Bless my dear Father and Brothers,
take care of, and guide Laura.

TUESDAY 31 I slept very late this morning. Very buisy until dinner
was ready packing and drawing off the pattern on Nannies swiss.
Aunt Patsy sat in my room. Just as we were going to dinner an
Ambulance with Yankee escort rode up to the gate. Mrs Perkins
coming for Nannie. Nannie and Helen with Laura ran to the Woods.
Then followed a scene which I trust I may never witness again—
such excitement and confusion. They scoured the woods for them,
but no where to be found. Nannie has not been back since, and I

---

21. Perhaps a reference to the Battle of Bermuda Hundred 21 May 1864, and the
Battle at New Hope Church in Georgia 25 May–4 June. Forrest had not met with any
Federal force since eluding Sturgis in May. Long, *Civil War*, 506–8; Jordan and
Pryor, *Campaigns*, 457–64.

expect is in Senatobia to Night. God guide & protect her. The Yanks staid about two hours & I think left disgusted with their trip, thinking until we told them, they had come for a little child. Mrs. Perkins left in anger, swearing vengenance on Tate and Helen. Poor Father it has broken him down, he is sick in bed. They are all ready and hope to get off by daylight. Have mercy my dear Savior and spare my poor old Father any more excitement—guide us aright—and protect and shield our household.

9

Refugees

1864 DIARY: JUNE

WEDNESDAY 1 Tate had me awakened at daylight this morning.
They had some trouble and confusion before we started. I drove my
Spring Wagon, with Tate, Bettie, Robert and Mammie as passen-
gers. Helen rode horseback on old McGruder. Uncle Elam, Willie
Perkins and Peter with the baggage went in the Wagon. We traveled
very slow, arrived at Col Perkins half past ten—with no accident,
and a very pleasant trip. Mr Reads wagon had been waiting since
daylight for them, so as quick as the baggage could be changed, they
started on for Dixie, and I hope are safe in Confederate lines to
Night. Nannie and Harison stoped at Mr Reids in Hernando last
Night, left at daylight. God forever protect her from the tyranny of
her Mother and the Yankees. Tis an awful step, but I trust it is right.
Mr Wilson came to Col Perkins some time after they had left, was
very much disapointed at not seeing them. He, Mr Crawford the
children and I spent a very pleasant day. Mr Wilson came some of
the way with us, we had an awful time from Horn Lake in a thunder
storm, arrived at home found Father composed & satisfied. We all
spent eve in the Parlor. Laura and I all alone.

THURSDAY 2 I slept late this morning. Laura brought me a cup of
Coffee to my room, which I enjoyed. We have had a very quiet day,
after the great excitement of the two days just passed. Very cloudy
& showery. I have made me a nice traveling sun-bonnet, and began
my white swiss waiste—did not get very much done to it. Not one
word from Hal yet—think [it] very strange, as she was almost sure
of coming yesterday morning. Joanna will go over to morrow to see
what is to pay. Anna Brodinax came over this evening for Miss Tarleton to see when we were going. Sallie Hildebrand came to get me
to take her Brothers in Jacksons Cavalry some things. Mr Wilson

and Mr Rutland[1] were here this morning, no late news, did not come in the house as we are in constant dread of another raide from the Yankees. Aunt Patsy, Father, Joanna, Sister Mary and I spent the eve together discussing passing events of our household. Frank and Sallie retired early—now Laura, Tippie Dora and I all alone.

FRIDAY 3 Laura awakened me this morning at daylight. Mr Wilson came to breakfast—had no later news than yesterday. We have every thing to be thankful for—our Armys have by the grace of God been victorious so far. Mr W. did not stay long after breakfast will return tomorrow. Joanna went over Nonconnah to day. Hal has not been able to get a horse yet, but expects to be along tomorrow. I hope she may for Father is so anxious for us to get off, did not hear any news from that direction. This has indeed been a gloomy day—cloudy and raining all day. Father spent the day in his big chair reading, "Small house at Allington".[2] Aunt Patsy, Sister Mary & I spent the day in Tate's room. I have almost finished my white swiss body. Sallie and Frank have been caged to day and right noisy. I wrote a letter for Marguerite after tea to her Mother in Holly Springs—the rest all in the Parlor. Laura and I alone except Tippie Dora who is nodding. I expect this is the last quiet night we will have for some time to come.

SATURDAY 4 This day has seemed like a month to me. I got up early and went to work to finish my white waiste, did not sew long before Hal, came, on her way down to Dixie. We have been disapointed in getting Dr Buntin [Buntyn][3] to go with us, and Johnie Armstrong is to be our escort to Pontotoc. Mrs Wren will be with us to Senatobia. Mr Seymour came this far with them but returned to Memphis. Mr Wilson came while they were here, did not have any late news, however we are confident of success. They are glorying over their victories from all points yet say nothing with regard to the price of Gold. We had to disapoint Miss Tarleton, Mr Wilson carried the news. Hal and I each have a spring wagon with our old Greys. I finished my waiste, my lunch fixed, and I believe every thing is ready to leave now. We all sat in the Parlor after tea. Father enjoyed the Music very

---

1. John W. Rutland of Henderson's Scouts. List of Scouts, CC.

2. Anthony Trollop (1815–1882), *Small House at Allington* (London, Leipzig and New York: n.p., 1864). The version Belle's father was reading may have been the one published serially in *Harpers* magazine between 1862–1864.

3. Dr. G. O. Buntyn, son of Geraldus Buntyn (1800–1865), a wealthy land owner in West Tennessee. Lenow, *Elmwood*, 104.

much. Sister Mary finished Helen's Bridal Gown, came out to the room with it to pack. Hal is asleep. Laura, Tippie Dora and I awake, I am very sad in thinking it is the last Night in some time.

SUNDAY 5 This day has seemed a week to me. We had a very late start from home. Hal was first to wake, the sun was shining then, Laura sound asleep. After some delay we had breakfast, bid all the servants and home folks good bye and got off at 8 o'clock. Poor Laura was greatly distressed. God guide her, and protect her from all harm—bless my poor old Father, and save him from such excitement as we are always exposed to. He came by Mr Hudgens and got Hal's things for her, met us at the burnt chimneys came with us over Horn Lake Creek, to see us safe, then went on back to go to Church. Oh! how my heart ached to see my poor hoary headed Parent leave me. Oh! God have mercy, have mercy. We did not get to Mr Boyd's until 12 o'clock, rested about one hour, have traveled very slow all evening.[4] Mr Wilson is with us, we ate dinner at Hurricane creek, having stoped for the Night at Mr Dennis's four miles below Hernando, a very nice place, and our horses well cared for. Sat up until 10 o'clock, very tired, and will certainly appreciate the nice clean bed. God bless my Fathers household.

MONDAY 6 After all of our agreements &c. about an early start we did not get off until 8 o'clock. A terible, terible day we have had. Cold Water almost out of its banks, and still rising—the slews [sloughs] swiming. Mr Wilson picked the way or we never would have gotten through. Arrived at Cold Water station[5] in time to eat

4. The route Belle traveled was described by Mrs. Meriwether in late 1863; "The road . . . was desolate and dreary; the farm houses on either side of the road were either in ashes or abandoned by their owners. We saw no animals on the way, not a horse or cow or sheep—silence reigned everywhere!" Meriwether, *Recollections*, 137. Mrs. Saxon was another woman who traveled the same route late in the war and found the area bleak and frightening. Saxon, *Reminiscences*.

5. Coldwater Station was a hamlet on the Mississippi and Tennessee Railroad, thirty-four miles south of Memphis and ten miles south of Hernando. Coldwater Bottom was described as a dark and dismal place with wolves howling and owls hooting. J. J. Rawlings, *Miscellaneous Writings and Rememberances* (Memphis: n.p., 1895), 22. General Grierson was another traveler along this road who wrote of it: "The face of the country between here [Memphis] and Hernando is flat and heavily timbered. Numerous small creeks intersperse the country, over which are thrown corduroy bridges poor in construction and not very safe. Beyond Hernando for about 8 miles the country is rolling until we arrive within 3 miles of Coldwater Station where the country becomes suddenly flat, and the creeks running through it are small winding, with steep banks. Here the timber is very heavy and the soil deep and mirey." Report of Benjamin H. Grierson to General Lew Wallace, 23 June 1862, *OR*, 17, pt. 1, 10; Map of Mississippi (Gulf–10), NA.

our dinner and feed [the horses]. Met with a Negro man, coming to
Senatobia, gave him part of our baggage, had to go twenty miles out
of the way, by Luxahoma to cross Hickey Hayley [Hickahala].[6] We
missed the road to Mrs Wren's home, had to travel until 8 o'clock,
through Senatobia bottom after Night, oh, how terible to think of—
we never would have reached here, had it not been for Mr Wilson's
kindness. Found old Mrs Arnold ready to receive us, where we are
all now ensconced. Mrs Wren fast asleep. Hal taking Chloroform. I
begged her not to but to no availe. I am all alone. Mr. Wilson and
John both retired. We have glorious news from Va. Gen Lee has
repulsed Grant, with heavy loss.[7] God grant it may be so. Traveled
two days and only 30 miles from home. God bless my poor old Father and his household.

TUESDAY 7 As usual we had a very late start. A very nice drive to Mr
Wallace's—arrived about 10 o'clock, found all home folks there.[8]
Bro Geo [Dashiell] and John Titus came for them in two Ambulances. Robin and Mamie both well, poor little Rob, I have been
grieved ever since I passed them, having caressed Mamie and not
him, I will make up when we meet again. They expect to leave tomorrow or next day. We have had few adventures in our travels to
day, rough roads. Mr Wilson has been extremely kind. We had some
difficulty in passing over Talehatchie [Tallahatchie River]—the ferry
boat had washed away, and we had a bad affair to get over in. We
are staying in Panola to Night with Mrs Dr Philips, a friend of Hal's.
She is very kind, and we were very fortunate in getting in. A very
hard rain after we got here. Mr Wilson went to Mrs Moors to stay
to Night. We have all made arrangements to start very early in the
morning, however I ought not to record our daylight starts. Hal is
suffering with tooth ache, has taken an opiate and sound asleep. God
bless all at home, my precious old Father, and Brothers far away.

WEDNESDAY 8 I think to day will be long remembered, a hard rain
before breakfast. Mr. Rodgers arrived just after, and had almost persuaded us to remain over until tomorrow, when Mr Wilson came up
and said it was imposible for him to remain, of course we could
never venture without him, so we packed up and left at 8 o'clock. I
never traveled such roads in my life—creeks swiming. As we neared

6. Hickahala Creek was one of the numerous watercourses that crossed the main
road between Memphis and Grenada. Map of the Gulf (West).

7. The Battle of Cold Harbor, 1–3 June. Long, *Civil War*, 512.

8. The Wallace home at Como was about seven miles south of Senatobia. Panola
was an additional ten miles. Map of the Gulf (West).

the City of Springport,[9] in passing a school house with the Children
at play, I greeted them with school, buttons, when all hands joined,
and I thought for a while Mr Wilson had a skirmish on hand, was
compromised however, when old Gray refused to pull the hill and
Mr W. had to come to our relief. We ate dinner there, which was
broken up by the hardest rain I ever was exposed to, we left the
scene in disgust and demoralized. Had a terible time, almost swam
Clear Creek. A rain and Night coming on we stoped 8 miles this side
of Oxford at Mr Bunch's, where Hal, Johny & I are now enjoying
the quiet of a room. Still raining. I never laughed as much, as when
I awoke and saw Hal's face swolen, completely disfigured, relieved
however. Mr W. left early with a book to read. After all the trouble
we have had a nice time.

THURSDAY 9 A bright and beautiful day, yet the roads very heavy, 8
miles from Oxford, hills all the way. Left quite early—were very
fortunate in getting to the place we did. Mr Wilson with his usual
kindness, assisted us greatly, in fact we would never have succeeded
in getting through had it not been for him. We arrived in Oxford
about 10 o'clock, stoped at the University[10] where Henderson's
Scouts were camped and put Mr W's bundles out. He very kindly
sent two Servants with us to take our baggage, and carry our horses
back to Camp. Indeed I do not know how Hal and I can ever repay
him for his kindness to us during this trip. Lt Carman & Mr Bacon[11]
came to the Wagon to see us, and get the late papers. Mr & Mrs Barr
were very glad to see us and have treated us as kind as our own
relations. Mr Wilson came round to see us this evening, we had a
very pleasant time. John went to Camp with him. Mr & Mrs Barr,
Emma, Hal & I spent the eve'ing alone. Hal & I slept all afternoon.

FRIDAY 10 We have spent a delightful day—did not get up in time
for breakfast. Mrs Barr sent it to the room. After breakfast, I cut,
of a piece of Calico I had, Emma a dress, and two Soldier shirts.
Did not sew any. Mr Wilson came this morning, Mr Cummins[12]

9. A small hamlet on the road from Panola to Oxford, ibid.

10. The University of Mississippi was chartered in 1844. A Federal soldier de-
scribed the town in 1864: "We found Oxford the county seat of Lafayette County,
Miss., to be a very pretty, well-situated and quite busy place. It is the seat of the State
University and of a Cumberland Presbyterian Female College." Maud Morrow
Brown, *The University Grays* (Richmond: Garrett and Massie, 1940), 1; Howard,
124th Regiment, 44.

11. J. S. Carman, Third Lieutenant and W. M. Bacon, Second Sergeant. List of
Scouts, CC.

12. Possibly Holmes Cummins, Adjutant of the Ninth Tennessee Cavalry. Mathes,
Old Guard, 68.

also—the latter staid to dinner. Mr Barr and all hands have been buisy trying to get us a Wagon, have not succeeded as yet. Wrote to Father this evening, and fixed a bundle of late Southern papers to send him by Johnie. We had just dressed to walk out to the University, when Mrs Goodman and Capt Scales[13] came, Mr Wilson & Mr Cummins also. We spent a delightful evening, but I always feel how sadly changed, how demoralized we are on the border when thrown in any society. Mrs Goodman is highly accomplished—I like her very much. Charlotte Ingram came over after tea. We spent a very pleasant evening. I think though she is too affected. No news from Tate, or any of the party yet. Hal & I have a delightful place to stay, and are content to await their arrival. Mr & Mrs Barr are very kind to us.

SATURDAY 11 Hal & I ready for breakfast, Mr Wilson and John came while we were eating for us to go out to the University. We had to wait some time for Mr Cummins. Lt McConnell, who has just returned from Helena with a flag of truce came to see us. I was very glad to see him—did not stay very long, before we had to start to fulfill our engagement. Mrs Hilgard gave us some delightful Music. The Labratory, Librarys &c were a great treat. Capt Scales accompanyed us also Lt McConnell. Mr Wilson & Mr Cummins staid to dinner with us, left soon after. Hal & I went round to call on Mrs Goodman, met with Capt Scales & Mrs Looney there. Spent a delightful evening. Hal went to bed soon after supper—poor Hal she is so easily discouraged, and has the blues to Night. Mr Barr & I sat up quite late, had a very pleasant time, although the rest had all retired. I found Hal nontalkative, and rather cross when I arrived in my room. Good news from Forrest. He has captured the Wagon trains, and completely routed the raide, which left Memphis two weeks ago.[14] God bless our dear Soldiers, and my poor old Father.

SUNDAY 12 Our news from the front to day is glorious. Forrest's vic-

13. Mrs. Walter Goodman, wife of General Chalmers A. A. G. Captain W. N. Scales, Co. D, Fifth Mississippi Cavalry. Jordan and Pryor, *Campaigns*, 686, 697.
14. The Battle of Brice's Cross Roads was fought 10 June 1864. General Sturgis left Memphis with a force of over 8,000 men and was completely routed by Forrest with less than half that number. A British officer thought it a most remarkable achievement, worthy of study by military historians: "He pursued the enemy from the battle for nigh sixty miles, killing numbers all the way. The battle and this long pursuit were accomplished in the space of thirty hours." Jordan and Pryor, *Campaigns*, 466–83; Garnet Wolsely, "General Viscount Wolseley on Forrest," Robert Selph Henry, ed., *As They Saw Forrest* (Jackson: McCowat- Mercer Press, 1956), chap. 1, passim; S. D. Sturgis, *The Other Side* (Washington: n.p., 1882).

tory is complete, captured 250 wagons,[15] the Yankees in full retreat
Bell's brigade close on the rear, capturing stragglers by the hun-
dreds. Willie Pope adt of 7th Tenn & Capt Tate of same both
killed,[16] no other casualties mentioned. Raining all day, no church.
Hal has had the blues all day. We both had a long nap before dinner.
I have spent most of the day reading, Lay of the last Nibelungers,[17]
which was loaned me from the University Library. Emma & I alone
in Parlor, when Mr Wilson came—spent the evening. Just at dark
Helen & Nannie, came riding up. John [Titus] & Lt McConnell
with them. They stoped at Mrs Barr's. John returned to Camp with
Lt McC. After tea Mr Wilson & John came over—we all have had a
delightful evening. Lt McConnell & Capt Wormsly came late. They
all staid very late, 12 o'clock. We had a nice lunch after we came to
our room. Nannie & Helen are sleeping on a pallet. Mrs Barr is so
kind. We think of going tomorrow. Oh! tis so happy to be in Dixie.
Poor Father, I wish he had all the good news to Night. God bless
him. Tate & Bro George broke down in Panola.

MONDAY 13 [The following entry is in a different handwriting] Nice
morning clear & rain ceased. Met Miss Belle E., Miss Hal R., Miss
Helen E. & Miss Nannie P. all looking pleasant and gay as larks.
They are en route for Tupelo and other important points in Dixie.
It is a gay party and I would be delighted to accompany them but
duty &c admonishes me not. Miss Belle says she feels sad. Wonder
why? I wish her sweetheart was here to accompany her. This would
make her feel cheerful I know. Who is the favored gentleman I wonder. Wish I knew for he is destined to be a happy man. From indi-
cations I fear my hopes for Capt H[enderson] must cease. The ladies
are now ready to start. Pleasant trip to you ladies & may each one of
you soon meet your sweethearts & have a gay & happy time not only
until you return but through life.

W.M. McConnell

15. According to Forrest's chief of artillery, General Sturgis's own headquarters
wagon was among those captured. In it were found the reports for the morning of 10
June 1864. Also captured were five new ambulances with medical supplies, sixteen
pieces of artillery, and twenty-one caissons. John Watson Morton, *The Artillery of
Nathan Bedford Forrest's Cavalry* (Nashville: Publishing House of the Methodist
Church, South, 1909), 184.

16. Lieutenant William Pope was among the first killed. Captain W. J. Tate of Co.
E, Seventh Tennessee Cavalry was killed as he pursued the retreating Federals. Jordan
and Pryor, *Campaigns*, 471, 479, 691.

17. *Lay of the Last Nibelungers*, Professor [sic] Lachman, trans. (London: Williams
and Margate, 1850).

We are camped 5 miles from Lafayette Springs,[18] no where to stay all
Night. Jim, Lt McConnell's cook, who is driving our baggage wagon,
cooked us a delightful supper—fried ham and eggs, Butter milk &
Corn bread. We threw heads and tails and decided not to go on to Night.
10 o'clock, after tea Jim cleaning up. Helen & John building a fire
in an old store which we are to inhabit. Nannie & Hal sitting over the
fire, I alone, writing a record of our adventures. Lt McC wrote for me
before leaving Oxford and I have no room—will recall all tomorrow.

TUESDAY 14 We had a little sleep last Night. Helen and Nannie fixed
their pallets in the corner—Hal and I were just in front of the fire,
an India-rubber blanket to lie on, a shawl for our pillow with only a
light mantle for covering we did not spend a very delightful Night.
John sat up in the corner and nod'ed. We all were up before daylight, our old store proved more comfortable than the open air. Our
poor horses did not have a mouthful. We had no breakfast. Started
on our journey at daylight, had a rough disagreeable trip to Pontotoc, distance 15 miles, which we accomplished by 11 o'clock. Came
by Mrs Duke's and left Hal, by the College[19] and got Willie & Andrew, met Bro Will [Kilpatrick] five miles from town. Mary, Eliza
and all were delighted to see us. We had a splendid dinner, slept all
after noon. Tate & Bro Geo arrived before sundown, came from
Oxford to day. Mary, Nannie & I slept together. Helen, Mary K,
Bettie and Ann on pallets. It is delightful and seems like home for
us all to be together.

WEDNESDAY 15 All up and ready for breakfast. Jim started for Oxford early. I wrote to Lt McConnell by him. John left for Tupelo,
came back this evening. Forrest's troops which have just achieved
such a victory are at Guntown will be in Tupelo in a day or two,
Forrest himself was there. Such sad news—our brave and christian
Gen. Leonidas Polk, was killed yesterday morning at 10 o'clock, by
a cannon ball, a stray shot, in a skirmish.[20] Oh! God have mercy on
our Southern land, drive the wicked foe from our soile, and we
humbly pray for thy mercy and peace. So many of our bravest and

18. Lafayette Springs was a post town on the eastern border of Lafayette County,
seventeen miles east of Oxford. Dunbar Rowland, *Mississippi*, 3 vols. (Atlanta: Southern Historical Publishing Association, 1907), 2:19.

19. Chickasaw College, opened in 1852 as the Presbyterian Collegiate Institute of
Pontotoc. "Chickasaw College" (clipping), unnamed, undated newspaper, vertical
file, Special Collections, MSUS.

20. Polk was killed instantly by a cannon shot near Marietta, Georgia, 14 June
1864. Ezra Warner, *Generals in Gray* (Baton Rouge: Louisiana State University Press,
1957), 243.

best have fallen. Bless and protect my dear Bros and return them safe to my poor old Father. We have all spent the day at home. Bettie took Mary & Robert visiting. Hal, Sina, Mary Martin & Capt Duke called this morning. Aunt Mary Gordon, Cousin Ginnie [Gordon], Mrs Clardy & little Annie [Gordon] called this evening.[21] We have spent a delightful day. God bless my dear Father and his household. Protect my dear Bros.

THURSDAY 16 Late risers this morning, but all ready for breakfast. John & Andrew went over to town after breakfast to get the Ambulances, We all spent the day with Aunt Mary Gordon, and a delightful time we had, Her home is as beautiful as ever.[22] Cousin Ginnie is so lovely, has a sweet little girl Annie. I dont know which enjoyed the visit most the Children or grown ones. I carried a Soldiers shirt to make but did not get much done. Music and conversation the order of the day. Cousin Ginnie has a splendid Piano. We had a hard rain and wind storm this eve, which delayed our return home rather late—arrived all safe and sound. After tea we all scattered to our rooms—rather fatigued. No news from the Army to day, and no news from home since we left. God grant that poor old Fathers life may be quiet, and spare him to meet his children once more. God bless my Bros, and oh! my Savior bless our Armys, and crown them with victory.

FRIDAY 17 A stupid and unhappy day for me—the rest have all enjoyed it. I was in a sad mood, sat in the Parlor alone, sewing most of the time, made a Soldiers shirt, none in particular. After finishing it, read three or four chapters in Macario [Macaria], am delighted

21. Mrs. Mary Walton Gordon, wife of Robert Gordon, was the sister of Andrew Jackson Edmondson's first wife. The Gordons' only son was Colonel James Gordon (1833–1912), Second Mississippi Cavalry, Armstrong's brigade, who went to Europe with Jimmie on the *Charlotte Clark*. Colonel Gordon's wife was Virginia Wiley (1836–1903). Their child was Annie Gordon (1836–1915). Mrs. Clardy was the wife of Thomas F. Clardy, chief surgeon, staff of Brigadier General Buford. Edmondson and Gordon Genealogy charts, EFP; E. T. Winston, *The Story of Pontotoc* (Pontotoc: Pontotoc Progress Printing Co., 1931), 148–50; Jordan and Pryor, *Campaigns*, 687. Although Belle makes no mention of it, Mrs. Gordon was suffering from cancer and had a breast removed later that summer. "Mrs. Gordon visited here today the first time Aunt Mary has left home since her breast was taken off." Frazor Titus diary entry, 8 Sept. 1864.

22. Lochinvar was in the path of Grierson's raid in April 1863. It was supposedly saved from the torch by the intervention of Captain S. L. Woodward, Grierson's adjutant. Mary Wallace Crocker, *Historic Architecture in Mississippi* (Jackson: University Press of Mississippi, 1973), 143–44; Dr. Forrest Tutor to editors, 30 May 1986; S. L. Woodward, "Grierson's Raid, April 17th to May 2d, 1863," *Journal of the United States Cavalry Association* 25 (1903–04): 690–91.

with it. There is one character in which I find much sympathy, will not mention until I live through it.[23] I was never so oppressed in my feelings, as in the last few days. I cannot define it, yet I feel I cannot rush quick enough to meet my fate—with a knowledge I will shudder when it overtakes me. God have mercy on my poor weary spirit, give me strength and patience to calmly see thy will not mine be done. Our news is not cheering to day. Oh! God we have suffered; we have endured patiently thy chastenings, if it can please thee, crown our two Armys, now in action with glorious victory, let thy smile brighten the sunny South with peace. Soften the hearts of our enemys, and oh! bless my dear Father and Brothers.

SATURDAY 18 Rather an eventful, and pleasant day, we made preparations early for a visit to Mrs Duke, but Bro George is always slow, and did not go for the Ambulance until late. We were all very much surprised to see Lt McConnell drive in it when it did arrive. We were delighted to see him, he drove us to where the prisoners were he was guarding, at the barbers shop. Bro Geo then took his seat. Mr Wilson was with him we were delighted to see him, had on his new Uniform, they did look so nice. Two detectives were the prisoners, one I have seen up on the lines. They all stoped at Mrs Dukes on the way out to Tupelo. Lt McConnell, Mr Wilson & Capt Wimberley[24] came in, did not stay long. John arrived from Tupelo, news Dashiell Perkins wounded, killed the Yankees who shot him, and saved his colors.[25] John Harris & Joe Park killed, how sad. Capt Henderson wounded.[26] Tate, Bro Geo, Nannie, Bettie & the Children all went out to Aunt Mary Gordons this eve. Hal, Capt Duke and Miss Miller were to see us.

SUNDAY 19 A delightful day we have had, although it is Sunday. Jim, Decatur and John went over to see Hal this morning. Nannie came in with Tobe Duke and went to Church, returned and spent the day

23. Augusta Jane Evans, *Macaria* or *Altars of Sacrifice* (Richmond: West & Johnston, 1864). The book was dedicated to the Confederate soldier, but one officer did not like it: "The lovers don't get married . . . . It is unnatural and unpleasant . . . a series of refined sentimentality." Cash and Howorth, *Nellie*, 177. Belle may have seen herself in the opening lines of chapter four: "From early childhood Irene had experienced a sensation of loneliness." Evans, *Macaria*, 36.

24. Probably Captain A. T. Wimberly, Co. A, Chalmers Consolidated Regiment. Jordan and Pryor, *Campaigns*, 699.

25. Dashiell Perkins was described as "brave as Caesar." A fellow soldier recalled seeing Dashiell "flaunt the colors in the faces of the enemy." Anna to My dear Em, PFP; John Milton Hubbard, "Private Hubbard's Notes," Henry, *They Saw Forrest*, chap. 4, passim.

26. No other mention of Captain Henderson's being wounded has been found.

with us. Robert came over and spent the day also. The boys came back to Dinner and we all had a gay time. Mr Wilson came over after dinner, he and Helen went out to Aunt Mary's to tea, Jim and Decatur went out to see Tate, but returned to Tea. John, Decatur and Jim all left for Tupelo about 9 o'clock, a beautiful Moonlight for their trip. Mr. Wilson staid very late, 12 o'clock, he, Helen, Mary and I sat out in the Moonlight and enjoyed it very much, he leaves at daylight for Oxford. Lt Mc did not return from Tupelo. We are hourly expecting Maj Crump & Eddie. Wrote home to day, sent letter by Mr Wilson. I hope to hear from home before leaving for Ga. God smile upon our Sunny land, bless my dear Father and Bros.

MONDAY 20 Mary, Helen and I were up bright and early, waiting breakfast for Bro Will, for fear he would lecture us about sitting up so late. Capt Duke brought Hal around early. I made the skirt to my Grenadine, Helen and Hal took a nap. Bro Will came to dinner and told us of another Yankee raide coming out of Memphis, after Forrest, of course we have no fears, for our success—but poor brave boys, how much they must suffer. No news from Maj Crump or Eddie yet. Kate Herron & Valley Huntington called. Bro Geo, Tate, Cousin Ginnie & the children came over this evening, did not stay long. Helen & Capt Duke went riding this evening. Hal staid until very late. I have been reading, Miss Evans last book—Macaria—I like it very much, though not entirely satisfied with the fate of some of the characters, have not finished it yet. We all chated for some time on the Porch after Tea. Bettie is sewing has one of Tate's candles, so I have an opportunity of reading again.

TUESDAY 21 I was up early this morning waiting for Capt Duke some time before he arrived. We started did not go far, before we had to run in to Mrs Martin's out of a hard rain. I was mortified for I had not called on Mollie.[27] We staid about an hour and spent it very pleasantly. Arrived at Mrs Duke's, Hal cut my dress for me, fited it, and help baiste. I never have any one to take an interest or help me with my sewing, and fully appreciate Hal's kindness. It has been rainy and gloomy all day, no chance for out door enjoyment, so Tobe & I against Hal and Capt Duke, spent the evening playing Euchre. Lt McConnell arrived from Tupelo about dark, unfortunate

27. For a discussion of the protocol of social calls that were an important part of female society in the South, see Elizabeth Fox-Genovese, *Within the Plantation Household: Black and White Women of the Old South* (Chapel Hill: University of North Carolina Press, 1988), 225–26.

with his prisoners, they having made their escape the Night before. Capt Duke & I, vs Hal and Lt Mc had a nice game of Euchre.

WEDNESDAY 22 I came home as soon as I ate my breakfast. Lt Mc came by to see Helen. We found Ebb Titus and Maj Crump, the latter arrived last Night, so we will have Helen's affair over to morrow. Ebb went over to Aunt Mary's for Tate, they all arrived double quick, had arrangements all made up with Maj C. Mary and I drove out to Aunt M. In the Ambulance. They were very buisy making preparations for the happy event. I finished my Grenadine this eve. Tate and her crowd returned to Aunt M. Maj C. and his Bro, Lt C called this eve.[28] Maj staid to Tea. Jim and Decatur arrived from Tupelo. No news from Eddie yet and I fear he will not hear in time to come. They all sat up so late, I retired, but Nannie with her loud talking awakened me. No news from the Army, Tate received a letter from home, all well, dated 10th the Yanks to breakfast for three mornings.

THURSDAY 23 A bright and beautiful day for Helen's bridal. The boys all left soon after breakfast. Hal came over with Decatur, went home to fix up her things to go to Aunt Mary's. Nan, and Helen went over before dinner. Mary, Hal, myself and Andrew and Willie went after dinner, Ebb driving us. Found all in readiness for the important event. Guests arrived late, we had a happy time in preparing. Hal & Jim, leading, Capt Morton[29] & I next, Mary & Capt Scruggs[30]—the last shall be first, so came Nannie & Lt Crump, then the bride & Groom. All in readiness, the Minister proceeded, and in a few moments Helen, my baby Sister was charged to the care of one whom I pray may make her life happy. My dear, my sainted Mother, we are now separated, long has the link of affection which you strove to bind together been fading. I was forcibly reminded of it in her marriage, by her preference for Nannie as first bridesmaid. Oh! God bless and guide my poor bruised, weary heart. Farewell Helen. I still had hope in our Mother's guidance until your test to Night. Annie Gordon & Willie Kilpatrick added a heavenly picture to the bridal train, in their part—Candle holders. Once more oh! God have mercy on me. Oh! have mercy on me.

28. Lieutenant Edward Hull Crump was with General John Hunt Morgan's command. He became the father of E. H. Crump, Jr., the "Boss" Crump of Memphis. W. D. Miller, "E. H. Crump: Family Background and Early Life," *Tennessee Historical Quarterly* 20 (1961): 364; Hamilton, "Holly Springs," 70.

29. Captain John W. Morton, acting chief of artillery, Morton's Battery, Forrest's Artillery Battalion. Jordan and Pryor, *Campaigns*, 690.

30. Captain E. R. Scruggs, Co. K, Seventh Tennessee Cavalry. Ibid., 692.

FRIDAY 24 A bright and lovely day, but one of the warmest I ever experienced. We were all up at 8 o'clock breakfast. Hal, Nannie and I roomed together, tried our fortune and did not go to bed until day was breaking—did not feel like I had any sleep at all. Helen was very composed, we went in her room as soon as Maj Crump went down. We all met in the Parlor after breakfast. Sina, Tobe & Jack all came out we had a nice time. Hal came home with them. Nannie, Mary, Robert and I came home before dinner, Decatur drove. I had a nap before & after dinner, therefore do not feel very sleepy, but I do think it is the warmest Night I ever felt. Bro Geo and Tate came home this evening to pack up, preparatory to leave in the morning. We have a house full to Night. Tate, Bro Geo and Rob in the Parlor, Nannie, Mary Mamie and I in our room. Mary & I made a pallet in the hall for Jim. John, Ebb and Decatur are enjoying it, from the way they are laughing & talking. Helen & Maj Crump did not come over this evening, are going over to Oxford in the morning. Poor Nannie is trying to fix her toe. The rest asleep. I am almost sufocating.

SATURDAY 25 The changes of life, how sad, oh! my heart how sad. A lively time until after breakfast, our little crowd began to scatter. Tate, Bro Geo, Nannie, Mamie, Rob & Bet all left for Tupelo. Decatur and Jim left with them, Ebb started for Camp below Aberdeen. Maj Crump and Helen called for a few moments, on their way to Oxford. I felt that my heart would break. May God guide and protect them both—grant their life may be happy, and no clouds gather in future over the bright present. Oh! Helen, my Sister, farewell, farewell. I have loved you, when you little dreamed, even a thought was for you. Mother, oh Mother hover near us, bind our hearts closer. God bless my dear Father, and his household. Mary and I have had a very lonely time. John left after dinner, failed to get a wagon. I ironed for the first time this evening. Hal and Capt Duke came over this evening, we will leave Monday for Tupelo. Poor Mary, she will then indeed be lonely. Bro Will and the boys retired early. Mary and I will soon follow suite. It is very oppresive—and oh! so lonely, so lonely. God have mercy on me.

SUNDAY 26 We had a late, and rather quiet breakfast, comparatively speaking. The little boys went to Sunday School and to our great joy and surprise Eddie and Jake Anderson arrived—came up to the Wedding, and knew nothing of it having taken place until after they came, both were greatly disapointed, and poor Eddie was really grieved. Oh! I can never cease to regret his not having notice of it. Jim Titus in his usual way, I fear was not punctual in sending the

Dispatch. Eddie is very anxious to go over and see Helen, but will not have time, goes to Tupelo with us tomorrow. Jake went visiting after dinner, has not returned yet. John & Decatur arrived from Tupelo this eve, after baggage but we had sent it on in a Government Wagon. No late news from any point. I feel real unhappy about leaving Bro Will and the Children, it will be so lonely, however the Children leave for their Grand Ma's Tuesday. Oh! God have mercy on my Father and his household. Bless my dear Bro.

MONDAY 27 Hal and I did not get an early start, she and I came in the Ambulance with John to drive us. Decatur and Capt Rodgers came in my Wagon, we had a very pleasant trip, arrived at Mrs Samples about 1 o'clock.[31] She took us in, and we feel very fortunate in getting here. Our room is very warm and disagreeable, but she is the nicest person about her household I ever saw, plenty to eat. We had a delightful time this evening. Our friends came out from Tupelo to see us—Maj Allison, Capt Ewing, two Mr Dunns, Thulus Beaumont & Jim Titus.[32] We had a happy time, they all left before Tea. Bro Geo, Tate, Nannie, Hal and I did not have a very lively time, it was entirely too warm. All came to our room early and I feel that I will sufocate. Eddie & Jake have not arrived yet. Poor Mary and Bro Will and the little boys, I know they are lonely to Night. God Bless my poor old Father, my dear Bros and oh! have mercy on our brave Soldiers—Crown them with Victory and give us peace.

TUESDAY 28 Mrs Samples our hostess, had us up very early. Bro Geo went to Tupelo after breakfast taking Robert with him. Oh! the heat is almost intolerable John came and brot Hal's and my baggage from Hd Qts, did not stay very long. Eddie and Jake Anderson arrived from Pontotoc before dinner, spent the day with us. I was never so warm and sleepy in my life, as after dinner this day. Our friends from Tupelo came out early this evening—Mr Galloway,[33] John, Decatur, Bose Pugh, they left about sundown, Eddie & Jake went in

31. Mrs. Samples lived just outside the town of Harrisburg on the Pontotoc-Tupelo Road. For a description of Mrs. Samples and her place, see Cadwallader, *Three Years*, 33–34; Map of route of cavalry expedition under Colonel Lysle Dickey, 13–19 Dec. 1862 shows the location of Mrs. Samples's home. RG 77:8, sheet 2 of 2, NA.

32. Major T. P. Allison, acting brigade quartermaster, staff of Brigadier General Tyree H. Bell's brigade, Buford's division, Forrest's Cavalry. Captain William Ewing, drillmaster, staff of Brigadier General W. H. Jackson. Captain R. F. Dunn, Co. F, Third Texas Cavalry; Lieutenant W. D. Dunn, Co. K, 19th regiment, Tennessee Cavalry. Jordan and Pryor, *Campaigns*, Appendix passim.

33. Captain Matthew C. Galloway, aide to General Forrest, founded the *Memphis Avalanche*, and was at one time postmaster general in Memphis. After the war he was co-editor of the *Memphis Appeal*; Henry, *Forrest*, 367.

also. Jim & Thulus Beaumont came out to Tea, we were having a
nice time, when Mrs Samples sent for us to retire. This rather
shocked us, but making the best of it, the boys in a laughing humor
departed. I am so undecided in my movements, Hal is flighty, never
of the same mind two hours. God guide me in the right path. I know
not to day, where to morrow will be spent. Bless My Father, and
Bros. Crown our Armys with Victory, oh! Give us success and peace.

WEDNESDAY 29 Nannie and Mr Pugh left for Aberdeen early this
morning.[34] Decatur came out, did not stay very long. Eddie and
Jake spent the day with us again. The order for them to leave to
morrow has been countermanded, and they are all delighted, their
horses are completely broken down since their march from Montev-
alo. Capt Barbour and Jack Doyle came to see us, we had a nice
time. Hal's Bro Frank[35] spent the day with us also. Hal & I made a
Soldiers shirt this morning—poor fellows I wish I could always have
it in my power to gratify their wishes. It has been a terible warm
day, and I have been unhappy, oh! so unhappy, so undecided about
my movement. I believe Hal has concluded to stand still until the
command is ordered to leave again. No news from home yet. Forrest
has changed his plans for the present, of course we know nothing of
their movements.

THURSDAY 30 Well, we have managed to exist through another terible warm day. Eddie and Jake spent the day with us again. Hal's Bro
Frank also. Gen Forrest reviewed the Artillery this morning, we did
not get to see them. Capt, now Maj Morton and Lt Blakemore[36]
called to see us. Bruce arrived to day from the Army of Tenn—Gen
Johnston, he was slightly wounded, and has thirty days leave. Hal
was delighted to see him and saved a trip to the Army, as he will
take Eddie's things to him. Robert went to Hd Qts with his Papa to
day. Hal and I took extra pains this evening in our dress but had no
calls. We heard the sad fate of two of our friends in Henderson's
Scouts, the Yankees hung them near Moscow. Mr Bonner and Lt
McConnell.[37] Oh! this horible, horible war. Our poor boys are look-

34. Dashiell was recuperating from his wound at his cousin's home in Aberdeen.
Perkins, "Record," 18.

35. Lieutenant Frank Rodgers, Ruckers Brigade, Chalmers division, Jordan and
Pryor, *Campaigns*, 689.

36. Lieutenant R. M. Blakemore, adjutant, Morton's Battery, Forrest's Artillery
Battalion. Ibid., 690.

37. Two of Forrest's Scouts were captured and killed, but their names were not
Bonner and McConnell. Reports from them continued in the pages of the *OR* until

ing for a battle every day, and expect to go in under the black Flag.
Oh! heavenly Father we pray and beseech thee to hear our prayers—
drive the Enemy from our Soile and give us peace.

---

the end of the war. Webster Moses to Nancy Mowrey, 26 June 1864, Webster Moses
letters, KHST; Stephen Starr, *Jennison's Jayhawkers* (Baton Rouge: Louisiana State
University Press, 1973), 304; the dead scouts' names are never given in the series of
letters exchanged between Forrest and A. J. Smith, *OR*, 39, pt. 2, 155 passim.

10

A Safe Haven

1864 DIARY: JULY

FRIDAY 1 It has been quite pleasant all day, a nice breeze, we spent it alone until this evening, several of our friends from Camp called, Col Rucker, Col Overton & Lt Rodgers from Ruckers Brig, Capt Severson, Capt Mason, Johnie and Decatur from Forrest's Hd Qts.[1] Maj Crump arrived from Oxford, he left Helen at Mrs Goodmans, she has a delightful home, and a nice horse to ride every evening. They all went back to Camp before Night except Maj Crump, and John & Decatur, they staid until bed time. We had a delightful time. I am charmed with my new Bro in law. Oh! my poor weary heart, how I long for some one to sympathize, to advise me, God have mercy. Bless my dear Father and protect his household, bless my dear Bros and Bros in laws. I wrote to Shallie Kirk to day. The 7th Tenn and McDonald's Batn have orders to move in an hour's notice. The Yanks are very strong in numbers, but God will bless us, and crown us with Victory, save our poor boys from privation and danger.

SATURDAY 2 We have spent a delightful day. Capt Barbour, Maj Allin and Lt Doyle spent the day with us. Robert went to Tupelo with his Papa. Hal's Bro Frank was to see us. Mr Pugh returned from his trip with Nannie, brought Mrs Galloway[2] and Miss Walington with him, he went on to Tupelo, Bruce went in the Ambulance with him. We had a gay time, Mrs Galloway is as lively as can be. Mr Galloway, Maj Crump and Bro Geo came out in the Ambulance this evening

---

1. Colonel E. W. Rucker, Rucker's Brigade, Chalmers's Division, Forrest's Cavalry. Major C. S. Severson, Chief Quartermaster, Forrest's Staff. Possibly Captain John Overton, Jr., of Rucker's staff, not his father Colonel John Overton. Jordan and Pryor, *Campaigns*, 685, 689.

2. Mrs. Galloway and Mrs. Forrest accompanied their husbands whenever possible. The practice of wives of officers staying near their husbands during inactive periods was common during the Civil War. Henry, *Forrest*, 367, 545n.

Belle Edmondson in her twenties. Civil War photograph on glass in a purple velvet carrying case. (Gift of Sidney and Lillian Newcomb)

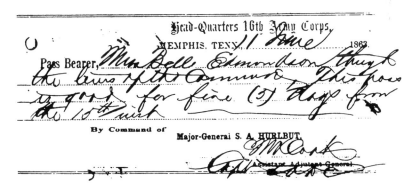

Pass used by Belle Edmondson to cross through army lines. (Courtesy of the Betty Lou Stidham Collection)

Waverley, "a real Southern mansion," where Belle refugeed in 1864. (Courtesy of Donna and Robert Snow and Mississippi State University Library)

Susan Young Johnson, one of the six daughters of Colonel Young of Waverley, ca. 1850s. (Courtesy of Donna and Robert Snow and the Waverley Collection, Special Collections, Mississippi State University Library)

Miss Em [Emily Esther Dashiell Perkins], Belle's friend and confidante, and Tate's sister-in-law. Postwar photograph. (Courtesy of Kate Pinckney)

Nannie Perkins, Miss Em's daughter and Helen's friend, dated on back 1871. (Courtesy of Kate Pinckney)

Postwar photograph of Belle with her friend Fannie Molloy. (Courtesy of Tate Dashiell Coggins)

Belle at seventeen with niece Minnie Anderson. (Courtesy of the Betty Lou Stidham Collection)

Jefferson Davis during his Memphis years, from Belle's photograph album, autographed on back: "To Miss Belle from her friend and faithful servant—21 May 1870." (Courtesy of Sidney and Lillian Newcomb)

Dr. Gratz A. Moses, Belle's fiance, in 1863. "I had a fine full likeness made for you." (Courtesy of Sidney and Lillian Newcomb)

Winnie Davis, "the daughter of the Confederacy," with Helen Edmondson Crump's daughter Mary Brodie Crump. (Courtesy of Sidney and Lillian Newcomb)

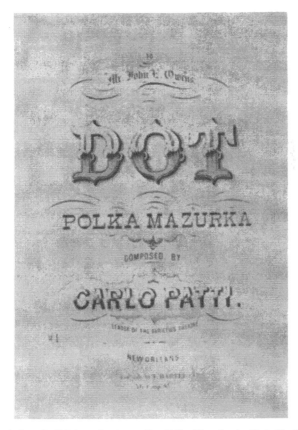

Sheet music from Belle's bound volume: *Dot Polka Mazurka,* by Carlo Patti, ca. 1860. (Courtesy of the Betty Lou Stidham Collection)

Younger sister, "gentle little Helen," who married Major Brodie Crump of Forrest's Command at Lochinvar in 1864. (Courtesy of Sidney and Lillian Newcomb)

Robert Walton Edmondson, Belle's half brother who lived near Waverley. (Courtesy of Charlotte Elam)

Mary Edmondson Anderson, Belle's widowed sister, mother of Minnie, ca. 1860. (Courtesy of Charlotte Elam)

James Howard Edmondson, the brother who went "privateering." (Courtesy of Charlotte Elam)

Postwar photograph of Belle's father in full Masonic regalia. (Courtesy of Charlotte Elam)

Older sister Tate of the "wild buoyant spirit," wife of Major George Dashiell of Forrest's Command. (Courtesy of Tate Dashiell Coggins)

Joanna Edmondson, an unmarried older sister, with Tate's son Robert and a slave boy.
(Courtesy of Charlotte Elam)

Prewar photograph of Belle. (Courtesy of the Betty Lou Stidham Collection)

from Tupelo. Poor Maj he is quite Sad that his honey Moon should so early be blighted—however Man proposes, God disposes. No late war news, nor any from home. The Yanks are moving slowly through the Country, rather shy of Forrest and his Company. I wonder when this horible war will be over, if the scenes now passing will be remembered. I must cease for to Night the Bats, are so bad, Hal, Bettie and I have already had a race with one, and hard to say which is the greatest coward.

SUNDAY 3 This day will be long remembered. Bro Geo & Brodie went to Tupelo early. Hal, Tate, and myself, with Bettie and the Children, started to Church at Tupelo in the Ambulance with Alfred to drive us. We got along very well until within a mile of Tupelo, had just passed through the Webfoot Cavalry Camp, saw them on parade and enjoyed the different scenes in Camp, reached the Creek, were undecided for some time whether to go over the bridge, or ford, the later seemed to be best, so we drove, and just entering the mud hole when the Ambulance upset with a terible crash. In a few minute fifty Soldiers ran to our rescue, and a Mr Harris, (did not learn his title) who was exceedingly kind. I was first out, Alfred jumped out with Robert as the Ambulance fell, Bettie kept Mary close to her, Tate went on top of Hal, they were all very mudy, no limbs broken. We went on to Hd Qts saw a great many friends, too late for Church, returned to dinner, Eddie & John Cummins spent the day with us. Capt Sheperd,[3] Capt Barbour & Maj Crump called this eve, we all went to Negro prayer meeting after tea.

MONDAY 4 To day is the Anniversary of the declaration of our forefathers independence, one year ago and a sad one for the happiness of our Southern Confederacy—Vicksburgh Surrendered by Pemberton to Grant. Many changes and sad days since that event, but thanks to a just and merciful God our hopes are brighter, than at any time since we have been struling for Independence. May the God of Battles defend our cause, protect our Armys from danger & disease, and crown them with glory and success. Tate, Hal, Mrs Galloway, Miss Walington & Mrs Samples all spent the day at Gen Forrest's Hd Qts. Bettie, Mamie & Rob of course Along. Maj Severson came for us. I do like him so much, he is so kind and attentive. We had a delightful day, Gen Forrest & Lady very kind. We saw all of our friends too numerous to name. Maj Severson brought us home this eve. Tate went riding on horse back with Bro Brodie. We heard

3. Possibly Captain William Sheppard, Co. I, Third Kentucky Regiment. Jordan and Pryor, *Campaigns*, 700.

Ferd Rodgers was not expected to live, Hal knows nothing of it. I pray it may be untrue. God bless my dear Father and Brothers. We spend the day in Tupelo again tomorrow.

TUESDAY 5 Jake Anderson & Ebb Titus came by this morning. Col Polk came out in Gen Forrest's Ambulance for us to go in and spend the day with Maj Severson & Maj Rambeaut [Rambaut]. We had a delightful day. The Miss Shurlak and Miss Bills of Jackson, Tenn were there.[4] We played cards, talked and had a gay time. All of our friends nearly, we saw. Ate dinner at three o'clock, and a more sumptous fare I never saw grace a table. We all talked a while on the Porch after dinner when our crowd came home to fix for a little dance, which we enjoyed very much, danced until two o'clock, and only got through with six setts. I played Euchre with Maj Severson, lost all except the last game, which I won him. We all like him so much. Gen Forrest was opposed to the dance, so none of his crowd were there. Majs Severson and Rambaut are splendid entertainers. I was shocked at the Miss Shurlaks deportments. Miss Clara Bills came home in the Ambulance with us. I never was so tired in my life, and the flees nearly devoured us. Mrs Galloway would not go. My setts were danced as follows. 1st Mr Pugh, 2nd Dr Cowen [Cowan],[5] 3rd Mr Beaumont, 4 Maj Rambaut, 5th Lt Rodgers, 6th Capt Barbour—the others, Maj Severson, Donelson, Rodgers & Scruggs were not danced—too late.

WEDNESDAY 6 Oh! I never was as sleepy in my life as this morning. Hal and Miss Clara ready for breakfast, I was not—went in after the rest had finished and got a Cup of Coffee. We all seemed dull and lazy this morning. John came in the Ambulance for Bro George and Miss Bills to go to Tupelo. Dr Cowan, Lt Dunn and Bro called. Maj Crump & Lt Rodgers came also, did not stay long. Hal and I came up Stairs as soon as we got dinner and went to sleep. Just dressed in time. Eddie & Bruce came over. Decatur and Bruce went to Tupelo, Eddie went back to Camp at Verona. Lt Rodgers came over after tea, they all have marching orders at 5 o'clock in the morning, do not know which way they are going, the Yankees are moving out towards Ripley.[6] God grant that our poor Soldiers may be spared,

4. Probably Clara Bills, the sister-in-law of Colonel Marshall T. Polk. Bills, Polk, Wood Papers, TSLAN. Major Gilbert V. Rambaut, chief commissary, Forrest's Headquarters Company, had been in the hotel business in Memphis before the war. Henry, *Forrest*, 104; Young, *Memphis*, 410; Jordan and Pryor, *Campaigns*, 685.

5. Dr. J. B. Cowan, a first cousin of Mrs. Forrest, was chief surgeon on Forrest's staff. Henry, *Forrest*, 82.

6. The fourth Federal expedition into Mississippi started south from Grand Junction, Tennessee, 5 July 1864. Generals Andrew J. Smith and Joseph A. Mower were in command with orders to "punish Forrest and the people." Henry, *Forrest*, 307.

and crown the Southerners with glory and success. Save my poor
Bro, oh! grant that he may nobly do his duty, but return safe. Bless
my dear Father and his household. Hal is waiting for me to tell her
fortune. Every body retired early to Night, disgusted with every
enjoyment except the soft folds of the arms of Morpheus. No late
war news. Answer to flag of Truce from Memphis, Washburn still
refuses to have any understanding with regard to the black flag.[7]

THURSDAY 7 All up this morning to breakfast—a very warm day.
Capt Ferd Rodgers came this morning, we were delighted to see
him, he is looking better than I ever saw him, although he is just
recovering from a terible sickness. Maj Rambaut & Maj Severson
also Bruce came out this morning to see us. Capt Rodgers went in
to Tupelo with them. Tate cut out Maj Seversons shirts so Hal and
I missed our nap this eve and sewed on them—Tate is making Capt
Rodgers. Maj Crump came over this morning, Robert went to Tupelo with him, they came back this evening. I received a letter from
home and one from Helen, all well. Capt Mason and Mr Beaumont
came out this eve. Tate and Mr B went riding on horse back. They
staid until after Tea. Our news from the Enemy is rather exciting
they are advancing in force, and our Armies are not many miles
apart, the command is expecting orders every hour. God grant they
may check the wicked foe, and drive them from our soile. Answer
to flag of truce. No black flag, but as near to Christian warfare as is
possible. Oh! God have mercy on our Army—crown them Victorious.

FRIDAY 8 We all were at our work early this morning—and would
have finished the shirts, but had orders to move. Mr Pugh came for
us with two Ambulances and a bagage Wagon. We packed and were
off in ten minutes time. Arrived in Tupelo at 1 o'clock, went to Gen

7. See *OR*, 32, pt. 1, 586–93, for the correspondence between Forrest and Washburn regarding the killing of two of Forrest's scouts and the use of the black flag at
Brice's Cross Roads. One Federal soldier wrote to his wife: "The arming of the Nig-
gers has in effect raised the *Black Flag*, and those who fight under *that* must bide the
consequences. Our men were foolish enough to go into that fight with 'Remember Ft
Pillow' for their battle cry, which being interpreted meant that no quarter asked nor
given." Onley Andrus to Molly Andrus, 28 June 1864. Fred Albert Shannon, ed.,
The Civil War Letters of Sergeant Onley Andrus (Urbana: University of Illinois Press,
1947), 87. A Confederate officer, Thomas A. Carter, wrote in his journal, when he
was wounded, that he thought the Negro troops would mutilate his body. He understood that they had sworn to show Forrest and his men no mercy. Journal of Thomas
A. Carter, typescript copy, CC. Mrs. Cordelia Stacy was still taking refuge at West
Point, Mississippi, about fifty miles from the battlefield. She wrote to her son that
Negro soldiers were shot after the battle. C. M. Stacy to James Hamner, 26 June
1864, Hamner Letters, MSUM.

Forrest's Hd Qts, every thing was in bustle, and hopeful in the coming campaign. Met with Gen Lee, who had just arrived on the cars,
I am perfectly delighted with him. If I had a heart to loose, I think
it would be in danger.[8] God bless both of them, spare them to our
Country, and crown them with Victory, in the battle which awaits
them. We ate supper with Maj Rambaut, it was delightful. We spent
a very pleasant evening, Maj Severson, Maj Rambaut, Mason, Beaumont and many other friends are as kind to us as Bros. We came up
to Col McCarty's put the children to bed, our friends spent the evening. Maj Crump and Eddie came to see us, we bid them all Good
bye, and will not see them again until after the battle. God grant
they may all be spared. The Yanks are at Ripley, moving slow, in
force, we have no idea when the battle will be fought.

SATURDAY 9 Not much sleep did any of our room, have last Night.
I did not close my eyes, the rest for only a few moments. Between
the flees and the bed bugs I spent a miserable Night. Hal and I
dressed long before day. Maj Rambaut, Capt Mason & John came
for us to go over for breakfast. We had a delightful Cup of Coffee.
Enjoyed our friends for a little while, then hurried onto the trains.
Met Mrs Forrest, the Gen, and her two companions, Miss Montgomery & Miss Grant. We did not get off for some time, Gen Forrest
had a fight with the Conductor before he would get off. Our trip was
tedious, disagreeable and warm, the Children suffered with heat
very much. Arrived in Columbus[9] at 4 o'c, stoped at City Hotel. Hal
and I have had a very pleasant room. Theresa Blennerhassett came
over and spent the evening with me. I was delighted to see her, oh!
how many bright and happy recollections her presence recalls, yet
alas my poor weary heart how sadly has life changed. Lt Anderson
came to see me this evening, bro't the sad news of Lt Lightners
death also of Len Eliots being wounded, he is a Missourian.[10]

8. Forrest, suffering with boils, asked Stephen D. Lee, recently promoted to lieutenant general, to take command of all forces. *OR*, pt. 2, 671.

9. Columbus, Mississippi, a town on the Tombigbee River, was a center of wealth
and influence. Its location, away from the main line of the Mobile and Ohio Railroad
by about ten miles, probably saved it from the series of destructive raids. A spur line
connected Columbus with Artesia depot on the main line. J. Frazer Smith, *White
Pillars* (New York: Bramhall House, 1941), 83. A crude map of the city of Columbus
is in the Grierson Papers, ISHL. See also, W. L. Lipscomb, *A History of Columbus,
Mississippi during the 19th Century* (Birmingham: Press of Dispatch Printing Co.,
1909).

10. Probably Lieutenant Charles W. Anderson, aide, A.A.G. and inspector general,
Forrest's staff. Leonidas Hooper Elliot, [rank unknown], Co. 3, 154th Tennessee Infantry, died 12 Feb. 1865 at Columbus, Mississippi of wounds received at the Battle
of Franklin. Jordan and Pryor, *Campaigns*, 685; Lenow, *Elmwood*, 114.

SUNDAY 10 A long, long weary day this has been for our little party. I went over to see Theresa directly after breakfast and staid until after dinner time. We had a long talk, she is a sweet girl, and I believe a good friend of mine. I did not get to bid either Bro Geo or Bruce, Good bye. Bro G. left for the front to join Forrest, and Bruce has recovered from his wounds and gone to report to Johnston, in Ga. Dispatches say the Yankees are in force, in Pontotoc on yesterday,[11] our boys will have some terible fighting. God grant they may be victorious, oh! heaven hear our prayers, spare our friends and Bro's, and shield our Gen's from danger, drive our wicked heartless enemies back to their own hearth stones, Smile upon; and prosper and bless once more our Sunny land. We had a hard rain this eve, Tate went to Church. Theresa came over. Our land lord is a very pleasant gentleman, Mamie is sick, he came up and sit with us a while. Hal & I sleep in Tate's room.

MONDAY 11 Tate, Hal and myself went over to see Theresa and her Sister after breakfast did not stay very long. Just fixing for a nice cool time when Miss Tabb, Miss Cannon and Sister and Mr Pugh called to see me. I was delighted with them, Miss Tabb in particular, they did not stay very long. We had some Candy made, Bettie went up to the Saloon and bought a large bowl of ice cream which we enjoyed very much. Had just fixed and began my sewing when Mr Sam Tate called, we all had to see him. After he left did not have time to fix again before dinner. Our land lord sent us a nice julep before dinner. Theresa came over and spent the evening with us, a very hard rain. Mr Pugh called and brought me a beautiful Magnolia with Miss Askews compliments. Capt Webb came for me to go to the Depot and assist in feeding the Soldiers of Neely Brigade, which are moving from Ala, to Forrests relief, only one Mobile Battery was there which we fed, the rest will be here in the morning.[12] A great many Ladies were ready, Theresa & her Sister I went with.

TUESDAY 12 A cloudy gloomy morning. Theresa came over early after breakfast for us to go with her to the Depot, and assist in feeding the Soldiers, Hal and Tate would not go. I went, Mr Pugh walked with me, I promised him if he would be a good boy, I would speak well of him, he is by far, one of the kindest young men I ever

11. The Federals were five miles north of Pontotoc on the evening of 10 July. John Allen Wyeth, *Life of General N. B. Forrest* (New York: Harper & Bros., 1899), 380.

12. Probably Thomas C. Webb, Co. B, Eighth Tennessee Cavalry, Jordan and Pryor, *Campaigns*, 692; Colonel J. J. Neely commanded a brigade in Chalmers Division which was sent dismounted from Alabama. A battalion of heavy artillery under Colonel Belzhoover came from Mobile, temporarily assigned to Brigadier General Hylan B. Lyon. Henry, *Forrest*, 319.

met. It repaid us for all of our labor and fatigue to see how the poor Soldiers enjoyed the food. They had nothing to eat since breakfast yesterday morning, their horses were broken down, they had to take the train here, did not get off until 4 o'clock this eve, will have to fight as Infantry. Our troops have fallen back to Okolona, the Yanks were in 15 miles of them to day. Our troops are confident of success, God grant they may be Victorious. Hal & I spent the evening with Theresa. The Dr McKim came to see Mamie, she is quite sick.

WEDNESDAY 13 Mr Pugh came round early this morning we made arrangements to start for Nannie in the morning Theresa was to go with me. Capt Tom Dashiell was to furnish the Ambulance.[13] Our trip had fully matured in preparations—but Tate give up the idea, so our trip has fallen through. Capt Dashiell came round after tea. Will send his Ambulance early in the morning. Hal, Theresa and I are going to spend the day with Bro [Robert Walton Edmondson].[14] I wish we were all going out to stay, but little Mamie is too sick. No news from Forrest yet we know they are fighting, God grant they may be successful, and spare the lives of our dear Soldiers, protect my dear Bro, and friends from danger. Theresa and Miss Wilkenson called this eve. Hal and I went to the Saloon and had a nice treat of Ice Cream, Robert was with us, Dixie prices are very high, but this rather startled us, $26. Mr Pugh attends the weding to Night. Miss Cozart of this place, to Mr Phillips of Nashville.

THURSDAY 14 Hal, Theresa and I got up very early and started for the Country, after running around first on one road and then another we finally arrived at Waverly just 7 miles above Columbus,[15] although we had traveled ten or twelve miles. We crossed the Tombig-

---

13. Captain Thomas Dashiell, paymaster, Forrest's Command, was probably related to George Dashiell. S. D. Lee to General Hardee, 6 Sept. 1863, *OR*, 30, pt. 4, 609.

14. Robert Walton Edmondson, Belle's half-brother, lived at Goshen, a plantation about nine miles north of Columbus. Kate Edmondson Johnson to Dorothy, 24 Jan. 1937; EFP; Lipscomb, *Columbus*, 50. Before the war Robert had been clerk of the U.S. District Court for the Northern District of Mississippi, and keeper of the books and records of the land office at Pontotoc. In 1866, he petitioned the government for the sum of $2725 to cover his expenses for transporting books and records from Pontotoc to Columbus and various places during the war to ensure their preservation. Petitions, 39th Congress, Committee 39A-Hi, NA.

15. The plantation and small community that grew up around it were named for the Waverley novels of Sir Walter Scott. The name is spelled variously as Waverly and Waverley. Colonel Young used the latter spelling in an 1857 letter to his daughter Lucy, while an 1856 map of Mississippi used the former version. Examples of both spellings occur in contemporary accounts. Except when quoting from sources that use the Waverly rendition, as Belle does, all references in these notes will adhere to

bee, rode up to Mr Young's[16] when he came out and insisted on our getting out, until he would send and try to find out where Bro lived, failed however, but we spent the day. Fa· , how strange, yet how delightful. They are a very wealthy family, a real Southern Mansion.[17] His daughters are very accomplished, and Miss Lou is a beautiful girl.[18] Such delightful Music, and an elegant dinner, our first peaches and Milk. We went to the Pond late this evening, to try to learn to swim.[19] Hal would not venture, Theresa and I tried it. I did not have any confidence in myself therefore did not make much improvement. Theresa was more successful. We had a delightful drive home, found Mamie well, and good news from Forrest.[20]

---

the Waverley spelling. George Young to Lucy Young, 4 Sept. 1857; A New Map of Mississippi (Philadelphia: Desilver, 1857), Waverley Collection, MSUS, cited hereafter as WC.

16. Colonel Young was noted for his "flowing courtesy" and good works. He was a trustee of the University of Mississippi from 1848–1870. F. A. P. Barnard, first chancellor of the university wrote about Young: "I found at a critical period in my life a most unwavering and influential friend . . . a friend of [his] fellow men, and an efficient promoter of all good works." Judge Orr, a contemporary of Young, described him as "a man of courtly and princely manners, refined, cultivated, hightoned, an aristocrat by birth . . . brave, discreet and conscientious." But another contemporary remembered Young in this way: "With Mr. Young there was a conflict between fame and fortune, but the decision was in favor of fortune. He dealt largely in lands and became very wealthy." F. A. P. Barnard to William Young, 10 Dec. 1880, printed in *Dilettanti* 4 (Winter 1958): 17–18; J. A. Orr, "A Field Trip from Houston to Jackson, Mississippi in 1845," *Publication of the Mississippi Historical Society* 9 (1906): 177–78; *Watkins Genealogy*, author unknown, loose page, n.d., n.p. [Mrs. Young was a Watkins], WC.

17. The mansion at Waverley was still new when Belle saw it. Begun in 1852, it was not completed until 1858. The architect was Charles I. Pond from St. Louis and the style was Greek Revival. Marble mantles and ornamental plaster work were made by Scottish and Irish craftsmen from Mobile. The park-like gardens were laid out by a German gardener. The mansion's furnishings were imported from Europe. Waverley had its own gas plant which produced light for the big house by burning pine knots in a retort. Lucy Young Banks manuscript written for a granddaughter, undated, WC; Smith, *White Pillars*, 92–94.

18. Lucy Watkins Young (1841–1933) was the youngest of Colonel Young's ten children. In 1870 she married Colonel James Oliver Banks (1829–1904), a Confederate veteran. Young Genealogy sheet, WC.

19. Among the amenities at Waverley were a brick bath house, swimming pool, and lily pond. Both the pool and pond were fed by pipes from an artesian well. Mrs. Charles B. Hazard, "The Old Plantation Home," *Confederate Veteran* (July 1921): 247–48, reprinted from *The Breeders Gazette*, n.d.; J. R. Atkinson and J. D. Elliott, Jr., *A Cultural Resources Survey of Selected Construction Areas in the Tennessee- Tombigbee Waterway: Alabama and Mississippi*, vol. 2 (Starkville: Mississippi State University, Dept. of Anthropology, 1978), 41.

20. The Battle of Harrisburg/Tupelo began with heavy fighting around Mrs. Samples's place at 7 A.M. 14 July 1864. The Confederates were repulsed at every point. "It

FRIDAY 15 Our dispatches from the front are very encouraging. Forrest is fighting the Enemy near Tupelo—nothing decisive, but we have repulsed them in every attempt to fight us. God grant our Army may be crowned with glory and success. Protect my dear Bro, and friends from all danger. The news from Virginia is glorious, God grant it may be true, our forces in three miles of Washington City and shelling the City.[21] Oh heaven smile upon our poor desolated South, brighten the hearthstones of our sad and lonely homes, drive our enemy back, take them in peace, we do not wish them any harm, but oh! grant our Sunny Land Victory and peace, bless my dear old Father, and spare him to us, for the days when our dear boys will once more bless our homes with their presence. After tea all sitting in our Room. Mr Crump [Brodie] sent Dis[patch]. "Yankees whipped & making for Ripley & Forrest after them"—thank God for this.[22] Letter from home poor Nannie Fletcher dead. Theresa & several Ladies called.

SATURDAY 16 To day Hal, Tate and myself set apart for returning our visits. Capt Dashiell kindly sent his Rockaway. Theresa and Miss Helen Goff came to see us, we started calling just at 11 o'clock, to see Mrs. Forrest first, she had just received a Dispatch from the Gen, he was slightly wounded in the foot.[23] We returned all calls. Bro came and spent the evening with us. Nannie and Dashiell came down from Aberdeen. Dashiell's wound looks very badly and I fear if he is not very prudent, he will be very unfortunate yet. Mr Pugh and I went out calling this eve, Dashiell, Tate, Nannie, Hal & I went over to see Theresa and her Sister after Tea. Oh! such a terible warm night I never experienced. Nannie staid in the room with Tate. Hal and I tried our room for the first time, I am almost suffocated with the heat.

SUNDAY 17 All ready for breakfast, one of the warmest mornings we have had. Theresa came over after breakfast to see if some of us would not go to Artesia on the train, to assist in attending to the wounded Soldiers. I fixed up my baskett, went by for Theresa & her

---

was all gallantry and useless sacrifice of life." Wyeth, *Forrest*, 396; Mathes, *Forrest*, 259.

21. General Jubal Early engaged the defenses at Fort Stevens on the outskirts of Washington and within view of the capitol 12 July 1864. George E. Pond, *The Army in the Civil War* (New York: Scribners, 1883), 11:69.

22. Although the Confederate forces were repulsed in an attack on the Union cavalry, they continued to pursue and harass the Federal army as it retreated back to LaGrange. Ibid.

23. Forrest suffered a debilitating wound to his foot in the fighting 15 July 1864. Henry, *Forrest*, 325.

sister we met the other Ladies at the Depot, arrived at Artesia did not wait long for the train. First two were loaded with Soldiers going to Demopolis to relieve Talegaga [Talladega] of the raid not [now] threatening it. Next two trains were loaded with our wounded, and oh! my heart ached to see so much suffering, we soothed and gave them every thing they wanted, returned to Columbus on the eve train. Col Crosslin [Crossland] of the 7th Ky was aboard destined for Columbus badly wounded.[24] We had a very disagreeable warm trip but a consolation in knowing we had soothed our Suffering Soldiers. Saw Capt Mason at Artesia, was delighted of course, spent the evening, took Tea with Molly Tabb, met my old friend Mollie at Artesia. Theresa, Mr Berry & Lt Watts called to see us. Bro George came to day. Dashiell improving.

MONDAY 18 I was very unhappy about no conveyance to go out to Bro's sitting in the Parlor after breakfast when our new made friend Mrs Reynolds[25] came in for Hal, Theresa and myself to go out and spend a few days with her. I accepted, Hal after we came to our room did not seem to like it, though I had no idea of anything of the kind when in Mrs R. company. Tate and Nannie both seemed distressed at Hal's departure, censured me for accepting the invitation. I can have no happiness it seems without so much unhappiness. We arrived at Col Youngs about 11 o'c. Miss Lou, who is one of the sweetest ladies I ever met, Miss Paine & Col Young greeted us cordially, and a happy day the rest was to me. Late in the evening we all went down to the Pond went in bathing, and had a gay time though some ridiculous scenes among the beginers. Theresa has more confidence than Hal or I therefore gets along better. I must confess I am really a coward in Water.

TUESDAY 19 A bright and beautiful morning—my heart seems as light and happy as the sunshine is lovely. I am perfectly in love with this charming family. Mrs Reynolds is so warm hearted and good. Though our acquaintance has been so short it seems we have always been friends, and Miss Lou, ah! how can I express the admiration I have for her, how beautiful, how lovely she is. I have never since the days of my childhood met with any Ladie I am so completely in love with—how my heart aches for a friend, just as Miss Lou is. If I only could gain her confidence there is something about her that reminds

24. Colonel Edward Crossland, Seventh Kentucky Cavalry was wounded 15 July in pursuit of the Federal troops. Jordan and Pryor, *Campaigns*, 700.

25. Sarah [Sally] Young Reynolds (1839–1910) was one of Colonel Young's daughters. In 1863 she married Colonel Reuben Reynolds (1820–1887), Eleventh Mississippi Regiment. Young Genealogy sheet, WC.

me of my dear, dear Mother. We have spent a delightful day. Mrs
James Young[26] called to see us, she sings exquisitely. Mrs Judivon
called also. We all went bathing again.[27] Theresa progresses rapidly
though Hal and I are still great cowards. Lou and I had a game of
Chess after tea. I cannot but be unhappy about not being at Bro. I
know I will be censured by all parties.

WEDNESDAY 20 Another happy and beautiful morning. Miss Lou
gave me some cotton to knit Eddie a pr of socks. I began them but
did not get much done—most of the time playing Bagammon, Chess
or having some Music, learned Miss L two pieces—"Brightest Eyes
Quickstep," "Rosebud Waltz."[28] She was very apt, but I fear her
swiming Scholar will ever be a drag to the art. Our days are as happy
as can be. Her Bro, Lt Watt Young,[29] came to day on short leave—
he is rather shy of Ladies therefor we have not seen much of him.
All went to the Pond again Hal was sick and could not go in. I
believe I am a greater coward every time I attempt it. Theresa is still
gaining confidence, and improving. Mrs Tom Young[30] & Miss King
were in bathing. I managed to float without assistance. Mrs Tom
Young and Miss King came round to see us after Tea, we had a very
happy evening. Hal and I did not agree very well. I bet I could finish
my sock, she bet I would not, so she put the gas out. I lit it again
and finished my sock.

THURSDAY 21 Still my happiness continues. I do dearly love Miss
Lou and Mrs Reynolds both. Mrs Hamilton[31] their Sister invited us

26. Emily Hubbard Young (1838–1910) was the wife of James Young. Their home
was in the Waverley community, WC.

27. The bathing attire for the ladies of Waverley may have been similar to that
described in *Harper's New Monthly Magazine*, June 1858: "Delaine flannel or . . .
bombazet with a fringe of buckshot covered with material of the dress, with pellets of
lead in lower skirt."

28. William Dressler, *The Brightest Eyes Galop or Quickstep* (New York: Dressler
Music Store, 1859); G. Marcailhou, *The Rosebud Waltz* (N.p.: n.p., n.d.); photoco-
pies of both, Music Division, LC, Washington D.C.

29. John Watkins Young (1826–1885), oldest child of Colonel Young, never married. Young Genealogy sheet, WC.

30. Georgia Priscilla Butt Young was married to Thomas Young. Their home, Tar-
awa, in the Waverley community, was similar to Waverley except for stained glass
windows in the cupola. Also known as the Hopkins place [one of Thomas Young's
daughters married a Hopkins], it sat vacant for years until it was accidentally burned
by rabbit hunters in 1918. Young genealogy sheet; Robert Snow to Jack Elliott, 13
April 1977, WC.

31. Anna Josepha Young (1830–1885), Colonel Young's eldest daughter, married
Alexander Hamilton (1824–1879) in 1857. Their home, Burnside, named for a Hamilton homestead in North Carolina, was part of the Waverley compound. After being

to Tea, we accepted. Spent the day so happy, all retired after dinner for a rest, got up early, prepared for the Pond. Mrs Reynolds and Hal did not go in, it was so much like rain. Lou, Theresa and I tried it. Theresa got along charmingly. I, poor me, I am a greater fool than ever. A shower came up so we had to hasten our pleasure. Began preparations for our visit as soon as we reached the house. We all five went in the Carriage. I never have spent a more pleasant evening, the Supper was Magnificient—every thing passed off so well. I have fallen in love with Mrs Hamilton, she is almost as sweet as Lou. There is some thing I cannot resist, in watching dear Lou, she is more like my Mother each day that I am with her. We staid until 12 o'clock, a beautiful Moonlight Night. Lt Watt rode home with us. Gen Johnston has been superceded by Hood, the latter having orders to fight immediately.[32]

FRIDAY 22 We all were ready for Columbus quite late, rather late in our breakfast after last Night's dissipation. I was really sad at leaving, so much happiness for my lonely life crowded into one short week. Met Col Porter of Gen Cheatham's Staff[33] at breakfast. We did not tarry long after our meal was finished, had a very dusty disagreeable warm ride to Columbus and my heart was indeed sad to part with dear "Waverly". Lou came in with us, oh! that dear sweet girl I do dearly love her. Theresa alighted first, we them came to the Hotel. Lou came and sat with us a while. I gave her my Photograph Album.[34] Telegrams—Hood fought and whiped Sherman— Grant has been relieved of his command,[35] by the interposition of our divine Father. Flags all at half mast, over the eventful news. God in his Wisdom will do all well. Went walking this eve with Theresa & Lucy Harris. Company after Tea and sat up very late. I am so unhappy, and no one to confide in, oh! God have mercy.

SATURDAY 23 I was never so sleepy as when awakened this morning.

---

unoccupied for many years, it was home to a Negro family when it accidentally burned in 1930. In addition to the the houses, the Waverley community had a post office, sawmill, commissary, cotton gin, tannery, smithy, and warehouses. Steamboats from Mobile stopped at its wharf. Lucy Young Banks manuscript, WC; Atkinson and Elliott, *Resources*, 41–43.

32. Hood replaced Johnston as commander of the Army of Tennessee 17 July 1864. John S. Bowman, ed., *The Civil War Almanac* (New York: World Almanac Publications, 1983), 215.

33. Colonel George C. Porter, Hardee's Corps, Cheatham's Division, Maney's Brigade. Organization charts, Army of Tennessee, 30 Apr. 1864, *OR*, 32, pt. 3, 866.

34. Belle's photograph album is extant. It belongs to descendants of her sister, Helen Crump.

35. No apparent basis for this rumor about Grant.

After breakfast I got my sock and knit all morning. Maj Rambaut and Mr Pugh came up in Tate's room and sat. Cousin Frazor [Titus] came for a while. The news this morning is glorious. Hood has attacked Sherman and driven his forces across the River with heavy loss on Yankee side. Hardee is in the rear and will give them a warm reception.[36] Did not get the evening Telegrams before leaving Columbus. Bro [Robert Walton Edmondson], Kate & Nannie came in, I returned with Bro. I am perfectly unhappy at the way in which Hal has treated me. I have no plans nor no idea when I will see one of them again. God be with me and guide me to do what is right. Theresa & Capt Triplett called this eve, Col Laynard also. Decatur arrived. Nothing reliable as to Grant's death. Bro, Kate & I had a very pleasant ride out. Sister Amirilla [Amarilla] and all the Children glad to see me.[37] All sat up late. Mrs. Smith & I occupy the same room. I am so undecided and unhappy. May God give us Victory, spare so much bloodshed, and give us peace.

SUNDAY 24 We all slept late this morning. Bro sent to Columbus for the news. A note from Bro Geo saying he and his crowd would leave for Tibby [Tibbee][38] in the morning. Nothing over the wires since we left yesterday evening. A note from Theresa, she is anxious I should come in & make another visit to Waverly. I am as unhappy as mortal can be at the manner in which Hal has treated me. I have no idea when or what will be my movements. I have no idea they will be to satisfy anyone else, but pray God may guide me right, and bless and brighten my sad path. Mrs. Smith, Sister Amarilla, Bro any myself with the Children have spent the day quite pleasantly. Sat up late after Tea. Mrs Smith and I are still roommates. Sam is improving very slowly, poor little fellow he looks dreadfully.

MONDAY 25 How very cold it was this morning. We must have had a great Victory in Ga—as this cool weather always indicates a great Southern Victory. No news over the wires again to day. It seems

36. Hood sent Hardee on a 15-mile trek south and east to attack the flank and rear of McPherson's forces between Atlanta and Decatur 21 July 1864. Bowman, *Almanac*, 216.

37. Amarilla Moore Ragsdale (1824–1878) married Robert Walton Edmondson in 1847. Of their ten children, five were living in 1864: Andrew Scott, Robert Yakely, Jane Katherine, Samuel G., and Hugh Clem. Kate Edmondson Johnson kept up a lively correspondence with other Edmondson family members over the years. Her letters tie together the generations and provide information and insights into the past. Unfortunately, no mention of Belle exists in any of her letters. Genealogy charts; Kate E. Johnson letters, EFP.

38. Tibbee, a station on the Mobile and Ohio Railroad between West Point and Artesia, Jordan and Pryor, *Forrest*, 403.

strange, but God grant we may be victorious. Our Enemy have every
advantage, yet in the God of battles we put our trust, and have faith
that all will be well. Mrs Smith returned to Aberdeen this morning.
Sister Amarilla and I spent the day mostly alone, Bro was off on the
farm. I did not quite finish my Sock, had a good nap after dinner.
Eddie arrived this evening from Gen Chalmers Hd Qts.[39] No news
from Ga or Va yet. Eddie is right sick, has not been well since the
fight. We all retired early. Katie is going to sleep with me, Rachel
will make her pallet in here also. I am the greatest coward in the
world—still undecided in my movements. I reckon Hal and her
crowd are happy to Night. May God soften my heart, I cannot
but feel bitter. Oh! guide and give me strength to bear my unhappy
fate.

TUESDAY 26 Ah! how sad and lonely days, are these now passing.
Eddie went to Columbus this morning, returned this evening, bro't
news of 25th from Ga—the Yanks were shelling Atlanta, nothing
decisive as to the fate of either Army in that State. Hood gave them
a bad thrashing, but from Telegrams since I fear our Victories cannot be followed up. God grant we may be blessed with glorious news
from there in a day or two. Nothing important from other points.
Tate and her crowd did not leave Columbus until to day. Robert was
sick yesterday and they could not leave. I heard through Theresa
from them. They spent last eve at Mrs Weavers. I am so unhappy I
don't know what to do—whether to go on home or not. Oh! my
heavenly redeemer guide me, teach my heart forbearance and for
pity lighten my trials. I finished one of Eddie's socks to day, had a
lovely nap this eve, consequently am not sleepy to Night. Received
letters from Capt Barbour and Shallie Kirk. We all sat up late. Oh!
heaven have mercy I am so unhappy.

WEDNESDAY 27 We all got up very early this morning. Bro & Eddie
had to go to Columbus, Eddie arrived in time for the train and left
for Okolona. Bro came back quite late this evening, bro't no reliable
news from any point. Yanks still shelling Atlanta. The raide seems
now to be pressing Jackson, Miss, in stead of our front, those on the
Charleston R.R. seem to be resting on their oares, watching, and
guided by movements in Ga. God grant their plans may be frus-
trated, and our arms Victorious. Cousin Frazor arrived to day and

---

39. n.˙ ·· the Battle of Harrisburg/Tupelo, Forrest wrote to General Lee suggesting
Chalmers's Division be sent to the area of Pikeville, a small town on the main road
between Houston and Aberdeen, to be fitted up, rested, and reorganized. Wyeth,
Forrest, 403.

has been quite sick all evening.[40] I am as unhappy as mortal can be. Bro opposes my going for some time. I have my plans made however, and have no idea of changing them. I have had so much to try me, I have no patience to argue the question, and trust there will be no more unpleasantness with regard to it. Oh! God give me strength to bear up.

THURSDAY 28 Another long, long weary day. I have been kniting very hard, to try and keep down my miserable feelings. Rachel very kindly offered to clean my head nicely. I accepted, so to Night I have one consolation, a nice clean head. Nothing important has passed to day, neither have we heard one word of news. Oh! it would kill me to live in the Country. Bro was very angry with me this evening because I would not consent to remain. I of course did not agree to any such arrangement. I am dependent on him however for a conveyance to Columbus, and he cannot take me before Sunday. God grant me contentment until then. I am going in opposition to my relatives advice. My life has not been one to make me bound by affection to obey. I cannot live thus. I am going I know not when. Oh! God guide and protect me. I will do my duty to myself, though the world condemns me.[41]

FRIDAY 29 I think without doubt, this is the warmest day I ever experienced. Knit all day finished Eddie's socks and Amanda washed them out for me—just finished them in time Eddie arrived from Columbus this eve, spent yesterday and part of to day, with Tate and the girls at Tibbee. They sent me no messages or regrets that I was not with them. I hope it will all be right. God be with me and guide me. No late news from either Army, Va or Ga. News of Kirby Smith's crossing the River from Trans Mississippi to this Department.[42] God is with us, and the light of independence now glimmering in the distance will soon burst forth with a halo of unfading light and glory. Sam was not so well, sent for Dr Brice, he came, bro't his daughter, Kate Brice, who is my room mate for to Night. Eddie, Brother and all of us sat up quite late talking. My dear Brothers how dearly I love them. God grant we may all be spared to meet once

40. Frazor Titus, weary of his exile from Memphis, spent his time traveling between homes in the Columbus, Aberdeen, and Pontotoc areas. When he found Belle at Robert's home, he wrote in his diary: "Belle E. Is here. My stay will be short."

41. On this date, Frazor Titus noted: "Some families are all gossips. One that shall be nameless has annoyed me greatly."

42. General Kirby Smith was ordered to transfer all of the infantry in Louisiana and Arkansas east of the Mississippi River in order to create a diversion. Castel, *Price*, 201.

more around the hearth stone of dear old Father. God bless and protect him.

SATURDAY 30 Bro and Eddie were undecided for some time this morning, whether or not I should return to Columbus. Eddie at last consented to bring me in. We had a warm disagreeable ride. Found Theresa at home and glad to see me. Eddie came round after dinner and sat with Theresa and I some time, poor Eddie I was so grieved to bid him good-bye, hope to meet him before he leaves for Camp. Lou Young came round to see us, invited us home with her which I of course did not refuse, Theresa also. We had a nice ride out. Dr Butts came with us. Her Bro Willie[43] is at home, we had a game of grab, did not last long. We then went down to the Pond and had a nice bath. I still have a great horror of the water. No late news from the Army to day. None from my friends at Tibbee. I was really sad at parting from my Brothers. Oh! heaven guide me and protect me from harm. Lou, Theresa and I are room mates to Night.

SUNDAY 31 This morning has been spent very quietly. Mr and Mrs Hamilton Lou's sister and her husband were here. Mrs H invited us when she left to visit her bath this evening, owing to our religious scruples not allowing us to go in the fish pond. The rain interfered with our plans. In the afternoon Lou, Miss Mary Lu and I occupied one bed in our room while Mrs Reynolds and Theresa had the other. I was the only one who succeeded in "making the trip" we started on—the other finding it impossible. For which non compliance of orders on their part I fully made up until I was awakened by the thunder not only in the Heavens, but in the bed beside me. We were interrupted in the midst of a highly intellectual conversation by the arrival of Miss Harris, Mrs Martin and Mrs Johnston [Johnson].[44] We dressed, spent a quiet evening and retired.

43. William L. Young (1837–1913) was a private in the Columbus Rifleman, Co. K, Fourteenth Mississippi Infantry. He was captured and imprisoned at Camp Douglas. After escaping from there, he was detailed "scout" for the remainder of the war. He may be the William Young on the list of Henderson's Scouts paroled in 1865. He and three of his brothers were graduates of the University of Mississippi. In later life he was known as "Captain Billy." He never married and lived at Waverley with another unmarried brother, "Major Val." They organized the National Foxhunters Association at Waverley in 1898. Major Val died in 1906, Captain Billy in 1913. Lipscomb, *Columbus*, 155; List of Scouts, CC; *the Historical Catalogue of the University of Mississippi* (Nashville: Marshall and Bruce Company, 1910), 14, 118, 129; "Val and Billy Young and Waverly," clipping, *The Chase*, 1938; editors' interview with Luke Richardson [Captain Billy's servant from 1903–1910], June 1979.

44. Susan Young Johnson was another of Colonel Young's daughters. Genealogy sheet, WC.

II

Life at Waverley

1864 DIARY: AUGUST

MONDAY 1 [This entry covers pages for August 1 and 2. It was written by Lucy Young.]

My Dear Belle

It has been such an "egrejus" long time since I saw you last, that I'm quite at a loss how to commence the many long yarns I have in store for you but as it's *utterly* impossible for me to communicate with you in any other manner than this, I must e'en put up with it—and narrate them as "gay and festive" as possible—but as *I* have been so very slow in writing thus far and it "waxes late" I will be compelled to leave for my next—what I have so auspiciously begun in this—and although it is of the greatest importance that you hear what I have to say *now*, I will pleasantly forbear and bid you my "gentle and puserlanermus cuss" a fond adoo—

Miss Belle Edmondson—a kiss

WEDNESDAY 3 Third anniversary of my beloved Mothers death. There are few more *sorrowful* times, in the experience of poor Children of earth—than round the *deathbed* of a loved and revered *Mother*[1]—one who has been indeed a true faithful Mother, whose life to us has consecrated the name—and left it on our hearts as a holy word—

FRIDAY 5 Our gay little crowd was broken up this morning—Theresa, Mrs Martin both returned to Columbus. Mrs Johnson went in with them to bring Mrs Forrest out to spend a few days—they have not returned, but for a heavy cloud which passed over this eve, and from all appearances was inclined to moisten mother earth about that point, we all would feel uneasy, that is our only consolation. So we a sleepy crowd retire early, with the hope of greeting them in the morning. Lou, Mary Poullain, Mr Will Young and I spent the eve-

1. Mary Ann Howard Edmondson (1800–1861) died after a visit to her daughter, Jane Kilpatrick, in Corinth, Mississippi, EFP.

ning together in the parlor, they knitting—he and I playing bagga-
mon. All together we have had a delightful day. Lou and Mrs Reynolds had company, Mary Lou & I had a nap—then a nice bath—not
much swiming. Lou sat on the bank, much amused at our fear of a
ducking—her country relations called and she could not venture in.
I have decided to not leave until I hear from Tate.

SATURDAY 6 We were all very uneasy all morning about Mrs Johnson the old driver arrived at 12 o'c with the news of trouble for them
on yesterday evening. Mrs Forrests girl was very sick, she could not
come. Mrs Johnson started out rather late, the heavy Storm which
we thought would disturb the quiet of Columbus overtook her, three
miles from Columbus, in this deep trouble the Carriage broke down,
so she had to return to the City had a terible time. No limbs or lives
lost however. Lou, Mrs Reynolds, Mary Poullain and I had a nice
quiet day. Col Young went to Columbus, left Mr Will Y. to attend
to the Mill, so we did not have much of his delightful Company. Mrs
Johnson & Dr Butts arrived with bad news from Mobile, the Yankee
fleet passed Forts Morgan & Gaines with loss of only one boat, the
Tecumsah.[2] God grant the City may be saved.

SUNDAY 7 A bright and beautiful day—no Church going from this
establishment. We all spent the day at home—hoping and praying
for the gloom which hovers over us to be dispelled, for the Safety
and success of our defenses of Mobile, the defeat of the raids which
are overunning our poor desolated land.[3] Give our armies Success,
and oh grant us peace. No late news from Mobile or any other point.
I received a letter from Hal, no news in it, am looking for her in a
few days. Lou, and all of us slept all afternoon, I suffered very much
with my ear all Night, did not sleep much and fear I am a great deal
of trouble to dear sweet Lou.

MONDAY 8 Day spent in kniting, [illegible] I slept very little last
Night, and to my distress kept the other Ladies awake—poor Lou
the task fell to her, to go down Stairs for Laudanum.[4] She is one of
the sweetest girls I ever met, I love her with my hearts warmest

2. The Battle of Mobile Bay, 5 Aug. 1864. The *Tecumseh* was sunk at 7:45 A.M.
Alfred Thayer Mahan, *The Navy in the Civil War* (New York: Charles Scribner's Sons,
1885), 3:244.

3. General Smith left Grand Junction, Tennessee 5 Aug. 1864 and moved down the
Mississippi Central Railroad. Forrest thought the movement was a feint to draw his
forces away from the rich prairie region around Okolona and West Point. Henry,
Forrest, 330.

4. Laudanum, a tincture of opium, was used by many women in the Civil War
era who became addicted through self-dosage. David T. Courtwright, *Dark Paradise,
Opium Addiction in America Before 1940* (Cambridge: Harvard University Press,
1982), 4.

affections. Mrs Hamilton was down to Tea, we spent a pleasant evening. My deafness is very disagreeable to myself and I suppose to every one else, having to enquire so often when addressed. The news from all points is not as encouraging as we hoped for—Mobile is teribly threatened. God grant our Armies may be Successful in defense of the City.

TUESDAY 9 I heard this Morning the sad news of poor Lt W. Tabb's death, he was killed in Ga in last Saturdays fight, in defense of Atlanta—how many desolated hearth stones, how long oh! Lord how long must we suffer. Nothing of importance having transpired to day. I will not continue the light, only to record my weary heart aches. Miss Judivon & Dr Judivon, called this evening. I excused myself on account of deafness. Mrs Young (Em) came, she came in the room where I was, and we had a nice little chat—enjoyed her delightful Singing after Tea. Mr Jim Young gave us some of Artemis best,[5] of course much laughter and enjoyment by all.

WEDNESDAY 10 Still no decisive news form any point except the Surrender of Fort Gaines.[6] This is a heavy blow, yet Morgan still stands to dispute their quiet entrance into the Bay. I am still as hopeful as can [be] of Mobile, they are now 30 miles below in the Bay, with every obstruction to impede their reaching the City. May the God of battles defend us from any further invasion by so wicked and sinful enemies as we have to contend with.

Mrs Hamilton spent the day with us to day. I could not have been much pleasure to her or any one else, as tis no company for myself to suffer for so many Nights with ear ache, then left deff. I am afraid to go in the bath, as my country relations may be offended and depart. Lou & I against Mrs Reynolds and Mr Will Young had a nice game of Cards after Tea.

THURSDAY 11 The cry is still no news from Va, Ga, or Mobile—all still holding their own but no advance from either side. Gen Dick Taylor has crossed the Mississippi with a heavy force. Forrest sent a great many Wagons to meet him, two Bateries to protect his march until they can form a junction.[7] The Yanks are still advancing at Oxford last accounts. Gen Chalmers fought them at Abbeville, fell

5. James Hamilton Young (1832–1899), Co. C, First Mississippi Infantry, may also be the James Young listed with Henderson's Scouts at the end of the war. Young genealogy sheet, WC; List of Scouts, CC.

6. Fort Gaines surrendered 7 Aug. 1864. Mahan, *Navy*, 245.

7. A rumor. General Taylor did not cross the Mississippi River until 5 Sept. 1864. Taylor, *Destruction*, 240.

back, our forces under Gen Forrest are at Lafayette Springs.[8] The
Yanks are in large numbers, yet we are confident of checking their
wicked course before they go much farther. A rumor that Gen Lee
had been sent to Ga, while our President was left in command of Va.
A nice game of cards after Tea, Lou and I were teribly beaten.

SATURDAY 13 [The first part of this entry is in Lucy Young's hand-
writing.]
The sun shone about as usual the birds sang gaily, I suppose, tho' I
didn't *listen*—a gentle breeze was stiring—entirely too gentle for the
temperature of the day. In fact the whole face of "nature" displayed
nothing more than a hot August day. I have managed to live through
it by "dint of a Squeeze". I ate breakfast, dinner & supper, knit
socks, played backgammon & cards—(at all of which I am profi-
cient—) pinched, beat, battered & bruised all of the white inhabitants—had my game ear looked into by a Confederate Surgeon. I
was dressed in my usual "flowery stile" at that time of day. I took a
bath but failed to get drowned—by reason of over caution—got
"egregiously" beaten at eucher & went to bed in a sprightly state of
mind. Tate and the girls have returned to Columbus, a note from
Tate to day. telling me to report to Hd. Q's. They will return home
in a few days. Lou like a good child wrote the first of to day.

SUNDAY 14 A bright and beautiful day. I did not come to Columbus
this morning. Mrs Johnson & Mary Poullain came in to Church,
brot me a note from Tate saying she would send Johnie out for me
this eve. Lou and I spent the morning alone, in the octagon.[9] Mrs
Reynolds writing to Maj Reynolds, Mr Willie Young making preparations to depart for Forrest's command. We had all just gone to
our rooms, and ready for a nap, when Johnie came. I concluded to
come in and make arrangements with Tate what to do. John & I had
a delightful drive in. Mary & Robert both look badly. Met Mr
Holmes just from home, left all well. Great deal of sickness in Memphis. Tate and the girls go to Macon on the train tomorrow morning.

8. Smith's advance force reached Oxford 10 Aug. 1864. Lyman B. Pierce, *History
of the Second Iowa Cavalry* (Burlington, Iowa: Hawkeye Steam Book and Job Printing, 1865), 109; Henry, *Forrest*, 332.
   9. One of the unique features of Waverley's architecture was its four-story stair hall
which terminated in a cupola. Although domes were considered Roman, not Greek,
some of the best examples of Greek Revival architecture were domed buildings, according to one architectural historian. Smith, *Pillars*, 93; Marcus Wiffen, *American
Architecture Since 1780* (Cambridge: Massachusetts Institute of Technology Press,
1969), 41. Belle was probably referring to the fourth floor of the octagonal cupola
with its sixteen windows that faced in all directions.

I have concluded to stay with Lou Young, will return tomorrow. I am almost crazy with my ear to Night. Parlor ful of company, I excused myself—and of all the miserable places, I have landed in it to Night. Hal, Nannie & I all in one bed, and the warmest Night imaginable.

MONDAY 15 Tate, Nannie, & Hal, with the rest of their crowd left for Macon on the 9 o'clock train. I left the Hotel after their departure and went over to Mrs Longs to spend the day with Theresa. My ear pained me teribly all day. I felt very badly after Tate left, but she promised to Telegraph me if they moved. Col Young sent for me about two o'clock. I had a lonely ride, met Duke about half way, he arrived safe with my trunk. Lou met me, and I was really happy to be with her again. We all went to bathe as soon as I arrived. Judge Clayton[10] came out, brot me a telegram from Tate, telling me to come to Macon immediately, they leave tomorrow for Grenada. I am almost crazy with my ear, so Col Young Dispatched "Not well enough to travel." I am suffering so much no sleep for me to Night.

THURSDAY 25 After my failure to remodel Lou's hat on yesterday, Mrs Johnson kindly offered to assist me, so she spent the morning making the crown. I then took it, finished puting it together and trimed it, after finishing, it looked quite nice—and Lou did not make so much sport over her Milliners misfortunes. I finished Maj Youngs[11] sock with Lou's assistance. We played backgammon, and altogether had a very pleasant day. Mary Poullain and I improved very much in our swiming. Col Young got back to day from his Plantation,[12] and is quite sick to Night from fatigue. Bad news from Va and Mobile. Fort Morgan surrendered and we have been defeated at Fredricksburg.[13] God grant the days may brighten for our poor bleeding Confederacy. No news from home yet.

FRIDAY 26 I had a regular seige to day with Mrs Reynolds hat, and I

10. Judge Alexander Clayton from Marshall County, Mississippi, was a member of the Confederate Congress and a district judge. In July 1864, the court was meeting at Macon, Mississippi. Henry Putney Beers, *Guide to the Archives of the Government of the Confederate States of America* (Washington: General Services Administration, 1968), 49.

11. Major George Valerious Young, quartermaster, Cheatham's Division. After the war Major Val was postmaster at Waverley. Report of Major General B. F. Cheatham, 20 Feb. 1863, *OR*, 20 pt. 1, 708; Waverley Post Office Account Book, 1897–1899, WC.

12. Colonel Young owned extensive land. His other plantation was listed as "Middle Place" in his ledger book for 1878, WC.

13. Fort Morgan surrendered 23 Aug. 1864. Mahan, *Navy*, 245. Belle must have been referring to Petersburg, not Fredricksburg. At Petersburg the Confederates

did not finish it. Mrs Johnson and I both failed to make a brim. I retreated to my room in disgust, the other girls were all enjoying a nice nap. We all went to bath. Mary Lou and I improved with much in swiming, not able to swim across the Pond yet. As usual we played Euchre after Tea, Lou and I were beaten only one game. No news of importance from the Armys.

SATURDAY 27 I began on the hat, immediately after breakfast, succeeded in forming a very nice brim, and Mrs Reynolds was pleased. I do not think I was cut out for a Miliner or hat maker. Poor Lou is loosing all her hair, and it really distresses me. I wish could remedy the evil. We all went to bathe, I improved a little in swiming, not confidence enough yet. Mr Clapp and Mr Chambers[14] arrived at Waverly this evening. Lou and I played against Mrs Reynolds and Mr Clapp at Whist. Spent a very pleasant eve, retired early and I venture to say Lou & I will enjoy it, as we did not sleep any last Night for the Musquitoes.

SUNDAY 28 Lou and I as usual too late for breakfast. We all spent most of the morning in the Octagon. Mr Clapp & Col Chambers making themselves very entertaining—I do like Mr Clapp so much. Lou and I came up stairs Lou occupied her time in writing to her Bro Vallie—I of course in sleeping. We had rather a discussion at dinner about Southern people taking the Oath of Allegiance to the Yankee Gov. Mr Clapp had the advantage of the discussion, his view being strictly against it.[15] The gentlemen returned to Columbus after dinner. We spent the evening in Slumber. Mr & Mrs Hamilton took Tea & spent the evening with us. I do feel so uneasy about home, no news decisive from any portion of our Armyies.

MONDAY 29 The day passed as usual—Waverly is always pleasant to me. Spent the day in knitting, backgammon, sleeping &c. We had a

---

under General A. P. Hill suffered losses of 1600 on 21 Aug. 1984. Bowman, *Almanac*, 2210.

14. Jerimah Watkins Clapp replaced J. D. Debow as general agent, Produce Loan Office, state of Mississippi with an office at Columbus in 1864. Beers, *Archives*, 115. Henry Chambers, member of the Confederate House of Representatives from 19 Feb. 1862 to 17 Feb. 1864, married the widow, Susan Young Johnson, 28 Feb. 1866. List of House of Representatives, *OR*, 4, pt. 3, 1188; Lowndes County Marriage Book 5, 356.

15. Dinner at Waverley was at three in the afternoon. Letter, unaddressed and unsigned, from Waverley, Hamner Letters. One of Mr. Clapp's neighbors in Holly Springs wrote that there were only two ways to get clothing in the late summer of 1864: to swear false allegiance or deal with a speculator. Cary Johnson, "Life within the Confederate Lines as Depicted in the War-Time Journal of a Mississippi girl" (M.A. thesis, Louisiana State University, 1929), 26 Aug. 1864 journal entry.

delightful time in the Pond, have not succeeded in swiming across yet. Good news from Va to day. Lee has had a great Victory, capturing 2,000 Yanks, killing and wounding large numbers. Report of the Siege of Petersburg being abandoned for the present. Nothing later from Mobile, Forrest or Ga. Lincoln is trying to arrange to send peace delegates, only for policy in the next election, of course we can never agree with him in our terms of peace.[16] No news from home. Had a nice game of Euchre after tea. Lou dear girl, I could but love you too well.

TUESDAY 30 Mrs Reynolds and Mrs Johnson went to Columbus this morning Col Young also. Lou, Mary L and I had quite a nice time although alone. The Miss's Burt called. Mr Clapp came out with Col Young on his way to Holly Springs. We all had a short bath this eve, as the Gentlemen wanted to go in. Mrs Young & Maj Henderson[17] took Tea and we all spent a very pleasant eve. I sat up very late writing to Capt [Thomas] Henderson.[18] No news from any portion of the Country.

WEDNESDAY 31 After all my sitting up so late, Mr Clapp went off and forgot my letter, or at least, I failed to awake in time to give it to him. We have had a pleasant day as usual, to me each day is delightful at Waverly—there is not much Variety—but tis always pleasant. We all together had a nice bath, although t'was very cold. I was really timid and foolish in the Water, tried to cross, but did not get more than half way, hope I will succeed some time. Still no news from home, and nothing different from the Army's.

16. The assault at Ream's Station, 25 Aug. 1864, cost the Federals 2742 men. A peace "pow-wow" took place at Springfield, Illinois, in the late summer of 1864, but Lincoln was not involved. The meeting was in opposition to the Lincoln faction. James C. Randall and David Donald, *The Civil War and Reconstruction* (Lexington: D. C. Heath and Co., 1969), 220.

17. Probably Colonel W. G. Henderson, McCulloch's Brigade, Fifth Mississippi, who lived at Okolona. Frazor Titus Diary for 1864; Andrew Brown, "The First Mississippi Partisan Rangers, C.S.A." *Civil War History* 1 (1955): 397.

18. Captain Thomas H. Henderson was named chief of scouts for the entire department by General Forrest 12 Aug. 1864. Circular, *OR*, 39, pt. 2, 773.

12

A Journey Homeward

1864 DIARY: SEPTEMBER

THURSDAY 1 Today is the first of Autumn. No falling leaves, or withering buds greet us—all is sunshine and happiness—fruit in abundance, and our bath as delightful as in Summer time. Mary Lou has more confidence in swimming, yet I can go farther. Poor Lou's relations were with her, and she could not indulge. We all enjoy life at Waverly, more than any place I have chanced to visit since the War. Gen Cheatham's Orderly[1] came to day for the horse's, the Maj & Gov have gone so no more horse back pleasure for Lou & I. Forrest has completely rid the Country above of Yanks, all bright in his Camp,[2] nothing deffinite from Va, Ga or Mobile. Lou and I redeemed our character to Night, in opposition to Mrs Reynolds and Mary Lou.

FRIDAY 2 To day has been one of the warmest I ever experienced. Lou and I buisy sewing on her dress. I finished the waiste, Lizzie the skirt and I think we will finish it tomorrow. No news from any point to day. Mary Lou joined Lou to entertain relations. Mrs Reynolds & Mrs Johnson went to Mrs Hamilton's—so Mrs Young and I had the Pond to our selves, and the water was delightful after this warm day. Lou & I beat again at Cards. 10 o'clock at Night—still suffocating. I dont know how we shall manage it through the Night.

SATURDAY 3 Oh misery how warm it has been. Heard this morning at the breakfast Table Gen Chalmers with his command would be at

---

1. Major General Cheatham commanded a division in the Army of Tennessee. Since George V. Young was on his staff, the horses at Waverley went to Cheatham instead of Forrest. Organization Charts, Army of Tennessee, 30 Apr. 1864, *OR*, 32, pt. 3, 866.

2. With 2000 picked men, Forrest made a spectacular dash into the heart of Memphis, almost capturing three Federal generals. The fear generated in the city succeeded in halting the fifth large Federal thrust into Mississippi. By the first of September, Forrest was at Grenada reorganizing his command. Henry, *Forrest*, 328–44; Mathes, *Forrest*, 281–82.

West Point to day, and have watched eagerly to hear news form home, as Maj Crump is with him, but alas have been sadly disapointed. I am very sad never to hear one word, it does seem they might find some way to send me word. Lou and I with Lizzie's assistance finished Lou's dress, and it fits really nice, and I am thankful. Mrs McGavrock and Mrs Hamilton called this morning. We all had a delightful bath, after the scorching heat. Lou & I beat Mrs Reynolds & Mary Lou badly at Cards. Mr Chambers sent the Ladies two latest novels, in which we all expect a great treat—Joseph 2d Court [*Joseph II and His Court*],[3] Ladie Audlies Secret [*Lady Audley's Secret*].[4]

SUNDAY 4 Another warm day, and much excitement in our family, for sympathy with a Neighbor and friend, whose only Son was wounded at Atlanta, and after four weeks suffering, this morning had his leg Amputated, reaction has barely taken place and very little hopes of his life. Lou is much distressed, and her exclimations of sympathy for poor Billy Burt[5] weigh heavily on my Spirits, although I am not acquainted with the young man. Mrs Hamilton received a note from her husband at West Point, he had seen Eddie & Maj Crump, said Eddie would be over to day, but alas I was sadly disapointed. No news from home yet. Maj Cheatham[6] arrived from Atlanta to day, seems very hopeful. God grant our Armies may be victorious.

MONDAY 5 I cut my foullard Silk and we have all been buisy sewing on it all day, Lou the Skirt, Ellen (Lou['s] P[ersonal] maid)[7] the

---

3. Clara Mundt [Luis Muhlbach], *Joseph II and His Court*, trans. Adelaide de V. Chaudron (Mobile: Goetzel, 1864).

4. Mary Elizabeth Braddon Maxwell, *Lady Audley's Secret* (Mobile: Goetzel, 1864).

5. The Burts lived in the Waverley community. Their home was less than half a mile down river from the Youngs. Their cemetery adjoined that of the Young family. Dr. G. S. Bryant to the *Aberdeen Examiner*, September 1940, clipping, Vertical File, Aberdeen Library, Aberdeen, MS.

6. Major J. A. Cheatham, chief of ordnance, Cheatham's Division, Army of Tennessee. Report of Major General Cheatham, 20 Feb. 1863, *OR*, 20, pt. 1, 708.

7. Colonel Young listed 137 slaves on the 1860 census. His sons Thomas, George V., and James owned between them eighty-eight slaves. Years later three of the Waverley slaves were mentioned in published sources. A servant of George V.'s was mentioned in the *OR*, though not by name, because he gave information to the enemy after the Battle of Chickamauga. Report of General James Garfield, 22 Sept. 1863, *OR*, 30 pt. 3, 778. Two ex-slaves from Waverley are in the pages of the W.P.A. Slave Narrative Collection, compiled during the 1930s. One was Clara Young who married a Waverley slave and moved there. She remembered the parties at Waverley and no bad times. The other was Ben Young, a slave who belonged to Thomas Young. He was "impudent" and after the war "became a white man hater and an incendiary

flounce, Mrs Reynolds and Mary Lou the Rosettes and I finished the waiste, we did not half finish the dress. Lou, Mary Lou and I went in the Pond early, I swam across, with Lou's assistance and got a terible ducking at floating. Heard from West Point, Eddie & Maj Crump will be down tomorrow. Maj Cheatham & Mary Lou played against Lou & I and we beat them badly. Mrs Johnson & Hamilton went to sit up with Billy Burt who I am happy to say is much better. Received a letter from Maj Price & Theresa Blennerhassett.

TUESDAY 6 Maj Crump, Eddie and Capt Daly,[8] in Company with Gen Chalmers and Staff came down from Tupelo [and] West Point, all stoped at Mrs Jim Youngs to tea, the first named came down here after tea—we all sat up very late—and spent a very pleasant evening.

WEDNESDAY 7 Our friends remained with us over to day, and we have had a very pleasant day—playing Cards, backgammon, chess, Music &c. All walked down to the pond this eve, of course did not go in bathing as the gentlemen were with us. We have all had some grand mistakes, if this horrid war lasts much longer we will all be so demoralized we cannot entertain Gentlemen, so accustomed we are to speaking free to each other.

THURSDAY 8 Maj C, Capt D and Eddie all left after breakfast for West Point. We have had comparitively a quiet day. No news of importance from any point.

FRIDAY 9 Very cool and delightful. I finished my foullard Silk—if the weather improves as fast as it has done for the last few days, I think I will soon be left high and dry in my white dress's. We had a call from some young Ladies of Columbus, Miss Jennie Ebert, Miss's Williams, Capt Martin, and our little friend Theresa. No news with them, nor have we heard any of importance to day. Lou, Mary Lou & I called on Mrs Young this evening. We had a game of Cards, Lou and I were not so fortunate, Maj Cheatham & Mary Lou ran very evenly with us.

---

politician." The account of Ben Young was written by Ed Hopkins, who was married to Thomas Young's daughter. George P. Rawick, ed., *The American Slave: A Composite Autobiography*, 19 vols., 12 supplements (Westport, Conn.: Greenwood Press, 1977), 10:2399, 2400. J. Frazor Smith had access to Colonel Young's diary for the year the mansion was being built. Smith commented on the domestic servants at Waverley who were "the aristocrats of the slave world." Smith, *Pillars*, 94. Information about the number of slaves at Waverley was obtained from Atkinson and Elliott, *Resources*, 34, who in turn obtained it from the 1860 U.S. Census.

8. Probably Captain E. Daly, Co. A, Twelfth Tennessee Cavalry, Forrest's Command. General Orders #13, 21 May 1864, *OR*, pt. 2, 615.

SATURDAY 10 To day has been rather warm and very idly spent by me. We have played Cards or backgammon most of the time. Lou and I beat Mrs Reynolds and Maj Cheatham badly after tea. No news to day, and nothing to write in my Diary. Of course 'tis always pleasant to me, I have always been happy since my stay at Waverly.

SUNDAY 11 Mrs Johnson, Mary Lou, Maj Cheatham and Woodie[9] went to Church. Lou, Mrs Reynolds & I spent the morning reading &c. All slept in the afternoon. Mr Clapp & Lucas arrived from Holly Springs, found his wife doing her own work, the Yanks made a complete wreck of every thing in their last raide.[10] Lou, Mary Lou & I went up to Mr Hamiltons after tea—had a very pleasant evening, and beautiful moonlight walk.

MONDAY 12 Lou and I went up to see little Willie Young,[11] he was better but quite sick last Night. Mrs Young came home with us and brought him. I sewed some on Mrs Reynolds dress, have spent the day quite pleasantly, and had a delightful bath in the pond. Maj Crump arrived just as we finished tea, and of course I have had a delightful evening. Lou and I beat Mary Lou & Maj Cheatham badly at Cards. Mrs R and Maj Crump played chess.

TUESDAY 13 Maj Crump, Maj Cheatham, Mrs Reynolds, Lou, Mary Lou and I have spent a very pleasant day. Eddie arrived from West Point this morning. Lou made him a beautiful Tobacco bag, Mary Lou made Maj Crump one. We all went in bathing, I swam across the Pond for the first time. Lou and I beat Eddie & Mary Lou at Cards. Mrs Reynolds & Maj Crump played backgammon. We sat up right late. I received a letter from Bro Will asking me to come and stay with Mary & the Children until he returned & of course will go, but have made no arrangements as yet.

WEDNESDAY 14 To day has been a sad one to many members of this household, or rather has terminated sadly to some. Maj Crump & Eddie left this morning for Grenada where Gen Chalmers command has been ordered. I am so unhappy to Night—my heart aches to see dear Lou in trouble. She had a long letter from Miss Sallie Sanders giving a rememberance of her Sister Prudie's last illness, Lou's dearest friend. I did not know her, but oh! Lou my hearts deepest sympathy is yours. Maj Cheatham received a letter from Ga bearing news of the death of one of his dearest friends, he left after tea—so

9. Woodie was the young daughter of Susan Young Johnson. Genealogy sheet, Waverley Collection.

10. Belle was referring to the Holly Springs Raid of 28 Aug. 1864. Summary of Principal Events, *OR*, 39, pt. 1, 3.

11. Willie Young, son of James and Emily Young.

we all came to our room. Lou, Sallie [Reynolds] & Mary Lou all reading. Oh! my poor weary heart when, when will it be at rest.

THURSDAY 15 To day has been quite cool, and we have spent it very quietly, sewing all morning. After dinner Lou, and I beat Maj Cheatham badly at Cards &c after Tea. We had a nice time in the Pond, but cold weather is fast approaching. I am very much afraid I will be left in my white dresses out of season. I received a long nice letter from Capt Henderson to Night, accompanying a Chicago Times, he gave me all the news,and I shall ever feel grateful for his kind rememberance on leaving with Forrest, with 40 of his best men for Shermans rear.[12] God grant some bright spot may cheer us from that brave little band.

FRIDAY 16 Autumn is fast approaching to day has been quite cool. We have spent the day as usual delightfully at Waverly. Cards being order of the day. A delightful bath, though rather cool. I made Maj Cheatham a nice Chess bag.

SATURDAY 17 Another cool day, spent very idly by all, playing Cards most of the day. This evening Mary Lou, Mrs James Young and I went in the Pond alone, Lou sitting on the bank looking on, both my friends had gone out I alone in, when a Company of Soldiers passed. I am sorry to say our Confederate Soldiers would so far forget themselves as to notice a Ladie in bathing, but more so to say those stoped and made several remarks loud enough to be heard. I was not uneasy knowing the Officers would keep them Straight. Lou & I are going to take a dose of Medicine as we are very much in Job's fix.

SUNDAY 18 All went to Church this morning except Lou, Mary Lou and I, we had a nice quiet time. I fixed poor Lou's afflicted head, and am greatly distressed she has taken that terible eruption. Mr and Mrs Hamilton came down to Tea. We all walked down to the Tombigbee, had a delightful drink from the Artesian well.[13]

MONDAY 26 Left dear Waverly at 9 o'c this morning. Mrs Johnson and Reynolds accompanied me, and to Night we find ourselves quietly ensconced at Mrs Henderson's.[14] I met many of my friends at West Point, Gen Forrest's Hd Qts are there. Mr Hamilton put us aboard the train, and fortunately I met with an old friend, Tub An-

12. Forrest had orders to destroy Sherman's railroads. Henry, *Forrest*, 350.

13. The artesian well, sometimes called "the overflowing well," was the source of water for the pool, pond, and cotton gin. Ehren Foster Pyle, "Waverley Mansion," manuscript written for the Farm Housing Survey Scrapbook, n.d. [ca. 1930s], WC.

14. The wife of Colonel W. G. Henderson,whose home was at Okolona. Frazor Titus was often a visitor. Frazor Titus diary for 1864.

derson who was guard on the train, he assisted us a great deal. We have spent the evening very pleasantly at Mrs Hendersons, she is a fine Musician and very accomodating. I miss my friend Lucy so much. Nothing very exciting transpired to day.

TUESDAY 27 Oh! how lonely this day has been to me. Mrs Johnson and Reynolds returned to Waverly on the 7 o'c. train. My Hack came soon after, when I left, and I do not think any one could have spent so lonely a ride as I did, no person except the driver. Mrs Henderson was very kind indeed to me. I arrived in Pontotoc about 1 o'clock, found Mary alone and delighted to see me. Very stormy and rainy, so I have not accomplished anything and made no preparations for my trip, but will certainly, if providence permits leave here Thursday morning. I sat up quite late writing to dear Lucy, so that I could send by the boy who drove me up and have mailed at Okolona.

WEDNESDAY 28 Well mercy on me if Pontotoc cant take the lead for dulness, and no way to get on!—I succeeded in getting $50 in G. B. from a Servant. Bro Will came home about 1 o'c, went over to Town and thinks perhaps I can get Mr Carr to take me over. Cousin Ginnie and Eddie Miller came over and staid a few moments only. No news on earth—and not worth while to write in my journal.

FRIDAY 30 Left Pontotoc 8 o'clock this morning, traveled very hard, but could not make the distance, had a very hard Storm about 3 o'clock got perfectly drenched, and oh! how I ached, could not prevail on Mr Carr to drive me on to Oxford, stoped at a miserable place 2½ miles from there, and oh, such filth, for any one pretending to civilization. I did not sleep an hour. Spent a wretched Night—could not eat such filth and went to bed hungry.

13

Return to Waverley

1864 DIARY: OCTOBER AND NOVEMBER

October

SATURDAY 1 Awakened at daylight, and all my hurrying could not get Mr Carr off until rather late. Reached my friends Mrs Barr's to breakfast, and spent a very pleasant day, but very impatient to get on—have not as yet succeeded in getting any conveyance.

SUNDAY 2 Awakened very late after a feverish, restless Night. Emma [Barr] and I started out to get a conveyance. Mr Bacon and Mr Alexander [Alexander] of Hendersons Scouts proved my friends, borrowed a buggy, and Mr Johnson [Johnston][1] one of their Company, Brother in Law of Maj Ingrams [Ingram][2] on Cheathams Staff bro't me safely to Panola—arrived here about 7 o'clock. Mrs Moore sick in bed but glad to see me, so Mr Johnston and I ate a hearty Supper and I am fixing for a hot toddy—think my cold will be relieved and save me from a spell. Got in too late, disapointed in seeing Gen Chalmers to Night.

MONDAY 3 Was rather despondent some time this morning. Gen Chalmers came at last, gave me a pass. Mr Lancaster [3] carried me to the train, where I met Brother Brodie coming up to Senatobia for

---

1. W. M. Bacon, Second Sergeant; W. L. Alexander, first sergeant; J. A. Johnston, private. William Alexander planned to write a history of Henderson's Scouts from material he obtained from Sam Henderson's daughter. He died before completing the project. Efforts to locate his papers have been unsuccessful. W. L. Alexander to C. P. Newton, 24 Mar. 1917; List of Scouts, CC.

2. Major John Ingram, A.A.G., Cheatham's Division. Report of Major General B. F. Cheatham, 20 Feb. 1863, *OR*, 20, pt. 1, 708.

3. There were three scouts named Lancaster among those paroled. This is possibly Sam C. Lancaster who was operating in the area. Sam C. Lancaster to General Chalmers, 29 Sept. 1864, *OR*, 39, pt. 2, 885.

Helen. We traveled on the horse cars—and of course were some time making the trip.[4] Helen did not come not a word from her. I am so impatient to go on but will have to wait here until she arrives. I wrote a long letter to dear Lou to Night. Maj C. added a postscript.

TUESDAY 4 Gloomy, Gloomy and dismal, raining all day. Maj Crump and I both impatient, but no Helen—he staid most of his time in Telegraph Office. Mrs Chalmers came and I had to share my room with her and Kate. I am so impatient to get home. Nothing of importance crowd continually passing.

WEDNESDAY 5 I arose rather delighted having an opportunity of going home, however we got started very late. Mr & Mrs Greenlaw[5] & I left Senatobia about 9 o'c got to Cold Water ferry where the Pickets would not pass us, without a special pass. Of course we were very much disapointed, but such is the fate of mankind, disapointments, reached Senatobia rather late in the day, found Gen Chalmers and his command at that place. Gen C had taken my place so I had to sleep with old Mrs Arnold. Eddie and a great many friends were with Gen C. They are ready for a raide some where—I think towards Memphis, as the lines North are closed.[6]

THURSDAY 6 Gen Chalmers kindly gave me a pass this morning, so I took passage in Dr Bullingtons Cart for home, had no trouble, as far as Hernando. Arrived there about 1 o'clock, was delayed some time in getting a driver to go on—finally got a little boy about 10 years old. We started off, but soon found obstructions, at Hurricane Creek two Miles above Hernando met with our Pickets, and they would allow no one to pass. Old Mr Nesbit was there and saw how disapointed I was and whispered to me if I would go back and get a Saddle he would assist me in running the pickets. I suceeded in getting every thing, [and] myself on one horse the little boy on the other, rode 16 miles after 4 o'clock, arrived at home by 8. Eddie arrived just before me. Oh! I was so happy, but no one glad to see me except Laura.

---

4. The railroads were in ruins. Horse cars provided transportation from the Tallahatchie River at Panola northwards. Robert C. Black, *Railroads of the Confederacy* (Chapel Hill: University of North Carolina Press, 1952), 222.

5. Possibly William B. Greenlaw, whose home in Memphis was used by General Washburn. Young, *Memphis*, 359. Greenlaw was one of the wealthy and influential citizens of Memphis who took the oath to protect his property and collect rents. H. Winslow to Major J. C. Dennis, 15 Mar. 1864, *OR*, 32, pt. 2, 634.

6. Chalmers's feint towards Memphis caused increased vigilance in the city and the area. It had the effect of keeping troops there who might have pursued Forrest. Henry, *Forrest*, 368.

F R I D A Y 7 To day has been passed at home, buisy enough with me—having all Laura's things to fix, and my own. Nannie and Sister Mary went to Memphis to try and get me out some things but have not returned. Eddie and all of us sat in Tate's room after Supper. Father made Eddie go to the Cotton Gin to sleep. He has not had much pleasure at home. I sleep in Sister Marys room with poor little Sallie. Oh! how my heart aches for those poor little Mother less Children. No Yanks, or any disturbance to day.

S A T U R D A Y 8 Hal came down this morning to spend the day with me. Helen, Laura and the bagage left about 10 o'clock. I will not go until Sister Mary and Nannie come. Eddie left this morning. Capt Forrest[7] came by for him a few moments after he left. Gen Chalmers got in six miles of Memphis, but found out the Yanks were too many, and retreated in good order.[8] Hal did not stay very late, says she is coming to Col Youngs this winter. Sister Mary and Nannie got home safe—got nearly all I wanted. Oh! I am miserable, poor old Father how my heart aches to leave him, yet all is ready to go bright and early in the morning.

S U N D A Y 9 Father came in Sister Marys room where I was sleeping before day and awakened me. I was all ready to start at daylight. The darkies and Aunt Patsy were the only ones up to bid me Good bye. Sister Mary was up also and helped me to get off. I had no appetite, though Bettie had a nice lunch, had to stop at Mr Hillstons and borrow a horse and leave Ginie. She could not pull us, had no difficulty after that. Father rode on the horse almost to Cold Water and Peter in the buggy with me. We bought corn for the horses and ate dinner about four miles below Hernando. Arrived in Senatobia about 4 o'c, stoped at old Mr Arnolds, Father went out to Mr Bowdrys after Tea to get a pass home from Gen Chalmers. Helen went out to Mr Wallace's.

M O N D A Y 10 I got up very early for fear of being left. Father went down and saw me safe on the train. I arrived at Como, and no Helen or baggage—concluded to get off. Mr Sledge carried me over to Mr Wallace's in his buggy. I found Father there, and Helen waiting for Maj Crump. Poor Father, oh! my heart aches to part with him. God forgive me and let me be blessed to see him once again. I feel like it

7. Forrest's brother and Forrest's son were both Captain Forrest. Mathes, *Forrest*, 356.

8. Chalmers's demonstration near Memphis with his small force convinced the authorities that they were the advance of a much larger force trying to capture the city. Ibid., 294.

will kill me—my poor aching heart, Father oh! Father, could I only
know you regreted my absence. Oh! God shield him and spare him
for my sake. He left early on his way home. May he have a safe and
speedy trip. Maj Crump arrived, so did Eddie.

TUESDAY 11 Gen Chalmers left this morning for Jackson, Tenn. The
day has been spent rather lazily by me. I have no heart for any thing.
We cannot go on until Thursday. No news.

WEDNESDAY 12 Nothing more to day than yesterday, still at Mr
Wallace's. Good news from Ga, if it only be true[9]—our Army will
certainly be blessed. All the Soldiers gone to Tenn and the Country
here is gloomy and deserted.

THURSDAY 13 Left Mr Wallace's very early in time for the train at
Como. Car crowded, we got aboard after much manuevering. An
unpleasant trip to Tallahatchie, reached the other train[10] in Safety,
were delayed some time in Panola to take a Battery aboard
(Thrawl's) [Thrall],[11] had a pleasant, but slow trip down, did not
reach Grenada until after Night. Mr Payne did not get the Dis-
patchs, so we had to hire an Ambulance, and come on out to his
house. I have an awful Cold, and my Night ride did not help it any.
I am comfortably ensconced in a room to myself. Laura only, shares
it. My heart aches teribly.

FRIDAY 14 Gloomy prospect for weather this morning. Bro Brodie
and Mr Payne went in to Grenada after breakfast came back to dinner, no news. Bro B. succeeded in getting an Ambulance, but no
Mules. I will have to exercise a great deal of patience—but I know
he is doing all he can—I am so grateful for his kindness and the
interest he has taken in me. This is a delightful family, and I am
thankful Helen has such a nice home. Bro Brodie has orders to move
to Jackson Tenn on Sunday. I have suffered very much with my cold,
but think it a little better to Night.

SATURDAY 15 My trip seems the plans are fully matured, but the
clouds are threatening, and I am very much afraid we will have bad
weather. If nothing happens, and God's will, I will leave for Ponto-

---

9. Hood and Sherman were skirmishing near Rome, Georgia, 10 and 11 Oct. 1864.
Bowman, *Almanac*, 228; General Johnston to Jefferson Davis, 27 Feb. 1864, *OR*, 32,
pt. 1, 476.

10. Across the Tallahatchie River where the bridge was out, as far as the Yalobusha
River southwards, to another destroyed bridge, trains with locomotives operated on a
limited schedule. Black, *Railroads*, 222.

11. Captain J. C. Thrall of Thrall's (Arkansas) Artillery Battalion. Troops in the
Department of Alabama, Mississippi and East Louisiana, 30 Sept. 1864, *OR*, 39, pt.
2, 888.

toc tomorrow. Bro Brodie got an Ambulance and Mules from Capt Mickle[12] and Mr Payne will send one of his boys to drive. My cold is much better to day. I wrote two letters home. The day has been spent very quietly, but pleasantly—still no news from the Army.

SUNDAY 16 Maj Crump was up before daylight and off for his trip to Tenn. I got up also but did not get off until 9 o'clock. Helen and I came to Grenada in the Carriage. I met the Ambulance at Capt Mickle's office, bid farewell to Grenada and my friends at 10 o'clock. Helen returned to Mr Paynes. I started on my journey to Pontotoc with Laura for a Companion, and old Uncle Thornton, Mr Paynes Servant for Driver. We had a very rough trip, got lost and to Night find ourselves only 20 miles from Grenada, at Mr Peirsons, five miles from Coffeeville.[13] No Ladie in the house. I have a nice comfortable room and do not feel afraid with Laura—hope Uncle Thornton and Mules are at rest also. Saw Dr DeHart in Coffeeville this evening.

MONDAY 17 Well! here I sit to Night 20 miles from Pontotoc—only traveled 24 miles to day, through the poorest Country, and worst roads I'll wager in Dixie—the celebrated Calhoun County. The people are dirty, miserable looking creatures, with no tastes, and scarcely any civilization, fortunately met with comfortable quarters for the Night—at Mr Sadler's, one mile North of Serepta. A little village, only the name, Banner we passed through about 4 o'c. Oh! mercy I would die if I had to live in such a Country. Our Mules did finely, but poor creatures I know they are as much rejoiced as we are to be over those bad roads. We were lost again to day, poor Uncle Thornton has very little idea of routes. I have a clean bed, and nice pine torch—with Laura's company will pass the Night very well.

TUESDAY 18 Arrived in Pontotoc after 12, broke down just under the big hill, below Bro Wills.

THURSDAY 20 Uncle Thornton started back to Grenada this morning, I reckon the Ambulance will last until he gets there. I was sorry to send it back to Capt Mickle broken but could not avoid it.

SUNDAY 23 I left Pontotoc this morning for Waverly—a very warm unpleasant ride, in a rough Dixie hack. (Spring Wagon) Arrived in Oklona just after sundown. Mrs Henderson received me very cordially, and I spent a very pleasant eve. Mr Hubbard, Mr Vassar and Mr Henderson being of the party.

12. Captain B. Mickle, assistant quartermaster at Grenada. J. R. Chalmers to H. C. Davis, 5 Aug. 1864, *OR*, 39, pt. 2, 757.

13. A town on the Mississippi Central Railroad in Yalobusha County. Black, *Railroads*, 222.

MONDAY 24 Up bright and early, Mr Henderson bro't me down to the Depot—had no trouble, but a very pleasant ride to West Point. Mr Hamilton, met me and oh! I am so happy to be with my friends once more. Lou and Grand Mother arrived just after the train, and after sitting a while with Mr Hamilton we started on our journey towards Waverly arrived before dinner. Mr Willie and Jimmie Young, Maj Cheatham & Maj [George Valerious] Young arrived soon after from the Brown place with the body of poor old Bevvie [Beverly?].[14] I of course am happy. Lu and I went in bathing but oh! twas miserably cold.

TUESDAY 25 Grand Mother left for Ga to day, Mrs Johnson went to Columbus with her. Lou, Grand Mother & I went up to see Mrs Hamilton. The day passed as usual always delightfuly for me at Waverly.

November

FRIDAY 4 To day is Lou['s] 22nd birthday.

SATURDAY 5 Lou and I spent the day with Mrs Hamilton who is dangerously ill. Mr Willie Young came after Tea, and sat until bed time. Mrs Tom Young, Lou and I sat up all Night, sent two messengers for Dr. Smith got [not?] back until daylight. She was over the sick spell, and the Dr's pronounce her out of danger.

MONDAY 7 Received two letters from home, one from Tate one from Sister Mary. All well.

TUESDAY 15 Capt Sanders & Ladie, Mrs Pat Hamilton arrived from Aberdeen. Miss Annie is as beautiful as ever, and has a beautiful boy.

14. This is possibly Beverly D. Young, Co. I, Eleventh Mississippi Volunteers, the only one of Colonel Young's sons to die in the war. At Gettysburg, Beverly was wounded in the leg above the ankle. He developed gangrene while a prisoner at David's Island, New York Harbor. He died 28 Aug. 1863 and was buried at Cypress Hill Cemetery, Long Island. There are poignant letters to Colonel Young from the northern doctors who treated him and from a friend who was also a prisoner. One doctor wrote that Beverly "made an impression on my memory from the courage he displayed during the operation & from his manly appearance & conduct." The doctors and the Watkins relatives living in Schenectady, New York, may have been able to arrange a transfer of his body during wartime to Mississippi. Patrick Mulvihill to Mr. George H. Young, 24 Aug. 1863; A. N. Brockway, Act. Assistant surgeon, U.S.A. to [Mr. Young], 1 Sept. 1863; John C. DuBois, M.D. to J. T. Simpson, 17 Nov. 1863. Letters printed in *Dilettanti*. Beverly's funeral may have been the reason for the visit of Grandmother Watkins from Georgia and for Major George V. Young's absence from the front. Beverly's grave is in the family cemetery at Waverley.

THURSDAY 17 My 24th birth day—I wonder if any one thought of me at home.

FRIDAY 18 Lou and I went to Columbus, saw Maj Rambaut, but no news from home. Saw Theresa, also Bro Geo then called on Miss Williams. A cloudy, bad day.

SATURDAY 19 Bro Geo came according to promise and spent the day with us. A miserable bad day, the boat sank, so he had to cross in a skiff.[15] [He] went back to Columbus.

SUNDAY 20 Mrs Sanders & Capt went up to Miss Em's [Young]. Col Mumford and Lt Young left this morning.

MONDAY 21 Lou, Mr Willie, Maj Cheatham and I spent the evening at Mrs Hamiltons. Capt Sanders & Lady, Mr Jimmie and Mrs Em, we spent a very pleasant evening.

15. A ferry was in service on the Tombigbee River near Waverley from the 1830s until well into the twentieth century. Atkinson and Elliott, *Resources*, 33.

14

A Wedding and Two Battles

1864 LETTERS

From Thomas Henderson

Near Como,[1] Jany 26, 1864

Dear Miss Belle,

Your kind report was recd & I am oblidged to you for it.[2] You will do so again if you can I know. Miss Helen, Capt Mrs Dashiell & family are all well. I have the pants on you sent down—fit first rate. You omited to send down the cost. I have got a few Green Backs on hand & you will please report the amount before they get away. I am mighty busy & have seen but little of the ladies yet, if the Yankees will let us remain here, hope to see more of them from this time forwd.

The 2 Bbs Salt are here, one damaged, what shall I do with them? We have no news of importance from the South. I send you latest papers. With kind regards to your Father & all the family I am

Your friend truly

Thos Henderson

1. Forrest established his headquarters the first of the year at Como, Mississippi, a depot on the Mississippi and Tennessee Railroad, forty-three miles south of Memphis. Henry, *Forrest*, 213.

2. Perhaps a report on Sherman's plans for the Meridian Expedition. As early as 11 Jan. 1864, Captain Henderson sent Forrest word that a Federal movement into Mississippi was planned. According to Captain Dinkins, Forrest was kept informed of what was going on in Memphis by scouts and private correspondents. (See Belle's letter to Henderson 8 Sept. 1863.) Henry, *Forrest*, 220; Dinkins, *Recollections*, 129.

From Helen Edmondson

At Mr R. Wallace's[3]—Panola Co
Feb'ry 4th 1864

Dear Belle:

I recon you begin to think as I am so long answering your note that Major Crump brought that I have forgotten entirely. But you have been to "Dixie" and know when you get to frolicking that writing is the last thing we want to feel compelled to do. And that has been my fix. There were so many in the house and were so pleasant. I was afraid to go off for fear some one would say something I would not hear. But all of them are gone now, and I have plenty time to write. We are anxious and did expect to start up home Monday. But we could not get "passes" and there is no telling when we will But don't be uneasy or look for us until you see us, we are doing very well. No one allowed to go up now but the couriers. By the way Capt Sam Henderson was here a day or two ago, and sent his best love to you and from also Capt Tom. Mr Harbut [Harbert] came this morning. I was so much in hopes we would get a letter, with the facts connected with Jack's disappearance, Father told us nothing.

Eddie and Dashiell are in the same Brigade and under "Chalmers". Eddie's horse is almost completely ruined since that "scout" on the river, but I believe Lieut McConnell has given him another. We heard this morning they were fighting at "Grenada'" but I don't know that there was any truth in the report or not.[4]

Your friend Major Crump has been very kind and attentive to me since his return from "Elm Ridge" and I think him quite a nice pleasant gentleman.

I am having quite a pleasant time. This is one of the nicest places I ever saw, and the family are always so pleasant with each other. Jim [Titus] came by and stoped to see us a few minutes yesterday. I don't hope anything more than he will have his place with Major Strange,[5] and I think he will. Tate fixed up all your things in one big bundle, and sent them on to Dr. Moses by Col Polke, just as soon as she got

---

3. For a description of the Wallace home at Como, see Dinkins, *Recollections*, 102, 121.

4. The Fourth Brigade of Chalmers's Division was ordered to Grenada to observe a movement of Federals up the Yazoo River. Young, *Seventh Tennessee*, 74–75.

5. Major John P. Strange, A.A.G., Forrest's Cavalry Department. Mathes, *Old Guard*, 196.

your letter. Will Moon was here last night but "Bob" has gone to "Europe".[6] Judge Clark is down here at Mr Irby's. I have not seen him yet.

I wish you would please write to me *all* about home, every thing. How the negroes take Jake's [Jack] leaving and just every thing that would interest you. Don't be uneasy about us, we will come home as soon as the "lines" are opened. I have been writing all day and am so tired I can't write any more now, and then there is nothing to write, or at least I am afraid I shall write something that I ought not. I will say this much don't look for us until you hear all this commotion, "fighting and rumors of fighting *is over*". Give my best love to all and please write soon. Accept the love of your

Affectionate sister
Helen

From Thomas Henderson

Hdqtrs, Panola Feby 7, 1864

Dear Miss Belle

Your several notes have been rec. I am very much oblidged to you for them. Have been so continually on the move could not respond. We left your Sisters at Mr. Wallace's. I was hurried off with Genl Forrest & did not get a chance to say goodby to them, which I much regretted. Say so to them for me. We are here, but how long we will remain is uncertain. The enemy are advancing from Vicksburg, also up Yazoo, & I have sent Scouts to Greenwood.[7] Should they come down in front we would have to move, but I don't think they will come this way, but go by Okolona &c. Lt McConnell has not returned from Miss bottom yet, but will go up in your section if possible when he returns. We had a gay time at

6. The Moon family lived in the vicinity of the Edmondsons at one time. Lottie and Ginnie Moon were spies and smugglers of contraband. Neither of them is mentioned in the Edmondson family papers. McCorkle, *Whitehaven*, 54–55; Harnett T. Kane, *Spies for the Blue and Gray* (Garden City: Hanover House, 1954), 263–81; "A Flashback into the Civil War with Virginia Moon," *New York World*, 18 Oct. 1925, Davis Collection, Filson Club, Louisville, Kentucky.

7. Three gunboats and seven transports were reported going up the Yazoo River in the direction of Greenwood. This was part of the cooperating expedition with Sherman for his Meridian thrust. W. N. Mercer Otey to Lieutenant General Polk, 10 Feb. 1864, *OR*, 32, pt. 2, 704; *OR*, 32, pt. 1, 3.

Wallaces & wished often that you were there. I send you late Southern
papers. Give my best regard to your Father & family.
Your friend truly
Thos Henderson
N.B.
These pants suited me finely & I am a thousand times oblidged to
you for getting them.

From Belle Edmondson to Mr. Perkins

Feb 25th 1864

Mr. Perkins[8]
Nannie informed me of your kind offer to take the letters I have for
the Army. Most of them are for Gen Breckinridge. I have tried to fix
them to give you as little trouble as possible, and I will be under lasting
obligations to you to carry them safe to the different commands. They
are for poor Mo. & Ky'ns from their homes. I know you have been a
Solider long enough to interest yourself in this cause. If it is in your
power please deliver them in person. You are in Johnston's Army. Polk
and I think Breckinridge too you will find at Meridian or near.[9] If you
don't go through Mobile please send by some reliable person. The car-
rier of this mail was captured it has had a hard time getting through.
With a blessing for both yourself and the package, a pleasant trip and
safe arrival I am as ever a true friend to all Rebels—
Belle Edmondson

From A. Campbell Edmondson
Cousin Belle
I am going below today. You can send your package over by Cam-
bridge or if convenient you had perhaps better bring it over yourself. If

8. Peter Pryor Perkins [rank and unit unknown] was the son of Colonel Perkins.
He and Nannie married at Elm Ridge 25 Oct. 1866. They were later divorced. Bible
Records, PFP; Marriage Book Four, Shelby County Courthouse, 219; see also W. K.
Hall, *Descendants of Nicholas Perkins of Virginia* (Ann Arbor: Edwards Brothers, Inc.,
1957).
9. Johnston's and Breckinridge's commands were at Dalton, Georgia. Polk's com-
mand was at Demopolis, Alabama. Maury's command was at Mobile. L. Polk to
General S. Cooper, 22 Feb. 1864; D. Maury to Lt. General Polk, 23 Feb. 1864; J. E.
Johnston to Jefferson Davis, 27 Feb. 1864, *OR*, 32, pt. 1, 338, 401, 476.

you think advisable you can if the (weather permits) take it as far as Col Perkins as I will be there by 12 o'c today.

Please send late papers—

I am most respectfully

A. C. E.

Feb. 28th 1864

From Emily Dashiell Perkins

Castle Garden, Feby 22nd

Murphreesboro   1864

My dear, dear Belle

Your very welcome letter was received a day or two since & but I was on the eve of starting to visit a friend, (a paroled Confed Col's family) would have answered immediateliy. To tell you how *much* pleasure it gave me, would only be to tell you what you, knowing my affection for you, must know. I had not heard you were married, but I had understood from Nannie you were gone South & probably would be, before your return—but your signature shows me you are not—& I fear Clouds have arisen in your heart's sky. If so, I *know* you are not to blame, but I can't write you all of this, but hope to talk to you about many things soon. I have hoped until heart sick—to be able to go to Memphis—but pecuniary disappointments have prevented. Quite a sum of money was expressed to me on the 13th of Jan which I have not heard from. It was Tate's [10] arrearsment of pay, and it will take some time to investigate it. I fear I shall not get it. I am now trying to raise money otherwise. Can't tell how I will succeed but if I do, I will be down soon. I wrote to Mr Pitzer Miller to know how I could succeed in getting boarders I think that the most profitable business one can engage in, & if he writes encouragingly I will go directly. I must have money. Trade is brisk here, every thing very high, but the whole country is desolated. Mr. Lytle's estates lying immediately around town have been entirely destroyed, I mean the timber and improvements. Negroes are in perfect rebellion, no one in the country dares correct them. I have just got thru humbling one. A few days ago since she spoke impudently to Emmie. I asked her why she did so, she refused to answer me. I thought I had taken up a shovel to knock her down, but twas the broom which I broke over her head. This morning Tate came down I sent him for her, & when she came in my room I locked the door & told her I intended whipping her & if she submitted quickly I would not tie her.

10. Not a reference to Belle's sister Tate but probably a Perkins in-law. The name Tate appears often in the Perkins genealogy.

She refused to be whipped. I told Tate to tie her, he succeeded then in getting the strap around her hands & knocked her down. I laid it on— till she yelled—& then she stopped & then till she promised she never would speak impudently or be otherwise than perfectly obedient to me. Now that Negro has been the torment of the house because, it has been thought *no one could* whip her. *She* said they shouldn't. I would have done it at any hazard, and if every one here would have done the same thing there would not have been half the trouble.

How much I am obliged to your for your kindness to my dear boy! I know he is clever & fine looking and my heart bleeds to know where he is—*but being in* may be bear himself nobly—honoring his Father's memory. This war has been a test of & trial of friendship & affection. I feel as much love, for those I did love, now as then. I know no differ- ence, but either the affection of others for me was not so strong as mine for them, or, that we are differently constituted, has caused great differ- ence in the *demonstration* on their part. I hope however, all will yet be well with all of us.

I imagine you in your office with Laura, Tip & Beulah—and very earnestly want to join you. My room here is off in a wing with a colinade between it & the main building, so that I enjoy full quiet. Emy has been quite ill the greater part of the winter, for 6 weeks we thought she would fall into rapid consumption. She is however recovering tho not yet able to go to school. She is a peculiar child. Reads Burns' poetry with as much Avidity as I would. I fear she is too much like you & I to be as happy as Nan generally is. I have to write to Nan & Tate besides other letters—so remembering Emmie's love to you dear Belle—your friend,

E. P.

When I know I can come & at what time I will write you immediately as I shall want to go out. My purse or inclination will not bear *many* days sojourn at the Gayoso[11] [Hotel] and I don't suppose I can hire a conveyance.

From Sue A. Bryan

Pontotoc Co.—Miss March 9th 64

My dear Belle

As it seems to be your good fortune to be the benefactress of the Soldiers in general I have a very great favor to beg in behalf of a noble hearted young Missourian it is impossible for him to hear from his home, or to let his Mother hear from him. He & two of his brothers

---

11. The Gayoso House in Memphis was one of the finest hotels in the South. Built to overlook the Mississippi River, it was completed in 1844. Young, *Memphis*, 85.

came with Genl Price to this state. Both his brothers are dead & his parents think that he too may be dead. Will you kindly arrange to have this letter which Major Allen [Allin] will give you mailed for me. And have the Post Office watched for one directed to me. And whenever there is a chance send it on & I will forward it. Do dear Belle do it if you please. You will have to furnish a stamp for which I will be greatly obliged. Mollie [Mary Anderson] & the children were well a day or two since. Give my regards to your Father, Tate & all if they are at home. Tell Betty Mother is very greatly obliged to her for the coffee she sent & will not soon forget her for it. She often talks of how kindly Betty used to nurse her, and sends this poor lone dollar in Greenback all she has and says she wants the worth of it in Coffee also, sent by the first chance. Her health is very feeble and she is very childish at times about her coffee. I am in haste as Maj Allin waits.

Your friend Sue A. Bryan

Kindness of Maj Allin

From Thomas Henderson

Oxford Mch 24, 1864—

Dear Miss Belle,

Your package & letter & also Mrs D.'s letter came safely to hand & shall be forw. by first opportunity, we have no mail facilities as far as Mobile now. I cant learn where Capt George [Dashiell] is, heard that he did not accompany Genl. F. I sent you one Southern paper by Mr. Pope, and two old ones now, all I have seen since I left Panola. I have no reliable southern news. I spent a day last week with Capt Sam & his good wife & children. She is delighted with the selections you kind Ladies have made for her & family & tryes to express her gratitude in accompanying letter to Miss Joe, in which she sends a few more orders. I fear we Hendersons, & Scouts are giving you all too much trouble, will have to take some one of us for pay. I for *one* am ready to reciprocate or pay up anyway in my power. Call on Mr Harbert for the money to pay for articles ordered. Lt McC. is up with Genl. F.[12] Hope and believe with his ten men will do good service. Again let me thank you for the

---

12. Lieutenant McConnell's part in the capture of Union City was acknowledged by Forrest. Mrs. W. M. McConnell to J. A. Clark, 18 Jan. 1917, CC; Jordan and Pryor, *Campaigns*, 409.

many papers sent. Genl. McC.[13] report is really good. With kind regards to yr. Father & all the family I am

Yr true friend, Thos Henderson

From Major T. Price

Selma Ala March 30th 1864

Miss Bell Edmonson

My dear friend; your very kind & welcomed favor of the 10 Inst was received a few days ago with enclosures to Dr Leonard & [*left blank*], which were delivered, & *forwarded* as directed. I assure you a letter never was received in a more opportune moment than was yours, for I don't think I was ever before more *thirsty* & *hungry*, for a letter than I was when yours came to hand. A thousand thanks for your efforts to hear from my wife on my account, though I am happy to be able to say to you that I have been more fortunate than you as I have received ½ doz letters from home within the last two months by flag of truce. My wife has been confined to her bed for six weeks with inflamatory rheumatism & was hobbling about on crutches when last I heard from her which was about a month ago. I am glad you did not send the ring & *other* things, hope you will just keep them until you get a first rate chance by some *reliable* person going through to St. Louis and then you can send them to Mr J B Semoine with [illegible] instructions to forward by *safe* hands from St. Louis to my wife. I am glad you wrote me about Mrs Dr Scott, I will write word to the Dr about her safe arrival at Memphis.

I have had some success in matters about which I told you and expect to accomplish more soon and know that I have your good wishes.

I hope you will remember me kindly to Miss Annie Perdue. I intend to write her soon—tell her that her friend Harry in the Trans Miss Dept was well when last heard from. I wish you had written me something about the note you sent me to be forwarded, I took it in person to the office immediately after it was received. So I wish I had some news to write you, but I am writing in great haste & with my mind full of business, and altogether I am well aware of the fact that I am writing a very uninteresting letter. We have no news here, every body, and everything buoyant & hopeful, all our armies in fine condition & spirits & we expect a glorious campaign this summer & spring & *perhaps* the end of the

13. A reference to Colonel McCulloch who was in temporary command after Forrest relieved Chalmers. McCulloch was never promoted to general. Henry, *Forrest*, 236.

war within the present year. I am a candidate for congress with Mr. [illegible] with good chance for election. If you see any of McCulloughs [McCulloch's] men make them promise to vote for me. Write soon & believe me very truly your friend

Thos H Price

From Thomas H. Price

Selma Ala April 5th 1864

Miss Bell
Dear Friend

I have the time to write you only a word by Mrs Flaherty who starts in a few minutes. I send a letter to Miss Annie [Perdue] which I wrote last night in answer to one just received from her. I did not know when I was writing it that I would have an opportunity so soon to send it. I wrote you about a week ago. No news here. Every body in good spirits & looking for active times in a military way very soon & if we can keep up our good fortune for a short time we think we will soon have peace. I heard Maj Hunt say a day or two ago that your Brother Jimmy had sailed safely from Wilmington & was by this time in Europe, he has received letters from Nassau is my understanding. Write me by first opportunity. Miss Annie said that a friend of hers would leave for St Louis in a few days by whom my package could be sent & that she would attend it &c in connection with you.

May God bless & protect you

Believe me very truly yours
in great haste Thos Price

From A. Curtis

New York Apl 1864

Miss Belle Edmondson
  Memphis   Tenn

It is now some 3 months since I recd a short note from a lady friend, Mrs. M. A. Van Hook of Selma, Ala. formerly of Columbus Miss, forwarded I presume through your hands, and to whom I was [illegible] by her, to write you what ever I may know or hear of her sisters husband Mr Geo W Van Hook of Columbus who has been missing since July 1862, having left his home for "Nashville", and not since been heard from. I immediately took such steps to find out what I could in regard to him by writing to parties at Nashville, and by advertising in the "Herald" of this city, in the hopes that the latter might reach some parties who could give me some information about him. But up to this time

I have not a line to aid me and I have now sent to "Nashville" to have an advertisement inserted in the papers there, trusting *it* may lead to hearing something of him, but Miss Edmondson, I very greatly fear from the length of time which has elapsed since he was last seen or heard from, that we shall never *see* him more, though I will pray for his beloved wife & children's sake, that he may be heard of, and how his last hours were passed, if happily, so far as his mental or physical state it would be a melancholy gratification—if not so—it may [be] well not to know anything. I saw an old friend from Columbus, who left there in Sept last, but of course he could not tell any thing regarding him. I would write to Mrs Van Hook, or to her sister in Selma, though I can tell them nothing to relieve their anxiety, or offer them any consolation in the hour of sadness and suspense. I can but faintly realize the distress of mind and agony of heart which the poor woman must undergo, or her feelings when she looks upon her little children and thinks of him who if living is yet dead to her and then may God support her, and may she find much consolation in the knowledge that he was a firm believer in the religion, and an humble and upright follower of, his Heavenly Master. I knew him, as well as Mrs V H intimately, perhaps as well as any other person, and can speak most highly of them and both the deepest sympathy of Mrs Curtis & myself are theirs. Should I learn in the slightest of Mr. Van Hook, I will advise you, in the meantime the contents of this letter can be forwarded to them, by you, if you think best to do so, *with our best love.*

May I ask you, if I should begin to write a letter or two to some friends (including our friends) in the South if they could be forwarded by you. If so I should feel very greatly obliged as I have not had an opportunity of doing so, since I was south now 3 years since.

Apologizing to you, Miss Edmondson for the length of this letter,

I subscribe myself
Your very obt servt
A Curtis

My address is
No 298 Water St
N.Y.

From Anne Kirk Fackler

Memphis, April 17th—64

My dear Husband

I have just had an opportunity to send out a letter and as usual, eagerly embrace it. Two months have now elapsed since my return home but still not one word from you. In the past week we have received six letters from the girls, Florence, Shall, Sallie, Ella and Sallie P. and not *one* of them mentioned your name! I do not know what to think. I only feel miserable and anxious, since that terrible shock in Mobile. God and my own heart only know the feeling of isolation and desolation that has weighed my heart down. I have only given way *once*—when Hurlbut ordered me to give up my home and I thought my children would be beggars. For a while I could only shed bitter, *bitter tears,* but my self-reliance which has now become my chief characteristic, showed me that it would never do to submit tamely. I must make a vigorous effort to keep the little all that was left. I succeeded in getting a *suspension* of the order, and in the meantime have taken two Federal officers with the wife and two children of one to board with me and so, I hope, the matter is compromised. While this sentence was still hanging over me, another order was sent to deliver up the carpets belonging to Genl Williams' parlour which I of course obeyed (like any slave) and feeling sure they were *now* acquainted with every article in my posseession.[14] I did not know what trouble would come next. This was soon followed by a letter from Mrs. Barrett, demanding that I should pay *her* half of Amanda's wages, as "upon reflection" she had concluded it was not right to let her hire herself. That threw me into a new disturbance for several days for, aside from the inconvenience it would put me to, I felt indignant at the order. I concluded to pay no attention to it after telling Amanda and finding she had no idea of giving up *her* "rights". So I have once more settled down into a quiet state of existence, endeavoring to keep a good boarding house, and make "both ends meet". How I shall succeed is yet to be proved, for taking the house just as Ma had been paid up for the month left me with only $75 that I had from the other rents, to begin on and I have had to borrow $50 already. I have Dr Summers & family in the front room (having had a door cut between them for their convenience), Mr & Mrs Goodwyn in the third front & Mr Leach & Mr Triplett in the back, while Dr Irwin occupies the back parlour and I & the children the second story back room & nursery. You see I have entered into the minutia just as if you were here and interested in my arrangements. Mr. Triplett told me yesterday he would have to find another place as it was too fatiguing for him to mount three pair of steps—he gave up the room downstairs for Dr Irwin as he preferred that and *could* dictate. I find them all very agreeable and perfectly respectful, so what I felt to be a hard necessity proves rather pleasant. Although their board

14. Perhaps a reference to the custom of the Abandoned Property Department seizing belongings of absent Confederates. Hallum, *Diary,* 279–80.

amounts to $410 which would *seem* quite sufficient to defray all expenses, but the prices here now almost equal Confederate prices and I had to hire an extra servant besides giving out my wash and boarding old Uncle John and a man of Dr. Summers. Our family only numbers *twenty-two!* with the *prospect* of an addition. I suppose by this time Ella is a happy bride. I should have dearly loved to be with her on the eventful occasion and I trust she will be as happy as she deserves, which is the *best wish* I could make for the best of girls. I sent her a package of *clothes* by Mrs. Lanier who went to Mobile. I have regretted so much that I did not get some for you before the wedding. *What did* you do? I hope it will not be long before I receive one of your good long letters reassuring my doubting faith, allaying my fears and telling me all about dear Ella and other loved ones. I do need something to cheer me up—I am growing old with care. As I read the girls' letters, overflowing with mirth, happiness & excitement I envied the feelings they enjoyed and it recalled a time when I too was light hearted and happy. Besides my anxiety and distress about you, I have an ever-present trouble in seeing how Papa does. He is more dependent upon me now, than I upon him and things grow worse every day. If he made any money in that auction business no one can tell what went with it. Ma paid all house-expenses with the board she received and all that has been sent to the girls was from the money for which her house was sold—that has been exhausted now, so I have no idea where they will get any clothing. He doesn't seem to give it a thought and did not know we sent the few articles by Laura Martin. Of course Ma is unhappy and denies herself every thing. Ma & Papa are staying at Sue's until they make "other arrangements"—no one knows what they will be. I hope the girls will not leave before they recieve Ma's letter advising them to remain. They would be miserable here. We heard from John a few days since. He was in the neighborhood at Capt E's. Ma sent him some clothes, as those she sent a month since were never delivered to him—$50 lost to her. He was very well and contented. The town has been in great excitement over Forrest's raids and every preparation made to defend Memphis. The taking of Fort Pillow & the blockade for a few days raised the price of provisions enormously. We have received invitations to Jennie Lou's & Mr Fontaine's wedding—at the First Presbyterian Church, the 21st April. Capt Cook was married to a Miss Buchan (a friend of Martha Bradford) at Calvary last Thursday. Genl Hurlbut gave away the bride & had a reception for them that evening—for which occasion *the carpets* were taken. I attended Church this morning—it was crowded as usual & plenty of Yankees. H. G. Smith walked home with me. He says he intends to write Shall a long gossiping letter. Ma's from her came last evening—dated the 27th March. Sallie intimated that she intended to get married, to whom? I will see that her *dress* is sent—if he is a clever man and able to provide for her. I wish Florence & Shall would do likewise. Dr Summers has just come in & says the river is blockaded by the Rebels above & below—that looks threatening. Turner & Kirk still go to school and improve rapidly. They send much love to "Pa" and "wish he would come home." I look forward to some distant day when *perhaps* you may return and take your place as head of the family, but that *eager* hope that sustained me so long has died out and I am quietly reconciled to my lonely life. Kirk was teasing me yesterday to have a trap door cut so he could go up on the roof for pigeons and when I told him I could not afford it he said "when Pa comes and makes some money I will get him to have it cut". So they talk as if they expected great pleasure when Pa returns. God grant they may be so blest! Mr Ayres & Mr Triplett went to Grenada last week & after the latter returned Mr Ayres was thrown from his buggy and badly injured. He sent word to Mrs. A. but as she was too sick to go Laura went with Mr. Triplett in a buggy down to see him. They returned yesterday having found her Pa much better & today Mr Triplett went out in a easy carriage to bring him home. He is certainly very kind hearted. He fell in love with Laura and begs me constantly to court her for him but, of course, she doesn't reciprocate. He thinks she is *previously engaged*. Jennie Pickett has gone South with Mary Warfield Jackson. Her Mother has been very ill since she left, but is better. I saw Mrs Griffin & Martha Bradford a few days since they were very well. I intend going out there tomorrow. Ma is busy getting Josie's dress made to send by Wm Carroll[15] to Montreal this week. Mrs Carroll at last succeeded in getting a permit for him to come in and she is going with her children to join Genl C in Canada. Josie's letters show a great improvement in her writing & composition since she went there. She says Mrs Porterfield (an old friend of mine) thinks she looks *exaclty* as *I did* when at school in Nashville. It seems as though Spring was never going to smile upon us here. The wind whistles now like winter and we still keep up big fires. The children all have dreadful colds & Kirk & Cal have sores on their face and heads, showing impurity of the blood. I sent them to Dr. Bevins who prescribed Potash & a salve, which has arrested the spreading of the eruptions in three days. Turner

15. General William Carroll, 154th Tennessee Regiment, was listed as unfit for duty in November 1862. His name disappears from the pages of the *OR* after that date. List of Officers detached from the Army of Mississippi, *OR*, 20, pt. 1, 508. Before the war he had been postmaster at Memphis.

brought an excellent monthly report and a prize book for Spelling of which he is very justly proud. I find Mr & Mrs Goodwyn the kindest of friends—they are like brother and Sister more than friends and seem to feel a deep interest in all concerning me. They expect to go North this summer on a tour. The children send love. Give mine to each of my dear Sisters and brothers, and all friends. I concluded you surely could not be at Etowah as Sallie did not allude to you and you could easily have written by the same person or else you were wholly indifferent. I will endeavor to believe everything before that and still pray for your health, safety and happiness. Your affectionate wife Anne[16]

Kiss darling little Jennie for me.

From Surgeon Joseph S. Lenard

Wayside Hospital
Selma Ala
March 29th 64

My dear Miss

Allow me to thank you most sincerely for the favor you have done me in forwarding my letters, and sending answers in return. Though a rough soldier cannot probably properly express his thanks for such uninterested kindness, let me assure you that an impression is thereby made on his heart and soul which cannot be easily erased.

I gladly avail myself of your kind offer to send other letters through for me. The one to Dr. Waters I enclose with this. I have asked him to forward some money to me. Will you be so kind as to send a note with the letter telling him of the safest plan for doing so.

He is a true southern man. Mrs. Hudson is very well. Pray excuse the liberty I have taken in addressing this note to you

Very Resfly
Joseph S. Lenard
Surg Wayside Hospital

Addressed: Miss Belle Edmondson
Near Horn Lake
Fav of Mr. Greenlaw of the Escort

---

16. One can only speculate why Belle had this letter among her papers. Perhaps Mrs. Fackler gave it to Belle to send south by one of the scouts, but before that opportunity, Belle learned of Mr. Fackler's death.

From Major Thos. H. Price

ORDNANCE OFFICE
TRANS-MISSISSIPPI DEPARTMENT
Selma, Ala., April 19th
1864

Miss Bell Edmondson

My dear friend, having an opportunity to write you a line by Mr Eldridge I hasten to do so without the hope of write[ing] you any news, or say anything that will interest you. Genl Forrest is creating more excitement than any body else and I suppose you hear from him oftener than we do. Every thing is looking very cheerful down in Dixie, and evey body looking forward to big news from Richmond, in Va, in a very short time, perhaps in a week or two. I have not heard from my wife since I wrote you last, in my last letter to her I told her that you had the package (pin &c) for her & that some of these times it would come to hand all right. I hope you will write me very soon, if not before write by Mr Eldridge when he returns. All of your friends & acquaintances this way are well. I have had frequent letters from the Trans-Mississippi Dept recently all well & in good spirits and looking forward to better times soon. We are hearing glorious news from over there now, a big victory is rumored, and indeed confirmed some what through the Federal papers; but as yet we had had no particulars. I hope this hurried letter will find you well and that you will write immediately to your friend and obed servt

Thos H Price

From Mrs. Pope to Lieutenant William S. Pope

Hernando May 22nd 1864

My dearest son,

I did not write to you by Neddy because I was too busy getting up clothes for him, & repairing the delapidations in your last summer's stock which I should have done during the winter. Tilly is quite well again. Do not disturb yourself about her little illnesses they never amount to any thing. The day after Neddy left I got out some fine blue cloth for your pantaloons. I am afraid it is a little too dark, but it is pretty and good. I am at a loss what to do about it whether to try to make them or send you the cloth, am inclined to the latter as you can have them cut to fit By the same person who bought the cloth. I had a letter from your father. He seemed to be in better health, & said some thing of taking a sea voyage in the fall. We are of course quite mystified.

I think we had better try to get him out here, though how to manage it I cannot think. He has done nothing at all since I left there. He wrote to us of the death of Mrs. Holmes Louisa's aunt. She died at Louisa's house of apoplexy on a visit. A strict blockade exists now, & all communications with Memphis is Suspended. I came in from Henrietta's today, having spent Friday & Saturday nights with her. She must have a lonely dreary time there & I do not think her situation safe at all. She has no servants but Tamar & Bob both dishonest & utterly unreliable. Her brother has never taken any notice of her at all, & Martha is away teaching School in the bottom. I have never heard or seen any thing of Mrs. Jones or Miss Emma since I left their house. I shall try to go & see them this coming vacation. Mrs. Jones had a son married recently— Rufe they call him. Hernando is awfully dull to Tillie, & she wants to leave here but where else to go is the question & how to get anywhere. Our school is very small & unprofitable & the people cold & inhospitable, but I am disposed to stay. Tillie wants to go to Mobile. I never hear from my mother & sister though I sometimes hear of them. Mr. Ward and his daughters came out of Memphis last week. They say Eliza Rawlings has married a widower with grown daughters, Mr. White brother in law to the Yankee fellow she was engaged to before the war. Write as often as you can & persuade Neddy to write. I am distressed that he does not. I persuaded him to buy a pistol here as he had not a good one, & to give me the rest of his money to buy him a horse, but have not heard of one worth buying within the compass of my means without touching on your investments, which I want to keep for you too, if you can get along without it, for as you say it will do to keep & something may turn up suddenly to make you & Neddy need it. I am afraid the drawers & undershirts I sent you wont hold out long, but I shall make some more by the time they are gone. I thought you had better wear them out than have new ones yet. I have some light calico shirts now for you & shall make you some more white ones. Have you heard any thing of the fate of Miss Hudson? I feel interested in her for the sake of her civility to you. God bless & keep you, my precious darling boy, my good, dutiful affectionate son. May his grace ever keep you what you are now to your idolizing.

Mother

Tell Neddy to write to us. I am afraid he will cease to love his Mommy & sister if he does not write sometimes.[17]

17. Perhaps Belle picked up this letter for Lieutenant Pope while in Hernando. Pope's death at Brice's Cross Roads may be the reason this letter was among her papers.

From Mary Anderson [unsigned, undated fragment]

. . . I had a note from Cousin M[at] who says of course the unfortunate affair places her in an unpleasant situation, but will not affect *her intercourse* with the family and *naught* can separate she and Frazor from us. She said Mrs Perkins had just been there talked and cried all the time about Nannie, seemed *almost heart broken*, Cousin M. said if she had not *known* better she would have thought from her [illegible] representations of the case that she was a deeply wronged woman. She vows vengeance on poor Tate, says she was demented that day or she would have taken Robert, declares she will have him *yet*. Alas *alas* she has brought much *anxious* dread among us and poor Nannie I can but deeply sympathize with her in this trying position. I dont think any one could possibly condemn or think her course unavoidable. I haven't heard a [illegible] of disapprobation—We hear that Dashiell was wounded I trust if so not seriously—with a safe opportunity Jo will send his boots. Eddie Millers are here too if we can only get them to him. Be sure to enquire for Eddie and Georges *safety* they are in this glorious campaign in Virginia.[18] God grant they may be spared through it. Let me hear from all the boys. Father says tell Brother he *must* send Aunt Patsy's servants a pr of cards immediately if possible. Tell Brother Mr Banks told me he would get his Harness for him but that I made no *collection* of *money* for him as I hoped I might. Give much love to all my friends—I hope Sina liked her bonnet let me know. Much love to Hal tell her to remember her *promise* to write. If Tate, Helen & Nannie are with you much love to them and ask them to write. Tell Tate all her things I [illegible]

[Written some time between June 10, Brice's Cross Roads, and June 23, Helen's marriage.]

From Mary Anderson

Elm Ridge June 26/64

Dear Belle

According to promise I will now attempt a note to you, knowing if nothing more of interest you would love to hear from Father. The life has been truly quiet here since you all left. [illegible] looks lonely so we all felt many times in this *monstrous* quiet. Father has not been well he

18. Probably a reference to the sons of Hugh Miller of Pontotoc. They were related to the Edmondsons through Andrew Jackson Edmondson's first wife. Their mother was Jane Scott Walton's sister. Genealogy charts, EFP.

has had two or three Chills but today with many doses of Quinine has thus far kept it off. I trust he will soon be up again. Three of our scouts were here this morning Mr Rutland, Mayfield & Palmers,[19] they brought us but little news. Rutland is a nice young man. Johnny Armstrong got here Friday and brought the letters which we were glad enough to get, the first we had heard since you *all* left. Johnny looked well but poor old Gray looked *teribly*. The Yankees came out every morning last week until Friday. Monday our scouts had been gone but five minutes when they came, then Thursday they came immediately *after* the Yanks were gone. The Yanks boldly confess that Forrest whipped them *embarassingly* but some say Sturgis sold his troops to Forrest, but Father told them "not a bit of it". They did us no harm and they were of the terrible 7th Kansas.[20] Another raid has gone out. God *have* mercy upon our brave Southern boys, shield and save them. When will this dreadful scourge cease? I hope you will make sufficient apologies to Pontotoc people for my neglecting this time[,] there was nothing of *neglect* but an *iron yoke* that prevented. Tell Mrs Gordon with much love how grateful we were for the comfort [illegible] and how *grieved* to hear the Yankees had taken it from old Mr Hogenwood by the time he reached Finley *Holmes's*. I will attend to her other things as soon as possible. Remember much love to all my *friends* there.

Laura sends much love to you and says she has done all that you told her and that she is trying to behave herself—that Tippie Dora has recovered her health. The Monday after you left I undertook the *tremendous* task of cleaning the *Locked* room!! One hard days work I tell you, but t'was *accomplished* and well done by *sunset*.

I hope Helen liked her gown, although I have *heard* not *one* word to *myself* from her. Tell Mary I've written to her several times I hope she will find *some* time to *reply*. I will write to her again next week. Since writing the above I've been over to see [illegible] Tell Hal all were well & Mr Clayton gave me a letter to send to her which I have done by the Scouts, it was not from any of the family. He said tell you all if you could wait two weeks longer he would come and go with you to *Johnston's Army*, this he said on the 20th so you may know how long to wait if Mr Clayton is a *minute man* I should think you might wait very pleas-

19. John W. Rutland and John S. Mayfield. The name Palmer does not appear on the list of scouts. CC.

20. Webster Moses of the Seventh Kansas Cavalry wrote to his sweetheart: "General Sturgis is considered a Copperhead and *some think he sold* his command, all are glad he is broken while we can not very well spare the men." Webster Moses to Nancy Mowry, 12 June 1864, KHST.

antly in old Pontotoc. We are anxious to hear from you again and hope you will be prompt and write.

[unsigned]

From Helen Edmondson Crump to E. A. Edmondson

Oxford
June 28th '64

My dear friend brother:

I have promised myself the pleasure of writing to you every day since my arrival here but have put it off from time to time when I begin to think I have treated you real bad. Now Eddie I may deserve a scolding, but just defer it until you are a bride and see if you will feel like writing to anybody on any subject.

You don't know my dear brother how anxiously I looked for you to come to my marriage and with what a heavy heart I gave up the hope that you would come even at the last moment. I was so anxious to have you for one of the waiters, and then to think you my "baby brother" could not see me married. Oh! it was too much. I did all I could to get the news to you, sent a dispatch, also a message but I know you did not get the news or you would have come.

We were married at Aunt Mary Gordon's and oh! such a nice time we did have. Only a few friends but enough to make it pleasant. I would write you a full description of the whole affair but I know Tate and Nannie will tell you or if you don't see them Maj Crump will.

I had anticipated a most delightful time while Maj C.'s "leave" lasted, but yesterday he received an order from old Genl Forrest for him to report immediately and he starts this evening for Pontotoc. Now this is the blighting of many bright dreams for the remainder of the time his "leave" lasted. And I don't know what I am to do, for although I am very, *very* pleasantly situated, I know I shall miss my husband and be extremely lonely. Eddie please come over and see me as soon as you can. I do want to see you so much and since I was so disappointed about your coming to my marriage my desire has doubly increased.

I hope you will see a great deal of Nannie and Tate this summer. I don't of course expect you can get a very long "leave of absence", to come over and see me but I want you to be with them.

Eddie, I hope you will be a great deal with Maj Crump and like him very much, if such a thing is done by gentleman. I hope you will love him. He has a good, big noble heart, and full of affection for your "baby sister". He is just as kind as he can be, and every word, every action, speaks of the deep and abiding love he has for me. When you *know* him you will be obliged to love him. He has but a few hours more to stay with me and I know you will excuse this short letter, and think I am perfectly right to stop writing and go talk with him. Goodbye my dear sweet brother. I hope we will soon be together again for a short time anyhow. Write to me often please. God bless you and keep you from harm and temptation. Goodbye once more.

Your own loving sister
Helen

From Helen Edmondson Crump

Dear Belle,

I have but a few minutes to write, but Maj Crump will write when he gets to Tupelo. I only write to ask you to get from William Hunt or tell Decatur to do it, out of Jimmie's papers, the diamond ring he gave me. Hal can tell you what kind of box the ring is in. Please attend to this and send it to me as soon as you can. I will write to you in a few days perhaps to morrow and write a long letter.

Best love to Hal & Tate. Write to me soon

Your loving sister
Helen

Oxford
June 29th

From Major Brodie Crump

Verona, Miss. July 1st 1864

My dear sister

Doubtless you will be much astonished to hear that I am at Verona,[21] so soon after parting with you en-route for Oxford; but I am here, "is a sad reality" and it will be some time I fear before I can see Helen again.

Tuesday just before dinner Helen & I were in our room writing to Elm Ridge when Mrs Goodman called out "come down here, I have news for you" and it was "By Genl Forrest's order you must report at once" JR Chalmers &c. I telegraphed him to try and get me off & let me know result, but he failed and I had to come. Andrew Mills & I started 11 o'clock Wednesday night took dinner at Judge Kilpatricks yesterday and have just got here this morning. I feeling rather mad & ill-tempered, at being ordered away from my precious darling wife, before the expiration of my furlough, so if my letter is not every thing it should be, please make all due allowances for it.

---

21. Verona, Mississippi, a small village on the Mobile and Ohio Railroad, about five miles south of Tupelo. Rowland, *Mississippi*, 2:856.

I left Helen at Mrs Goodman's in Oxford, and very much pleased with her, & as snugly fixed up as possible, which was a source of great comfort to me, feeling she was with a friend during my absence; which of course will be nearly all the time. You saw our vehicle & train the morning we parted with you, so it will not surprise you that we were until 2 ½ o'clock PM Sunday getting to Oxford. We never could get up a trot for on level ground the old horses couldn't do it, and going down hill we were afraid the old horses would fall down if they struck a trot, so we made them walk. Altogether it was the gayest bridal tour, I reckon, that ever has been made in these Confederate States, or "any other" and I intend to get Dr Barnett of our staff to draw a series of illustrations of it, entitled the "Bridal Tour of the guerills" and I'll show it to you.

Helen had heard nothing further from Elm Ridge since the 18th which you saw at Mrs Gordons, but I reckon she has by this time, and I will write you again as soon as I hear through her from Joanna & your father, telling you all in her letter about them, and you must keep me posted as to your whereabouts and write me every time you feel like it or have the time, and I'll try to interest you with all the army news. I am going to see Tate this evening and will not close this letter until I see her. Mary Kilpatrick & the children started from home yesterday morning and their father said they were a very gay party indeed.

I never was as thunderstruck in my life when I was ordered back here, not married a week! and half of my furlough still left! but for Helen's sake I tried to put a good face on it, and told her it must be some thing very important; but it seems that Genl Chalmers unwittingly brought it about in this way. The Brigade Commissary who was to act in my place was detained behind one day & the Genl telegraphed up to Tupelo asking that Capt Mason[22] be temporarily ordered to report to him, whereupon Genl Forrest who was afflicted with boils and in a furious way generally, telegraphed back "order Maj Crump back immediately" and so it was done and miserable "man that I am", I had to start the next day. As soon as I found out how it was I felt that "I was sold" most completely and all by an error, for Genl C was very much chagrined that he should have been the cause of it; for the very next day the man who was to represent me came in, and I was no longer needed, but Genl Forrest "had ordered it & no one dared to say nay". It is very doubtful when I can get another furlough or rather the remainder of my wedding one, and I will try to bring Helen over here on a short visit if the army

22. Major R. M. Mason, quartermaster, Forrest's staff. Jordan and Pryor, *Campaigns*, 689.

dont move us away from here, & then I want to know what Tate intends doing—

Write soon to Care Genl Chalmers HdQrs

Truly Your Brother

Brodie

From Helen Edmondson Crump

Oxford

June 30th 1864

My dear Belle:

From the very formidable size of the paper I expect you will take fright at it and run away and not read your letter. You will think I am going to talk "bride talk" tell you how extremely happy I am, how much in love, what a good husband I have got that he is better than any body else and finally wind up by saying I would die if I couldn't have him. I am not going to write of any such stuff, for it will not please any body but Maj Crump and my self. I am only going to write a family letter, and thought this size would look more sociable and home like than a smaller size sheet.

Belle don't you think Genl Forrest sent a dispatch, (an order) here day before yesterday for Maj Crump to report at Hd Qrts immediately and he left as soon as he could make his arrangements. Now I think it was too much. His "leave of absence" was only half gone and had been granted by Genl [Stephen D.] Lee too. But never mind this is only one of the many troubles we poor "military widows," have to put up with, and I shall be satisfied if this is my worst. He had intended to write to you every day since we got here, but being a "young blushing bride" he could not "screw up" his courage. No I ought to be ashamed to talk that way, when I know it was business that kept him from writing. But the last thing he promised was, that he would write to you as soon as he got to H'd Qrts. I sent you a short note by him to forward you and for fear it will not reach you, I send my order here, I want you to go to W. R. Hunts and get out of Jimmie's papers that diamond ring he gave me and please send it to me as soon as you can. Decatur can tell you whether the papers are in Selma or Lagrange [Georgia] (I think Selma tho') and Hal can tell you what kind of a box it is in. Please attend to it for me if you can.

Belle I asked Maj Crump about Sissie Cox and he says she did have a baby and what was more he was there the night it was born, but that he did not know it for sometime afterwards. I think I shall call him "Granny Crump" hereafter when I see him. Don't you remember how

Sister Mary and I teazed you and Eddie for going to the "cow borning"? Well I think this is another clear case of "grannyship."

I have not heard another word from home since I saw you except one of the scouts said only three Yankees had been on a raid & taken breakfast at "Elm Ridge" for three or four mornings. Mr Wilson is the only one of the scouts that has called as yet and he only once. I went over to see Capt Henderson the morning after I got here and after that he sent me some papers, and that is the sum toto of my communication with the scouts.

I am invited this evening to go around to Mrs Barrs, and take tea with a few friends. I expect a nice time but fear I shall feel quite lonely without my Maj to encourage and help me along, when I get embarassed.

He gave me a splendid riding horse for a bridal present and we had two mighty nice pleasant rides.

Have you heard from Eddie and where was the poor dear boy all the time I was hunting him? I do hope he will get off so he can come over and see me.

I am very pleasantly situated indeed much more so than I expected. But Mrs Goodman is so kind and agreeable that [illegible]

I have written two long letters this morning and have another to write and I know under the circumstances, you will excuse me from writing any more.

Give my best love to Hal and tell her to please write to me soon. I shall look for the letter. Remember me to all my friends you meet in the Army. Accept a large share of my love for yourself and do please write soon to

Your devoted sister
Helen L. Crump

Miss Belle Edmondson
Care = R. W. Edmondson
Columbus, Miss
Please forward if necessary & oblige—Helen C.

From Andrew Jackson Edmondson to E. A. Edmondson

10 July 1864

My Dear Son

I received yours by Mr McMahon some days since but felt so unwell & dissatisfied with the way things have been going on for some time that I could not write. I got a letter from Mr Kil[patrick] a day or two since and he praised you so much that I am forced to write unprepared as I am to write all I wish to say. My health has not been good since you were at home but am now I hope on rising ground that will be permanent. We have to thank P Miller[23] that we have a shelter to cover us as Mrs P [Perkins] met him on her way to Gen Washburn the day after she was here [May 31] for a Guard to come out & destroy everything we had. He prevailed on her to wait & think what she was doing so she has gone home without doing any thing. I have been so harassed about that affair that it almost makes me sick to hear the name of Perkins. I may get over it after while. My Son you appear to have the blues too in relation to being turned out of your position[24] as I dont know enough of the course that such things take these times I cant say any thing in relation to it only I hope if you have been wrongfully treated it will not cause you to forget your duty to your Country whose Soldier you are & I think the private is the most honorable position in the Army & it gratifies me more to hear of your doing your duty in that position than any to which you could be called to fill but I hope I would be Proud of you in any position. If Jimmy has written me any letter since he left I have not received it. Mat [Martha Titus] got a letter from him at Liverpool and dated Sixth of June he was low spirited & we need not be surprised if he came home with out doing any thing. Bob Moon had just got there the day before he wrote had left his [wife] at her fathers & been spending his time in Canada. I knew when he went with Jimmy who would have the work to do. Enough of this however. I never wanted him to go into the thing & would not be Sorry for it to fail. We are having a pretty hard time here old Washburn is pretty hard on the Secesh has proposed 40 of them to travel on the Cars as Guarnity [guaranty?].[25] We still manage to get Something to eat but are very lonesome since the Children left. Our crop prospects good needing rain. All are well & the darkies behaving as usual Joe [Joanna] fixing to make you a Suit of Jean [jeans]. I dont know that I have any thing else to write that would interest you. May the blessing of heaven be with you & protect you in all your danger.

Your affectionate father
And J. Edmondson

23. Probably Pitser Miller.

24. E. A. Edmondson was listed as a lieutenant on Forrest's muster book as of 22 Mar. 1864. General Forrest's Muster Book 1861–1864, original copy, CC. It was a common practice to allow the men to elect their own officers. Randall and Donald, *Civil War*, 326.

25. As a result of attacks on the trains along the Memphis and Charleston Railroad, General Washburn ordered forty of the most prominent secessionists placed in exposed positions on the trains. *The Memphis Bulletin*, 7 July 1864.

From E. A. Edmondson

In Camp Verona Miss
July 16th 1864

Dear Bell

I left the front yesterday evening after all the fighting, for the day, was over and came to Tupelo, almost dead with fatigue & hunger & thirst, and this morning came to this place as everybody said there would be no more fighting, that the yankees were retreating, rapidly towards Ripley & we would be unable to catch them.—And my horse was completely riden down so I limbered to the rear.

Our fight up here was not so successful as we hoped. But *Lt Genl* Lee is blamed with all.[26] As for myself I think him the most complete *humbug* we have in Genl's Uniform. I do believe if Genl Forrest had had command he would have whipped those Yankees well, but as it was I think we lost in the operation a great many good and brave soldiers. It was poorly planned and badly executed (as well) affair as any since the war. I have never [seen] Forrest's Cavalry so badly cut up in my career. No more you will hear it all in time—for I have some business for you to attend to. I am just as dirty as if you had taken me and rolled me in the dirt for a half a day, and I want you to send me some clean clothes and my jacket that is at Brothers. I have clothes on that I have worn since I saw you all last. I would like for you to send me some by the first opportunity. There will be some one coming up that you can send by, I mean that Jacket and some shirts.

I am not well to day and would I think feel better if I had some clean clothing, to take a bath and put on.

Tell Miss Hal that Capt Ferd & Frank were all right on day before yesterday, I saw them. Give her my best Love as also Tate & the children. With much Love for yourself

I remain most Affectionately
Your Brother
E A Edmondson

send those things to Genl Chalmers Hd Qrs.

From Theresa Blennerhasset

Columbus July 26 [1864]

Dear Belle

Your note has just been handed me, your *sister, Hal & Nannie* left here this morning—Robert had a slight attack of croup which prevented

---

26. Conflicting opinions exist about which general was at fault at Harrisburg/Tupelo. For more information, see John W. Morton Scrapbooks, CC.

their starting yesterday morning as they intended—this morning however he was well enough [illegible] I was there before they left. They
were all invited to Mrs. Weavers last night and went—there were only
[illegible] other young ladies asked—I too had an invitation but did not
go. Hal told me this morning she had received a note from Lou Young
yesterday—I believe it contained nothing more than a pressing invitation for her to return and stay there until she went home. She went
home with your sister this morning. I have heard nothing myself from
Lou or any of them and have formed no plans for going out unless something unforseen occurs after you come in I doubt if this visit will be
made. I have heard nothing from Lucy Harris. I suppose she would
send me word before going [illegible] of course when you are so close
by, would not go unless you were here to go with me. I hope after you
come in we may be able to go. [illegible] Helen Goffe and I went to see
Mrs Forrest yesterday. We had the pleasure of seeing the Genl too, he
says he suffers a great deal from his wound but hopes to be able to join
his soldiers next Monday. The only military news is that the Yankees
are near enough I think to throw shells in. Gen Price Yankee dispatches
say has gone into Missouri with 51,000 men.[27] Gen [illegible] has been
sent over here. I will take [illegible] of them for you. I send you two
letters, one from Shallie that was entrusted to me with a short note. She
did not leave Selma until last Saturday. Belle please dont talk of going
home so soon. I am anxious now that Mrs. [illegible] is not going with
you to her sisters [illegible] I am afraid if you go home as you speak . . .

[unsigned fragment]

From Shallie Kirk

Selma July 22nd/64

My dearest Bell,
   At last I have heard where you are to be found, and hasten to answer
your *most welcome* letter, which was received more than a week ago,
having been a long time on the way. You cannot imagine how delighted
I was to hear from you again, for I was very much afraid the Yankees
had carried out their threat of sending you to Alton. I had a hearty laugh
over Nannie's escape from her Ma. I am so glad she got away. Now Bell
tell me what you have done with my trunk you wrote that you would
send it—to Mobile to Mr Jones, he had left there for the neighborhood

27. A rumor. Price had been seeking permission to cross from Arkansas into Missouri with an expedition. It was late August before his campaign began. Castel, *Price*,
199–203.

of Memphis taking Mollie & the girls, so I wrote to a gentleman there to get it out of the express office & send it to me at Marion did not answer, I telegraphed but again received no answer, I then went to the express office here & got them to telegraph the office in Mobile, the response was, 'no trunk here'. I leave tomorrow with Mrs Hudson for Memphis, and if you have not sent the trunk yet, send it to Fannie Molloy at Marion Ala; she will keep our things & pay Mr Jones, & will know what to do with the others; I hope they are not lost. I have been in Selma bout a week waiting for that trunk before starting, as I wanted to dispose of the things, & get the money to take home with me. I left Marion with Ed, to go to Macon Ga, on a visit to him there; but when I reached here Mrs Hudson begged me to say, & go with her to Memphis; & as I was anxious to get there I complied. Mr Jones expected me to stay at Marion until he could return, & he would then take me, but I thought I would surprise them all by getting there almost as soon as they do. I suppose you are with Theresa! How is the little girl? tell her I would give a great deal to see her before I go in, & I am nearly crazy to see you! why didn't you come to Marion, instead of stopping at Columbus? You know Lou & I both want to see you. I looked for Lou down this morning, but she hasn't come, I feel really disappointed. I dont know how I will get along without you at home. Bell make haste & come back, old Hurlbut has gone, & there will be no danger now. & I do *want* to see you *so much!* I have a thousand things to tell you, that I can't write; meet me some where on the way, I go by Meridian, Jackson & Canton. Can't you get to one of those places as soon as I do? Please! Give my best love to Mrs Dashiell, Nannie & Hal; I must close, but not because I have nothing more to say, but, because I have so much. I can't write it all, & so won't attempt it. Good bye dearest Bell, come home soon; Mr Hudson is hurrying me to stop & eat a watermellon. My love to Theresa & her sister. I will enclose this letter to her so that you may certainly get it. You ought to go & see Fannie, she is so anxious to see you. Well good bye as———I was called down in the Parlor just now to see a lady, & who should it be but old Lou & her Pa. They have just left after spending several hours with me. One of my sweethearts that I caught in Marion also came to say good bye, & concluded to remain & go part of the way with me tomorrow. Maj Price has just left came to say good bye & bring some letters, one to you which he insists on my *taking* to you, as he says I will be certain to see you before I get home. If I do not, I will mail it at Canton. Can't you telegraph me at Canton & tell me what you did with my trunk? I will be there Tuesday. I wish you would

[letter ends, no signature]

From Tate Dashiell

[ca. August 14, 1864]

Dear Belle

We got a dispatch from Maj Rambaut this morning to meet them today at Artesia to go to Macon but too late to leave on the train so we will not leave until in the morning. John [Titus] is here with ambulance and if he don't leave this evening wil send him out and you can use your own pleasure as to whether you come in. I don't know what our chances are to get a place in Macon, and if you had rather and are pleasantly situated you can stay with Miss Lou till we start home. I don't know until this raid passes when we will go. I have not had a line from home since I saw you but heard through brother that Mrs P[erkins] had been out again with a squad of Yankees and made her threats. I think it will be best if you don't go home. Father is in so much trouble. Nannie is going back to her [Mother] for she says she can't stand to see us suffer *so* much for her. If John don't have to leave I will send him out but that will be my only chance. You can act as you think best about joining in [illegible]. I am under many obligations for my [illegible]. You must not think anything of it if John is [illegible] for everything is in confusion with us. He has all the horses, negroes, ambulances, [illegible] under his care and may have to leave this evening and it is the only chance to send. The children are better this morning.

Your loving sister Tate

Love to the Ladies and thanks for their kindness to you.

Bibliography

I. MANUSCRIPTS

Privately Held Manuscripts
Edmondson Family Papers
Perkins Family Papers
Frazor Titus Diary for 1864

Official Mansucripts (National Archives, Washington, DC)
General Records, Department of the Treasury (RG56)
War Department, Cartographic Records (RG 77)
War Department, Collection of Confederate Records (RG 109)
War Department, Records of the Provost Marshall General: Citizens
    File; Scouts; Guides; Spies (RG 110)
Treasury Department, Special Agencies (RG 366)
Cartographic Department, Department of the Gulf (RG 393)

Other Manuscripts
John Houston Bills, Robert Hancock Wood and Marshall Tate Polk Papers, Tennessee State Library and Archives, Nashville, Tennessee
Maude Morrow Brown Papers, Mississippi Department of Archives and History, Jackson, MS
Stephen A. Brown Collection, Special Collections, Mississippi State University, Starkville, MS
George Cadman Papers, Southern Historical Collection, University of North Carolina, Chapel Hill, NC
Civil Register, State of Alabama, Alabama Department of Archives and History, Montgomery, AL
Confederate Collection, Tennessee State Library and Archives, Nashville, TN
Jefferson Davis Collection, Filson Club, Louisville, KY
Jefferson Davis Papers, Nannie Mays Crump Collection, Library of Congress, Washington, DC
Jefferson Davis Papers, Special Collections, University of Alabama, Tuscaloosa, AL

Lyman C. Draper Notebooks and Correspondence, Wisconsin Historical Society, Madison, WI

Belle Edmondson Diary for 1864, Southern Historical Collection, University of North Carolina, Chapel Hill, NC

Edward Fontaine Papers, Special Collections, Mississippi State University, Starkville, MS

Franklin Female College Catalogue, Mississippi Department of Archives and History, Jackson, MS

Benjamin H. Grierson Papers, Illinois State Historical Library, Springfield, IL

James Hamner Letters, Special Collections, Memphis State University, Memphis, TN

Andrew Hickenlooper Collection, Cincinnati Historical Society Cincinnati, OH

H. H. Huhn, "Biographical Notes" Scrapbook, Local History Room, Memphis and Shelby County Public Library, Memphis, TN

John Merrilees Collection, Chicago Historical Society, Chicago, Il

Webster Moses Papers, Kansas State Historical Society, Topeka, KS

Necrology Scrapbooks, Missouri Historical Society, St. Louis, MO

Thompson-Pound Papers, Special Collections, Mississippi State University, Starkville, MS

Martha Titus Diary—1873, Special Collections, Memphis State University, Memphis, TN

Waverley Collection, Special Collections, Mississippi State University, Starkville, MS

II. GOVERNMENT PUBLICATIONS

U.S. Congress, House of Representatives, "Expenditures from the Chickasaw Fund," H.R. 65, 27th Cong., 3rd sess., 1843.

The Official Military Atlas of the Civil War, comp. by Calvin O. Cowles. Washington: Government Printing Office, 1891–1895.

U.S. Navy Department, *Official Records of the Union and Confederate Navies in the War of the Rebellion* 30 vols. Washington: Government Printing Office, 1894–1922.

U.S. War Deaprtment, *The War of the Rebellion: A Compilation of the Official Records of the Union and Confederate Armies* 130 vols. Washington: Government Printing Office, 1880–1901.

III. NEWSPAPERS

Memphis Daily Appeal, 1863–1864

Memphis Bulletin, 1863–1864

Memphis Commercial Appeal, 1933–1934
Memphis Press Scimitar, 1937

IV. UNPUBLISHED MATERIAL

Bristow, Eugene Kerr. "Look Out for Saturday Night: A Social History of Professional Variety Theater in Memphis, Tennessee, 1859–1880." Ph.D. dissertation, University of Iowa, 1956.

Dinges, Bruce J. "Making of a Cavalryman: Benjamin H. Grierson and the Civil War Along the Mississippi, 1861–1865." Ph.D. dissertation, Rice University, 1978.

Chisman, Margaret Sue. "Literature and the Drama in Memphis, Tennessee to 1860." M.A. thesis, Duke University, 1942.

Farrow, Kathryn. "Nonconnah Bottoms: Reminiscences and Legends," Local History Room, Memphis and Shelby County Library, Memphis, TN.

Furtell, Robert F. "Federal Trade with the Confederate States, 1861–1865, A Study of Government Policy." Ph.D. dissertation, Vanderbilt University, 1950.

Hamilton, William Baskerville. "Holly Springs, Mississippi to the year 1878." M.A. thesis, University of Mississippi, 1931.

Hooper, Ernest Walter. "Memphis, Tennessee: Federal Occupation and Reconstruction, 1862–1870." Ph.D. dissertation, University of North Carolina, 1957.

Johnson, Cary. "Life Within the Federal Lines as Depicted in the War-Time Journal of a Mississippi Girl." M.A. thesis, Louisiana State Univeristy,1929.

Lash, Jeffrey Norman. "Stephen Augustus Hurlbut: A Military and Diplomatic Politician." Ph.D. dissertation, Kent State University, 1980.

V. BOOKS

Aaron, Daniel, *The Unwritten War: American Writers and the Civil War.* New York: Knopf, 1973.

Adams, G. W. *Doctors in Blue.* New York: Henry Schuman, 1970

Anderson, Ephraim M. *Memoirs: Historic and Personal, Including the Campaigns of the First Missouri Confederate Brigade.* St. Louis: *Times Printing Co.*, 1869.

Atkinson, James R. and Jack D. Elliott, Jr. *A Cultural Resources Survey of Selected Construction Areas in the Tennessee-Tombigee Waterway: Alabama and Mississippi.* Mississippi State: Department of Anthropology, 1978.

Bakeless, John. *Spies of the Confederacy.* Philadelphia: John B. Lippincott Co., 1970.

Baldwin, Joseph C. *The Flush Times of Alabama and Mississippi.* San Francisco: Sumner Whitney and Co., 1883.

Bayard, Samuel J. *The Life of George Dashiell Bayard.* New York: Putnams, 1874.

Bearss, Edwin C. *Decision in Mississippi.* Jackson: Mississippi Commission on the War Between the States, 1962.

Bettersworth, John K. *Confederate Mississippi: The People and Policies of a Cotton State in Wartime.* Baton Rouge: Louisiana State University Press, 1943.

Bevier, Robert S. *History of the First and Second Missouri Confederate Brigades.* St. Louis: Bryan, Brand & Co., 1879.

Biographical and Historic Memoirs of Mississipi. 2 vols. Chicago: Goodspeed Publishing Company, 1891.

Black's Medical Dictionary. 35th ed. 1987.

Black, Robert C. *Railroads of the Confederacy.* Chapel Hill: University of North Carolina Press, 1952.

Bowman, John S., ed. *The Civil War Almanac.* New York: World Almanac Publications, 1983.

Boyd, Belle. *Belle Boyd in Camp and Prison.* Ed. Curtis Carroll Davis. New York: Thomas Yoseloff, 1968.

Brown, Maude Morrow. *The University Grays.* Richmond: Garrett and Massie, 1940.

Buck, Irving A. *Cleburne and His Command.* Ed. Thomas Robson Hay, 2nd. ed. Jackson, Tennessee: McCowat-Mercer Press, 1959.

Cadwallader, Sylvanus. *Three Years With Grant.* New York: Knopf, 1955

Capers, Gerald M. *The Biography of a River Town: Memphis, Its Heroic Age.* Chapel Hill: University of North Carolina Press, 1939.

Carter, Hodding. "A Proud Struggle for Grace." Thomas C. Wheeler, ed. *Vanishing America, Twelve Regional Towns.* New York: Holt Rinehart and Winston, 1964.

Carter, Samuel. *The Final Fortress: The Campaign for Vicksburg, 1862–1863.* New York: St. Martin's Press, 1980.

Cash, William M. and Lucy Sommerville Howorth, eds. *My Dear Nellie: The Civil War Letters of William L. Nugent to Eleanor Smith Nugent.* Jackson: University Press of Mississippi, 1977.

Castel, Albert. *General Sterling Price and the Civil War in the West.* Baton Rouge: Louisiana State University Press, 1968.

Clark, Thomas D. *A Pioneer Southern Railroad: From New Orleans to Cairo.* Chapel Hill: University of North Carolina Press, 1936.

Cogley, Thomas S. *History of the Seventh Indiana Cavalry.* LaPorte, Ind.: Herald Company Printers, 1976.

Connelly, Thomas L. *Army of the Heartland: The Army of Tennessee, 1861–1862.* Baton Rouge: Louisiana State University Press, 1967.

———. *Autumn of Glory: The Army of Tennessee, 1862–1865.* Baton Rouge: Louisiana State University Press, 1971.

———. *Civil War Tennessee: Battles and Leaders.* Knoxville: The University of Tennessee Press, 1979.

Coppock, Paul. *Memphis Sketches.* Memphis: Friends of Memphis and Shelby County Libraries, 1976.

Corliss, J. Carlton. *Main Line of Mid-America: The Story of the Illinois Central Railroad.* New York: Creative Press, 1950.

Courtwright, David T. *Dark Paradise, Opium Addiction in America Before 1940.* Cambridge, Mass.: Harvard University Press, 1982.

Crocker, Mary Wallace. *Historic Architecture in Mississippi.* Jackson: University Press of Mississippi, 1973.

Cunningham, H. H. *Doctors in Gray: The Confederate Medical Service.* Gloucester, Mass.: Peter Smith, 1970.

Dana, Charles A. *Recollections of the Civil War.* New York: D. Appleton and Co., 1902.

Daniel, R. E. *Recollections of a Rebel Surgeon.* Austin: Von Boeckman, Schultze & Co., 1899.

Daniels, Jonathan. *Prince of Carpetbaggers.* Philadelphia: J. B. Lippincott Company, 1958.

Davis, Reuben. *Recollections of Mississipi and Mississippians.* Boston: Houghton, Mifflin & Co., 1890.

Dinkins, James. *Personal Recollections and Experiences in the Confederate Army.* Cincinnati: Robert Clark Co., 1897; reprint ed., Dayton, Ohio: Press of Morningside Bookshop, 1975.

Dorlund's Illustrated Medical Dictionary. 26th ed. Philadelphia: W. B. Saunders Company, 1951.

Downing, Alexander C. *Downing's Civil War Diary.* Edited by Olynthus B. Clark. Des Moines: the Historical Department of Iowa, 1913.

Dugan, James. *History of Hurlbut's Fighting Fourth Division.* Cincinnati: E. Morgan Co., 1863.

Elam, Charlotte E., Margaret I. Ericksen and Ruth H. Wyckoff. *Gravestones Inscriptions From Shelby County, Tennessee Cemeteries.* Memphis: Milestone Press, 1971.

Evans, Augusta Jane [Wilson]. *Macaria.* Richmond, Va.: West and Johnson, 1864.

Faulkner, John. *My Brother Bill.* New York: Trident Press, 1963.

Fidler, William Perry. *Augusta Jane Evans*. University: University of Alabama Press, 1951.

Folmar, John Kent, ed. *From That Terrible Field: Civil War Letters of James M. Williams*. University: University of Alabama Press, 1981.

Foote, Shelby. *The Civil War: A Narrative*, 3 vols. New York: Random House, 1974.

Fox-Genovese, Elizabeth. *Within the Plantation Household: Black and White Women of the Old South*. Chapel Hill: University of North Carolina Press, 1988.

Furness, Clifton Joseph. *The Genteel Female*. New York: Knopf, 1931.

Gailor, Thomas Frank. *Some Memories*. Kingsport, Tenn.: Southern Publishing Inc., 1937.

Gottschalk, Louis Moreau. *Notes of a Pianist*. Edited by Jeanne Behrend. New York: Knopf, 1964.

Graf, Leroy P. and Ralph Haskins, eds. *The Papers of Andrew Johnson*. 7 vols. Knoxville: The University of Tennessee Press, 1967–.

Grant, Ulysses S. *Personal Memoirs of U. S. Grant*. 2 vols. New York: Charles L. Webster & Company, 1892.

Hall, William K. *Descendants of Nicholas Perkins of Virginia*. Ann Arbor: Edwards Brothers, Inc., 1957.

Hallum, John. *Diary of An Old Lawyer: Scenes behind the Curtain*. Nashville: Southwestern Publishing House, 1895.

———. *Reminiscences of the Civil War*. Little Rock: Tunnah and Pittard Printers, 1903.

Hazen, W. B. *A Narrative of Military Service*. Boston: Ticknor & Co., 1885.

Halpin, T. M., comp. *Memphis City Directory, 1866*. Memphis: Bingham, Williams and Co., 1866.

Headley, John W. "The Confederate Secret Service," *The Photographic History of the Civil War*. Ed. Francis P. Miller. 10 vols. New York, Thomas Yoseloff, 1911.

Hearn, Lafcadio. *Occidental Gleanings*. Edited by Albert Mordell. Freeport, Me.: Books for Libraries Press, 1925.

Henry, Robert Selph. *As They Saw Forrest*. Jackson, Tenn.: McCowat-Mercer, Inc., 1956.

———. *"First With The Most" Forrest*. Jackson, Tenn.: McCowat-Mercer Press, Inc., 1944.

Historical Catalogue of the University of Mississippi. Nashville: Marshall and Bruce Co., 1910.

Holliday, Carl. *A History of Southern Literature*. Port Washington, N.Y.: Kennikat Press, 1906.

Howe, M. A. DeWolfe. *Home Letters of General Sherman*. New York: Charles Scribners Sons, 1909.

Howard, R. L. *A History of the 124th Regiment, Illinois Volunteers from Aug '62–Aug '65*. Springfield, Ill.: H. W. Bokker Co., 1880.

Hunt, Gaillard, comp. *Israel, Elihu and Cadwallader Washburn*. New York: McMillan, 1925.

Johnson, Robert U. and C. C. Buell, eds. *Battles and Leaders*. 4 vols. New York: Century Co., 1884–1887.

Jones, Archer. *Confederate Strategy from Shiloh to Vicksburg*. Baton Rouge: Louisiana State University Press, 1961.

Jordan, Thomas and J. P. Pryor. *The Campaigns of Lt. General N. B. Forrest, and of Forrest's Cavalry*. New Orleans: Blelock and Co., 1868; reprint ed., Dayton: Press of Morningside Bookshop, 1973.

Kinchen, Oscar A. *Women Who Spied for the Blue and the Gray*. Philadelphia: Dorrance and Co., 1972.

Kane, Hartnett, T. *Spies of the Blue and Gray*. Garden City, N.J.: Hanover House, 1954.

Keating, John M. *History of the City of Memphis and Shelby County, Tennessee*. 2 vols. Syracuse, N.Y.: D. Mason and Co., 1888. Second volume by O. F. Vedder.

Kennerly, William Clark. *Persimmon Hill, A Narrative of Old St. Louis and the Far West*. As told to Elizabeth Russell. Norman: University of Oklahoma Press, 1948.

Kerr, Elizabeth. *Yoknapatawpha*. New York: Fordham University Press, 1969.

Klein, Herman. *The Reign of Patti*. New York: Century Co., 1920.

Law, Sallie Chapman Gordon. *Reminiscences of the War of the Sixties between North and South*. Memphis: Memphis Printing Co., 1887.

Leckie, W. H. and Shirley A. *Unlikely Warriors: General Benjamin H. Grierson and His Family*. Norman: University of Oklahoma Press, 1984.

Lewis, Lloyd. *Sherman, Fighting Prophet*. New York: Harcourt Brace and Co., 1958.

Lenow, Joseph, comp. *Elmwood*. Memphis: Boyle and Chapman, 1874.

Lindsley, J. B. *The Military Annals of Tennessee, Confederate*. Nashville: Lindsley and Co., 1886.

Lipscomb, W. L. *A History of Columbus, Mississippi during the 19th Century*. Birmingham: Press of Dispatch Printing Co., 1909.

Long, E. B. and Barbara. *The Civil War Day By Day*. Garden City, N.J.: Doubleday & Co., Inc., 1971.

Lonn, Ella. *Salt as a Factor in the Confederacy*. New York: W. Neal Co., 1933.

Lord, Walter, ed. *The Fremantle Diary—Being the Journal of Lieutenant Colonel James Arthur Lyon Fremantle*. Boston: Little Brown and Co., 1954.

McCorkle, Anna Leigh. *Tales of Old Whitehaven*. Jackson, Tenn.: McCowat-Mercer Press, 1967.

McDonough, James Lee. *Chattanooga—A Death Grip on the Confederacy*. Knoxville: University of Tennessee Press, 1984.

Magness, Perre. *Good Abode: Nineteenth Century Architecture in Memphis and Shelby County, Tennessee*. Memphis: Towery Press, Inc., 1983.

Mahan, Alfred Thayer. *The Navy in the Civil War*. New York: Charles Scribners Sons, 1885.

Malone, James H. *The Chickasaw Nation*. Louisville: John P. Morton and Co., 1922.

Massey, Mary E. *Bonnet Brigades*. New York: Knopf, 1966.

Mathes, J. Harvey. *General Forrest*. New York: D. Appleton and Co., 1902.

———. *The Old Guard in Gray*. Memphis: S. C. Toof, 1887.

Meriwether, Elizabeth Avery. *Recollections of My 92 Years, 1824–1916*. Nashville: Tennessee Historical Commission, 1958.

Miller, William P. *Mr. Crump of Memphis*. Baton Rouge: Louisiana State University Press, 1964.

Morton, John Watson. *The Artillery of Nathan Bedford Forrest's Cavalry*. Nasvhille: Publishing House of the Methodist Church, South, 1909.

Owens, Mary C. [Stevens]. *Memories of the Professional and Social Life of John E. Owens*. Baltimore: J. Murphy and Co., 1892.

Parks, Joseph H. *General Leonidas Polk, CSA*. Baton Rouge: Louisiana State University Press, 1962.

Pattee, Fred Lewis, *The Feminine Fifties*. New York: D. Appelton-Century Co., 1941.

Pierce, Lyman B. *History of the Second Iowa Cavalry*. Burlington: Hawkeye Steam Book and Job Printing Co., 1865.

Pond, George E. *The Army in the Civil War*. New York: Scribners, 1883.

Quaife, M. M., ed. *Absalom Grimes: Confederate Mail Runner*. New Haven: Yale University Press, 1926.

Rable, George C. *Civil Wars: Women and the Crisis of Southern Nationalism*. Urbana: University of Illinois Press, 1989.

Randall, James G. and David Donald. *The Civil War and Reconstruction*. Lexington, Mass.: D. C. Heath and Co., 1969.

Rawick, George P., ed. *The American Slave, A Composite Autobiography*. 19 vols. Westport, Conn.: Greenwood Publishing Co., 1972

Rawlings, J. J. *Miscellaneous Writings and Reminiscences*. Memphis: n.p., 1895.

Reid, Whitelaw. *After the War: A Southern Tour.* Cincinnati: Moore, Wilstach & Baldwin, Publishers, 1866.

Richardson, Albert Deane. *The Secret Service, the Field, the Dungeon, and the Escape.* Hartford, Conn.: American Publishing Co., 1865.

Ross, Ishbel. *Rebel Rose: Life of Rose O'Neal Greenhow, Confederate Spy.* New York: Harper and Brothers, 1954.

Rowland, Dunbar. *Mississippi, Comprising sketches of Counties, Towns, Events, Institutions, and Persons.* 3 vols. Atlanta: Southern Historical Publishing Association, 1907.

Saxon, Elizabeth L. *A Southern Woman's Wartime Reminiscences.* Memphis: Pilcher Printing Co., 1905.

Scharf, J. T. *History of St. Louis City and County from the Earliest Period to the Present Day.* 2 vols. Philadelphia: Louis H. Evarts and Co., 1883.

Scott, Ann Firor. *The Southern Lady: From Pedestal to Politics 1830–1930.* Chicago: University of Chicago Press, 1970.

Shalhope, Robert E. *Sterling Price, Portrait of a Southerner.* Columbia: University of Missouri Press, 1971.

Shannon, Fred Albert, ed. *The Civil War Letters of Sergeant Onley Andrus.* Urbana: The University of Illinois Press, 1947.

Simon, John Y., ed. *The Papers of Ulysses S. Grant,* 14 vols. Carbondale: Southern Illinois University Press, 1977–.

Smith, J. Frazer. *White Pillars, Early Life and Architecture of the Lower Mississippi Valley Country.* New York: Bramhall House, 1941.

Smith, Solomon. *Theatrical Management in the West and South.* New York: Harper and Co., 1868.

Sparks, H. W. *The Memories of Fifty Years.* Philadelphia: Claxton, Remsen & Haffelfinger, 1872.

Spencer, James, comp. *Civil War Generals.* Westport, Conn.: Greenwood Publishing Co., 1986.

Starr, Stephen Z. *Jennison's Jayhawkers.* Baton Rouge: Louisiana State University Press, 1973.

Sturgis, Samuel D. *The Other Side as Viewed by Generals Grant, Sherman and Other Distinguished Officers. Being a Defense of His Campaign into Northeast Mississippi in the Year 1864.* Washington: n.p., 1882.

Taylor, Richard. *Destruction and Reconstruction: Personal Experiences in the late War.* ed. Richard B. Harwell. New York: Longmans, Green and Co., 1955.

Throne, Mildred, ed. *Civil War Diary of Cyrus F. Boyd.* Iowa City: State Historical Society, 1953.

Vandiver, Frank E. *The Civil War Diary of General Josiah Gorgas.* University: University of Alabama Press, 1947.

Vilas, William Freeman. *A View of the Vicksburg Campaign.* Madison: Wisconsin Historical Commission, 1908.

Walker, Peter F. *Vicksburg, a People at War.* Chapel Hill: University of North Carolina Press, 1960.

Warner, Ezra. Generals in Gray. Baton Rouge: Louisiana State University Press, 1957.

Wiffen, Marcus. *American Architecture Since 1780.* Cambridge: Massachusetts Institue of Technology Press, 1969.

Williams' Memphis Directory, City Guide and Business Mirror, 1860. Memphis: Cleaves and Vaden, 1860.

Winston, E. T. *Story of Pontotoc.* Pontotoc, Miss.: Pontotoc Progress Printing Co., 1931.

Woodward, C. Vann, ed. *Mary Chesnut's Civil War.* New Haven: Yale University Press, 1981.

Wyeth, John Allan. *Life of General N. B. Forrest.* New York: Harper and Brothers, 1899.

Young, Bennett H. *Confederate Wizards of the Saddle.* Boston: Chapple Publishing Co., 1914.

Young, John P. *Seventh Tennessee Cavalry.* Nashville: Barbee and Smith, 1890.

———. *Standard History of Memphis, Tennessee.* Knoxville: H. W. Crews and Co., 1912.

Young, Mary Elizabeth. *Redskins, Ruffled Shirts and Rednecks: Indian Allotments in Alabama and Mississippi.* Norman: University of Oklahoma Press, 1961.

VI. PERIODICALS

Anderson, R. B. "Secret Service in the Army of Tennessee." *Confederate Veteran* 21 (1913): 21–22.

Bonner, Sherwood. "From '60 to '65." *Lippincott's* 18 (October 1876): 500–509.

Brown, Andrew. "The First Mississippi Partisan Rangers." *Civil War History* 1 (1955): 371–399.

———. "Sol Street, Confederate Partisan Leader." *Journal of Mississippi History* 31 (1959): 155–173.

Camm, William. "War Diary, 1861–1865." Fritz Haskell, ed. *Journal of the Illinois State Historical Society* 18 (1925–1926): 830–950.

Castel, Albert. "Fort Pillow: Victory or Massacre?" *American History Illustrated* 9 (April, 1974): 4–10, 46–48.

Davis, Curtis Carroll. "The Spy Memoir As a Social Document." *Civil War History* 10 (1964): 385–400.

DeBow, James D. B. "Editorial Miscellany." *DeBow's Review* 27 (July 1859) 112–118.

Fishel, Edwin C. "Mythology of Civil War Intelligence." *Civil War History* 10 (1964): 344–353.

Forbes, Stephen A. "Grierson's Cavalry Raid." Illinois State Historical Society *Transactions* (1907): 99–130.

Hesseltine, William B. "The Mississippi Career of Lyman C. Draper." *Journal of Mississippi History* 15 (1958): 165–180.

Hoard, Henry. "Scouting About Memphis." *Confederate Veteran* 20 (1912): 207–209.

Mendenhall, Marjorie S. "Southern Women of a 'Lost Generation.'" *South Atlantic Quarterly* 33 (1934): 334–353.

Miller, William D. "E. H. Crump, Family Background and Early Life." *Tennessee Historical Quarterly* 20 (1961): 360–364.

Orr, J. A. "A Field Trip from Houston to Jackson, Mississippi in 1845." *Publications of the Mississippi Historical Society* 9 (1906); 177–178.

Parks, Joseph H. "A Confederate Trade Center under Federal Occupation: Memphis, 1862–1865." *Journal of Southern History* 7 (August 1941): 289–314.

———. "Memphis under Military Rule, 1862–1865." *East Tennessee Historical Society's Publications* 14 (1942): 31–58.

Steukrath, G. H. "Memphis, Tennessee." *DeBow's Review* 27 (Aug 1859): 235–39.

White, James. "Papers of Prominent Mississippians." *Publications of the Mississippi Historical Society* 5 (1902): 265.

Woodward, Samuel. "Grierson's Raid, April 17 to May 2d, 1863." *Journal of the United States Cavalry Association* 14 (1903–04): 685–710, 94–123.

Index

Edmondson, Isabella *(continued)*
flight from home, 136–87; at Waverley, 158–87 *passim*; postwar friendship with Jefferson Davis, xiii; death of, xxiv
Edmondson, Col. James Howard, xvi, xviii, xxxi, 10, 21, 21*n27*, 23–26 *passim*, 34, 59, 65, 72, 90, 125, 196, 207, 211
Edmondson, Jane Scott Walton, xxix, 204*n18*
Edmondson, Joanna H., xxxi, 19*n22*, 29, 48, 85–120 *passim*, 194, 204, 211
Edmondson, Kate, xxxi, 164, 164*n37*, 165
Edmondson, Mary Titus, xxxi
Edmondson, Aunt Patsy (Martha S. Buchanan), 131, 134, 183, 204
Edmondson, Lt. Robert, Jr., xxix
Edmondson, Robert W., xxxi, 158, 158*n14*, 160–67 *passim*, 204, 210
Edmondson, Robert Yakely, xxxii
Edmondson, Samuel Gholson, xxxii, 166
Edmondson, Thomas Ridgely, xxiv, xxiv*n34*
Elder, Sam, 23
Eleventh Tennessee Cavalry (C.S.), 34*n5*
Elliot, Leonidas Hooper, 22, 26, 156, 156*n10*
Elm Ridge, x, xxiii, 18*n22*, 29, 189, 191*n8*, 207, 208, 210
Enterprise, Mississippi, 26, 26*n46*
Etowah, Georgia, 60
Ewing, Capt. William, 149, 149*n32*
Eyrich, Albert, 58–59, 59*n4*, 60, 71–72
Eyrich, Julian, 98

Fackler, Anne K., 23, 87, 96, 97, 97*n20*, 104, 116, 117, 197–201, 201*n16*
Fackler, Calvin M., 59–60, 60*n5*, 127, 127*n10*, 197–201, 201*n16*
Farmer, Henry, 11–12
Farrell, Capt. W. T., 108, 109, 132
Farrow, Mr., 112, 112*n10*, 119, 124, 125, 134
Ferguson, Henry, 28, 82, 82*n6*
Flaherty, Mrs., 116
Fletcher, Nannie, 29, 160

Floyd, Capt., 123, 124, 126
Fontaine, Noland, 117*n25*, 199
Forrest, Col. Jeffery, 87, 87*n19*, 90, 90*n3*
Forrest, Gen. Nathan B., 20–67 *passim*; death of brother, 87–90; relieved Chalmers, 98–99, 100–34; Brice's Crossroads, 141–51; at Tupelo, 153–65; wounded in battle, 160; Memphis raid, 174–75*n2*
Forrest, Mrs. N. B., 152*n2*, 153, 154*n5*, 156, 160, 168, 169, 213
Forrest, Capt. William, 183
Forrest's Cavalry, 34, 34*n5*, 189*n5*, 212
Fort Donelson, Tennessee, xix, 34, 34*n6*
Fort Gaines, Alabama, 169, 169*n2*
Fort Henry, Tennessee, xix
Fort Morgan, Alabama, 25, 25*n42*, 169, 169*n2*, 172, 172*n13*
Fort Pemberton, Mississippi, 16*n14*, 95
Fort Pickering, Tennessee, 64, 68
Fort Pillow, Tennessee, 112, 112*n13*, 113, 114, 199
Fourth U.S. Cavalry, 90, 92
Frank, Whitney, 93, 93*n11*, 104*n37*
Franklin, Mrs. Anne, 126
Franklin Female College, Holly Springs, Mississippi, xv
Freeman, Mrs., 14, 15, 46, 58
Frelligh, Mrs. Rebecca, 16, 21, 27, 37, 41, 47
Friars Point, Mississippi, 71

Galloway, Capt. Matthew C., 149, 149*n33*
Galloway, Mrs., 152, 152*n2*, 153, 154
Garro, Miss, 23, 24
Gates, John W. (scout), 114, 114*n18*
Gayoso Hotel, Memphis, 193, 193*n11*
Germantown, Tennessee, 64, 103, 127
Gettysburg, Pennsylvania, 53, 55
Gibbert, 97, 117, 117*n25*. *See also* "Dutch"
Goff, Helen, 213
Goodman, Mrs. Walter, 141, 141*n13*, 152, 207, 210
Goodwyn, Mr. and Mrs., 198, 201
Gordon, Annie, 144, 147
Gordon, Col. James, xxxiii

Made in the USA
Lexington, KY
11 November 2010